FEMINIST PEDAGOGY

A *National Women's Studies Association Journal* Reader

Feminist Pedagogy

Looking Back to Move Forward

EDITED BY **Robbin D. Crabtree**
David Alan Sapp
Adela C. Licona

The Johns Hopkins University Press
Baltimore

© 2009 The Johns Hopkins University Press
All rights reserved. Published 2009
Printed in the United States of America on acid-free paper
9 8 7 6 5 4 3 2 1

The Johns Hopkins University Press
2715 North Charles Street
Baltimore, Maryland 21218-4363
www.press.jhu.edu

ISBN 13: 978-0-8018-9276-9
ISBN 10: 0-8018-9276-7

Library of Congress Control Number: 2008934991

A catalog record for this book is available from the British Library.

Special discounts are available for bulk purchases of this book. For more informa-tion, please contact Special Sales at 410-516-6936 or specialsales@press.jhu.edu.

The Johns Hopkins University Press uses environmentally friendly book materials, including recycled text paper that is composed of at least 30 percent post-consumer waste, whenever possible. All of our book papers are acid-free, and our jackets and covers are printed on paper with recycled content.

Contents

FEMINIST PEDAGOGY

Introduction: The Passion and the Praxis of Feminist Pedagogy

ROBBIN D. CRABTREE, DAVID ALAN SAPP,
AND ADELA C. LICONA

The term *feminist pedagogy* refers to a particular philosophy of and set of practices for classroom-based teaching that is informed by feminist theory and grounded in the principles of feminism. But such a seemingly straightforward definition does little to illuminate the history, practices, influences, and complexities of feminist pedagogy. Both words in the term have multiple meanings.

Perhaps no word and few concepts have been as contested as *feminism.* At once a seemingly narrowly gendered term and a comprehensive almost-totalizing philosophy, feminism encompasses ideas about the importance of women and women's experiences, histories of social movements seeking gender equality, a philosophy of humanism that works as a lens for understanding the entire human condition (not just that of women), and a critical analytical method that interrogates the relationships among gender, sex/uality, race, class, the environment, and power, often using misogyny as an organizing principle to explain inequalities and injustices in these realms. All of these understandings of feminism, and the multidisciplinary literatures that explicate them, inform feminist pedagogy.

Similarly, the term *pedagogy,* still unfamiliar to many practicing teachers, refers broadly to the art, craft, and science of teaching. Of course, this vague definition does not even hint at the politics of knowledge that are critical to understanding the practice and outcomes of teaching, the roles of educational institutions in maintaining social orders, or the complex power and identity dynamics in any given classroom. Commonly understood to be components of pedagogy are (1) curriculum, or the knowledge and content that are taught; (2) instruction, or the preferred modes of teaching and prevalent interaction patterns in teaching and learning contexts; and (3) evaluation practices, or the methods for, criteria used in, and values that guide the assessment of student performance. In addition to these components, A. Luke and Luke (1994) define pedagogy in relation to culture, focusing on the ways schools have been sites where social orders are organized, replicated, and reified. Pedagogy, it seems, is as much about social hierarchies and the ideological and political dimensions of education as it is about classroom practices. Feminist pedagogy, then, can be seen as a movement against hegemonic educational practices that tacitly accept or more forcefully reproduce an oppressively gendered, classed, racialized, and androcentric social order.

Although the terms *feminist* and *pedagogy* are both contested in the academic literature, consensus has emerged over the past few decades that, as feminists, we must critically engage in dialogue and reflection not only about *what* we teach but also about *how* we teach. Feminist pedagogy is a set of assumptions about knowledge and knowing, approaches to content across the disciplines, teaching objectives and strategies, classroom practices, and instructional relationships that are grounded in critical pedagogical and feminist theory. It is an ideology of teaching as much as it is a framework for developing particular strategies and methods in the service of particular objectives for learning outcomes and social change.

The actual practices of feminist scholars and women's studies teachers in relation to these definitions of feminist pedagogy are in need of continued study. In 1992, for example, Julie Brown published a report for which she surveyed two hundred teachers affiliated with women's studies programs. The results indicated that at least half of the respondents usually lecture in class, with only an eighth of them using student-facilitated group discussion and other participatory pedagogical strategies in their teaching repertoires. Her analysis also indicated that most of the teaching practices related to disciplinary norms, rather than having any clear connection to the teacher's feminist principles. One respondent actually questioned the relevance of the survey, intimating that since she wasn't teaching a women's studies course that semester, there would be no way for her to practice feminist pedagogy. Other responses were even more troubling, with an eighth of respondents indicating that there is "no such thing" as feminist pedagogical theory, and others questioning the legitimacy of studying pedagogy at all, in one case claiming that "people study pedagogy because they can't handle real theory" (p. 59).

Though published in the early 1990s, this survey points to a general lack of understanding of feminist pedagogy and the presence of attitudes and classroom practices that are not consistent with feminist principles. It is particularly noteworthy that these misunderstandings were prevalent among self-proclaimed feminists and women's studies teachers.

Given Brown's findings, it should not be surprising that a cursory perusal of more contemporary articles and book chapters that use the co-terms *feminist pedagogy* reveals discussion that variously focuses on curriculum reform, analysis of girls' and women's experiences in educational environments, teaching about women, teaching feminist ideas, and teaching done by self-identified feminists, as well as feminist concerns with the processes of teaching and learning. We would argue that merely teaching a women's studies or women-focused course or identifying personally as a feminist is not an indicator of feminist pedagogy. Thus, it is necessary to explicate the characteristics of feminist pedagogy in all its complexities to understand how the rubber of feminist theory and its principles hits the road in our teaching practices, classroom dynamics, and student-teacher relationships.

Roots of Feminist Pedagogy

One important stream of feminist writing about pedagogy brings a feminist perspective to the analysis and practice of what is known as *critical pedagogy* (or *liberatory pedagogy*, using Paulo Freire's original term). Feminist pedagogy has much in common with Freire's (2000) ideas about education and classroom practices, while also bringing an important critique to his work (and that of his intellectual disciples, most of whom are men, such as Henry Giroux 1997; Peter McLaren 2000; and Ira Shor 1996). Like Freire's libratory pedagogy, feminist pedagogy is based on assumptions about power and consciousness-raising, acknowledges the existence of oppression as well as the possibility of ending it, and foregrounds the desire for and primary goal of social transformation. However, feminist theorizing offers important complexities such as questioning the notion of a coherent social subject or essential identity, articulating the multifaceted and shifting nature of identities and oppressions, viewing the history and value of feminist consciousness-raising as distinct from Freirean methods, and focusing as much on the interrogation of the teacher's consciousness and social location as on the student's (see, for example, Weiler 1991).

Other roots of and important philosophical influences on feminist pedagogy can be found in the progressive education movement in the United States (see the writings of John Dewey [1916], for example), which emphasized experiential learning, social responsibility, and a reclamation of the civic mission of education in a democracy. While there are links to other social and educational movements, our review of the central characteristics of feminist pedagogy reinforces the idea that it is a unique approach with its own set of assumptions about teaching and learning, a commitment to certain kinds of classroom practices and interactions, and a set of explicit objectives, all of which are grounded in some kind of gender-based analysis of power, social structures, and educational contexts.

The growing body of literature on feminist pedagogy has posed and attempted to answer the following questions: What do we teach and why? How do we teach and why? How does what and how we teach impact our students and our communities (e.g., Munson Deats and Tallent Lenker 1994)? Typical topics explored in this literature include the revamping of curricula and courses to focus more on women's lives and experiences (e.g., Laskey Aerni andMcGoldrick 1999) and the exploration of approaches to teaching common women's studies courses, such as the introductory (often general education) women's studies course or courses on women writers, women's history, or gender/sexuality. Much of this literature has focused on course content primarily and secondarily on issues arising from classroom dynamics, such as ambivalence about teacher authority, student resistance, and diversity issues, with a tertiary concern for connections between classroom teaching and community action (e.g., Cohee, Daumer, Kemp, Krebs, Lafky, and Runzo 1998; Holland and Blair 1995; C. Luke 1996; Maher and Thompson Tetrault 2001; Mayberry and Rose 1999).

Feminist pedagogy is more than teaching about women or teaching feminist perspectives. Feminist teaching is a reexamination and reimagining of what happens in *any* classroom, indeed of the relationships between teachers, students, education, and society. In the following section, we offer a brief discussion of several of the most prominent tenets of feminist pedagogy.

Characteristics of Feminist Pedagogy

Feminist pedagogy arises from feminist social practice (Cohee et al. 1998). Consciousness-raising, social action, and social transformation are explicit goals of feminist pedagogy that are rooted in the desire to transform thought into action. Based in the principles of feminism and the material history of feminist organizing and consciousness-raising, then, feminist teaching is predicated on ideas about empowering individuals within a larger project of social change. As such, feminist pedagogy explicitly acknowledges and foregrounds the undeniable history and force of sexism and heterosexism in society.

Feminist pedagogy emphasizes the epistemological validity of personal experience, often connected to notions of voice and authority. Through a critique of the ways traditional scientific and academic inquiry have ignored or negated the lived experiences of women, feminist pedagogy acknowledges personal, communal, and subjective ways of knowing as valid forms of inquiry and knowledge production. Feminist pedagogy questions the ways traditional knowledge production and received knowledge serve particular interests and social configurations of power through the systematic exclusion or oppression of particular classes of people. It emphasizes accountability for the use of knowledge (see, most notably, Belenky, Clinchy, Goldberger, and Tarule 1986; see also Lather 1991).

Feminist teaching uses an ethic of care (Gilligan 1982); some have even used the word *love* (see, for example, hooks [1994, 1995, 1996], who explores the erotic nature of teaching, and Wallace's [1999] psychoanalysis of practicing feminist pedagogy). Feminist teachers demonstrate sincere concern for their students as people and as learners and communicate this care through treating students as individuals, helping students make connections between their studies and their personal lives, and guiding students through the process of personal growth that accompanies their intellectual development. This process includes a special care for female students, inside and outside of the classroom, and a commitment to advancing and improving the educational experiences, professional opportunities, and daily lives of women.

Feminist pedagogy is marked by the development of nonhierarchical relationships among teachers and students and reflexivity about power relations, not only in society but also in the classroom. The vision of egalitarian and empowering communities of learners who share a sense of mutual and social responsibility manifests itself in participatory classroom structures and dynamics, collaborative evaluation, and respect for individuals and differences (Shrewsbury [1987b] takes up these issues as her primary focus; see also Crabtree and Sapp 2003).

Critical analysis of the educational environments within which teaching takes place is likewise important, including recognizing the ways schools and classrooms have been hostile environments for girls and women and monitoring the evolving status of female students at all levels of education (e.g., Munson Deats and Tallent Lender 1994). Feminist teachers also engage actively in the exploration of how *who* we are within these environments necessarily impacts *what* and *how* we teach. This approach includes an explicit commitment to address the intersections of gender, race, ethnicity, class, and sexuality not only in the content of the discipline but also in the dynamics of the classroom (see Macdonald and Sánchez-Casal 2002). Teachers who subscribe to a feminist pedagogical approach develop teaching strategies that resist reinscribing dominant cultural notions about gender, race, sexuality, and class and deliberately problematize essentialist terms and constructs that have historically marginalized individuals and groups that have functioned to oppress a full range of human experience.

There is an explicit attempt to name and reflexively shift the dynamics of power and powerlessness in the classroom and in the complex relationships among students (and groups of students), between students and teachers, and as part of this process, to understand the experiences of and constraints on differently situated teachers in the complex web of institutional power structures (also see Maher and Thompson Tetreault [2001] for an analysis of gender and race privilege in the classroom context).

Feminist pedagogy links classroom-based teaching with opportunities for application in communities through social action using strategies such as service-learning, feminist-action research, and other methods of engaged and community-based learning. This tenet is about recognizing the links between the personal, including the individual's educational experience, and the political, including working to understand and change the collective social reality. The phrase "the personal is political" validates the political nature of women's individual experiences and voices and acts as a reminder that theory and intellectual inquiry have a responsibility to society (e.g., Novek 1999).

With respect to objectives and outcomes, feminist pedagogy seeks not only to enhance students' conceptual learning but also to promote consciousness-raising, personal growth, and social responsibility. It offers teachers and students alike the intellectual skills to expose ideology and complicate the concept of authority, that is, to participate in contesting and realigning gender politics in society. It provides teachers and students with a language of critique that allows them to analyze differences among social groups and how they are constructed within and outside the academic setting, as well as their own roles in various forms of domination, subordination, hierarchy, and exploitation.

Feminist classrooms create environments where students and teachers examine relationships of power in culture, where dichotomies of either-or can be rejected and replaced with the ability to problematize common-sense viewpoints, discover similarities within difference, and learn to understand phenomena through multiple lenses (Shrewsbury 1987b). It should not be superfluous to add that feminist pedagogy is not simply about learning the theory and applying it in a classroom, but it is also, more important, a way of living both professionally and personally.

Despite compelling arguments in support of practicing feminist pedagogy, many teachers find that putting feminist theory into practice raises a number of pedagogical challenges and dilemmas (Crabtree and Sapp 2003). These, in turn, create a gap between what feminist teachers believe is the best educational approach and what they actually manage to practice in their everyday experiences. Those challenges bring additional political and professional consequences for teachers who practice feminist pedagogy, which could prove detrimental to their success in the academy, a social context where innovative teaching is often neither valued nor rewarded. The articles selected for inclusion in this volume explore the characteristics of feminist pedagogy and reveal many of the ambivalences, contradictions, and risks inherent in feminist pedagogical practice.

The Volume: Feminist Pedagogy in Action

This volume brings together theoretical and empirical articles, critical essays, and personal reflections on classroom practices published in *The NWSA Journal* from 1989 to 2002. The collection illustrates trends in the development of feminist pedagogical theory, a range of applications in classrooms across many disciplines including in women's studies classrooms, a variety of teaching contexts, and the process of teacher reflection on methods of putting pedagogical theories into action (or *praxis*) that accompanies feminist thinking about teaching. Among the hundreds of articles published in *The NWSA Journal* since its founding, there have been dozens that have explored some aspect of teaching. This reveals much about feminist scholars and feminist scholarship; that is, teaching is central to our lives and our politics. But instead of choosing articles that explicated approaches to teaching in this or that discipline, or to teaching in this or that educational context, we decided to focus on articles that explicitly investigated teaching practices and processes with a preference for articles that both explored intellectually and revealed narratively an engaged feminist teacher praxis, or the cycles of grounded theorizing, action/experience, and critical reflection that are the hallmarks of feminist teaching.

Although this volume is organized into discrete sections, the ideas explored in this collection of essays are anything but separate. Articles that purported to be about feminist and pedagogical theory, for example, inevitably drifted productively into stories from classrooms and authors' revelations about themselves as teachers and as feminists. Similarly, articles that offer classroom strategies and practical advice inevitably connected these back to theory, to feminist activism, and to the embodied personal narratives of teaching. So while this messiness made identifying an organizing principle for the collection challenging, it also reflects accurately and honestly the nature of feminism itself: the personal is political is theoretical is pedagogy is activism is teacher praxis is personal.

Part I: Feminist Pedagogical Theory and Praxis

The articles included in the first section center on theorizing feminist pedagogy. While we believe the project of theorizing a feminist pedagogy is the foremost concern of the authors in this section, there is also included much that is personal, both in the examples from the authors' own classrooms, and in the reflexive structure employed in many of the essays.

Dale Bauer's (1990) chapter, "Authority," originally appeared in a section of *The NWSA Journal* called "Feminist Bywords," offering short treatments on terms that had become foundational to feminist inquiry. We include Bauer's article because it engages directly and succinctly with one of the most central concepts and dilemmas in feminist pedagogy. Whether related to the struggle of women, other feminists, and members of historically underrepresented groups to be recognized as "authorized speakers," or in the dance/danger inherent in reimagining teacher authority in the feminist classroom, this issue is universally faced by feminist teachers and scholars. Bauer's piece reminds us that the struggle to gain and share authority in our own classrooms (not to mention in our departments and relationships more generally) has been the subject of much debate and controversy in feminist writing over the decades.

Bauer concludes her chapter with a challenge to all of us: "Why not think of *claiming* authority as an emancipatory strategy?" (p. 25). While such a strategy is familiar in the sense of *authoring*, or writing from a place of authority, it remains troubled in the context of the feminist classroom, where women's authority is wrought with layers of complexities, from the question of women's authority to teach, to the ways students challenge a female professor's (and particularly a feminist professor's) authority, to a teacher's own struggles with how to create an empowering classroom for students—ostensibly by reducing teacher authority—even as she is trying to gain legitimacy in her institutional culture. As Bauer's brief musings on authority establish, and many of the other essays in this volume continue to explore, the question about and controversy over notions of authority remain extremely salient.

The chapter by Pamela Caughie and Richard Pearce (1992) continues the discussion of teacher authority, as the authors explore resisting the "dominance of the professor." This article was originally written as a dialogue, using the two professors' approaches to teaching the writings of Virginia Woolf, in particular *A Room of One's Own*. The main point of the dialogue (and our reason for including their essay) emerges about two-thirds of the way through the piece as the authors contemplate the relationship between narrative authority and classroom authority. Woolf provides an apropos context for exploring this relationship. Given that one author is a woman and the other a man, the dialogue explores the ways the gender of the teacher affects how feminist pedagogues' management of classroom authority is an extension of their investment in/with institutional authority.

One disturbing, though not at all surprising, revelation is that male, and perhaps some female, students tend to accept feminist ideas more readily from male professors than from female ones. While this assertion remains ripe for empirical inquiry, the dialogue leads the two authors through a valuable discussion, demonstrating individual teacher praxis as well as useful theorizing about teacher authority. The authors conclude that one way of resisting the dominance of the professor is to make the pedagogy part of the class and to self-reflexively subvert these gender polarities by explicitly interrogating them with each other and the students. This article illustrates that in feminist classrooms, the pedagogy we use is (or should be) as much a part of course content as the disciplinary subject matter.

Becky Ropers-Huilman's (1999) chapter completes the discussion about teacher authority. She uses the threads of power and caring that have been woven throughout the literature on feminist pedagogy to analyze three scenes from her own classroom. Her interrogation of a teacher's choices about the use of power and the complex process of empowering students is evocative. More than the previous two chapters, this one begins with an explicit discussion of what it means to engage in feminist pedagogy, reviewing what had become known by 1999 as the literature of feminist pedagogy. She then reveals the challenges therein, in part by situating her reflections in a framework of poststructuralism. She notes that "a feminist poststructural approach to education would involve a conscious effort to recognize and utilize the positions that one embodies as a participant in feminist education, with the caveat that we cannot always know the effects of the actions that we choose" (p. **51**).

Ropers-Huilman illustrates her theoretical and philosophical discussion with reflections on three teaching experiences at different points in her career, concluding with a summary of the lessons she learned. Ropers-Huilman reminds us that, while the literature on feminist pedagogy is useful, it does not always provide easy or certain answers about putting it into action.

Debbie Storrs and John Mihelich (1998) then take up another of the dilemmas that have become so important to feminist thinking, teaching, and activism. In their chapter, "Beyond Essentialisms," the authors confront the problem of who should teach what to whom. They question the premise that only those who have experienced gender oppression (and their unstated assumption is that this group includes only women) have the knowledge and right to teach about it. Storrs and Mihelich then dismantle this premise, arguing that "a politics of experience essentializes both students and instructors and presumes singular notions of identity" (p. **64**).

The authors argue that the absence of male instructors in most women's studies curricula implicitly reifies the status of males as the invisible center, as the genderless norm against which women are studied as deviant, as "other." Moreover, they note that this structural reality and conceptual problem typical in most women's studies programs, and thus reinforced for students and teachers alike, results in male professors' being excused from taking responsibility for their gender privilege in women's studies courses. It also denies men the opportunity to teach topics that are personally relevant to them and students the opportunity to explore these issues with a variety of differently situated faculty members.

Using their team-taught course as an illustrative case study, the authors show how their interactions with each other become implicated in the course content in positive as well as problematic ways, and how they debunk essentialized constructions of the "nature" of gender and sexuality as well as assumptions about who can and should teach what. There is plenty in this article to evoke debate among readers, and it is interesting to view it in the context of the chapter that occurs previously to it in this volume, as the authors attempt to neither claim nor forfeit authority based solely on their individual identities or experiences.

A chapter originally published in 1995 by sal johnston takes up similar problems in the context of teaching a course on sexuality in a religiously conservative environment. In "Not for Queers Only," johnston develops a postmodern feminist pedagogy, where it is essentialist notions about sexuality, rather than about gender, that are deconstructed and reminds us that teaching *is* activism, disrupting yet another unproductive distinction in/between our professional and personal lives, especially when we are teaching in reactionary contexts. Another argument johnston makes and demonstrates persuasively is that theory must affect our pedagogy. As some of the previous authors have, johnston effectively questions the feminist epistemic privilege granted to experience and instead argues for a politics of affinity and action. Thus, according to johnston, all students are invited to claim/learn (or minimally understand) antioppression stances even for groups and issues that are not "theirs."

The chapter contains many concrete examples of how postmodern and feminist theories inform choices about and approaches to course content, as well as the teacher's own behavior in the classroom and the kinds of assignments the teacher assigns and grading the teacher does. We are reminded that "if we want our pedagogical practices to resist heterosexism [or fill in any other oppressive system], then we must avoid rearticulating the logic that underlies it" (p. 91). This chapter goes a long way in addressing critics of postmodernism for its apparent apolitical stance, and johnston concludes that the exigency of questioning and analyzing essentialist constructions of sexuality, gender, and race is directly related to the fact that the social and political agenda of the Right is dependent on them.

The final chapter in this section, by Maralee Mayberry and Margaret Rees (1997), demonstrates the integration of most of the issues raised so far: the ways feminist principles challenge traditional epistemology, the goals of women's studies programs and in particular their interdisciplinarity, the theory and practice of feminist pedagogy, and the role of teacher praxis, all in the context of a feminist critique of science and science education. The title of the article is exactly what the article is and does: "Feminist Pedagogy, Interdisciplinary Praxis, and Science Education." There is plenty of pragmatic advice in this essay for readers interested in reimagining science instruction from a feminist perspective, and it is explicit in its emphasis and very well grounded in feminist pedagogical theory and principles. Mayberry and Rees clearly illustrate a feminist approach to science education as they help us both to deconstruct and to create productive dialectical relationships for reconsidering what science education could be. The authors include personal narrative as well as student voices in their chapter, further demonstrating feminist practice.

All of these chapters illustrate the difficulty of separating pedagogical practices from course content and curriculum from philosophy and theory. This differentiation is, and should be, more difficult for feminist pedagogues, precisely because it is based on the feminist principles discussed at the beginning of this introduction: what we teach and why and who we are in our own institutional contexts and the larger society must be taken into consideration in the development of our pedagogical theory and practice.

Part II: Pedagogical Practices in the Feminist Classroom

In this section, the authors move more toward the practical and offer a number of perspectives on specific pedagogical techniques, how they relate to feminist pedagogical theory, and how they are used in specific contexts. While this set of chapters is decidedly more pragmatic in intention, there remains an ongoing (though usually quite concise) effort to articulate the nature and values of feminist pedagogy, as well as a commitment to critical reflection on teaching and reflexivity about teacher roles, practices, and experiences.

Estelle Freedman (1990) begins this section by looking at a common pedagogical technique: the small group discussion or activity. She begins her chapter by recalling the consciousness-raising groups of the 1970s women's movement and her own experience with this method as a student in that decade. While the use of small groups in the consciousness-raising tradition might seem obvious to many feminist pedagogues today, Freedman explains that what is common in some contexts may still be innovative in others. In fact, she articulates compellingly how and why small group pedagogy was considered extraordinary at Stanford University in the 1980s. Her discussion, by weaving her reflections and analysis with student voices, is a reminder of why small group and consciousness-raising pedagogy remains an important part of feminist teaching.

In addition to a discussion of the specifics of how she used consciousness-raising groups in her classes, Freedman incorporates a good deal of attention to gender, race, class, sexuality, violence, and activism issues as to how these were addressed in course readings, group discussions, and student reflections on their own learning. Freedman's piece (re)inspires us to (re)commit to this pedagogical practice, and particularly to trust our students more in the learning process.

As a useful extension to Freedman's chapter, Julia Wood (1993) offers concrete methods for feminist teachers to facilitate group and whole-class discussions to ensure that diverse voices are heard. Based on work she developed for teaching gender and communication, Wood brings valuable conversational techniques to the classroom setting. Using reflective writing followed by structured conversational exercises, Wood shows how gender orientation (not sex) predisposes particular interpretations of what others say and, therefore, particular conversational moves. While Wood's chapter reports an analysis of gendered conversational patterns as they manifest in her classroom, the techniques she uses to guide students through active and reflective listening can be used by any instructor in any classroom. These techniques can also be taught as a way of helping consciousness-raising and small group participants listen to and hear diverse voices in that context and to reflect on their own communication behaviors.

Saundra Gardner's (1993) chapter on teaching about domestic violence is concerned with creating a safe environment for class discussion. While her reflections focus on her experiences teaching about sexual and domestic violence, the issues she explores related to student anger, hopelessness, and despair are also relevant to many courses in women's studies curricula and to teaching feminist perspectives in myriad subject areas. This chapter operates primarily at the descriptive level, as Gardner explains her choices, what has occurred in her classroom, how these experiences have led to revisions in course content and teaching strategies, and how this has had an impact on her and her students. The lesson to be gleaned from this chapter is how to create classroom environments that are relatively safe and empowering for students and teachers.

In their chapter, Mary Margaret Fonow and Debian Marty (1991) explore another familiar teaching practice: the use of panels to bring particular perspectives into the classroom, in their case the perspectives of lesbians. The discussion engages us in a valuable exploration of the dialectical tension between the feminist epistemological privileging of personal experience (i.e., to understand the lesbian experience you must hear from "real lesbians") and the poststructural deconstruction of essentialism (i.e., sexual identity is fluid, and there is no such thing as a "real lesbian" as a distinct or essential category).

In a chapter in the previous section, johnston explains the use of lesbian/gay/bisexual panels has been eschewed in johnston's course on sexuality to disrupt the privileging of experience as a reification of essentialism. Fonow and Marty attempt to engage the same questions and issues, but with a different result. In particular, they note the ongoing need for identity politics even while we deconstruct and destabilize essentialist identities and subject positions. Feminist pedagogues will find this article to be evocative as they reflect on their own decisions about if and how to use guest panels in the classroom.

Another common assignment in women's studies classes is the social action project. In this concise chapter, Suzanna Rose (1989) explains her use of the protest as a teaching technique as a way to promote feminist activism. Her objective was to help students move from focusing largely on intellectual and personal growth and toward developing their motivation to produce social change. The chapter explores an experiment she used in an upper-level feminist theory course and provides useful insights into how to facilitate student application of learning through the activist project—as grounded in the issues that are salient to the *student*—and the impact on the student's sense of self-efficacy. She also provides important caveats about risks to students and teachers who engage in this pedagogical activity.

We include Annis Hopkins' essay, originally published in 1996, to close this section, because it is in many ways future looking; that is, she challenges feminist pedagogues to consider how to develop engaged feminist teaching practices in online environments. Hopkins acknowledges the apparent paradox for feminist teachers: how do we produce personal, interactive, caring learning environments using distance education? How will this differ from traditional educational methods, which have historically been grounded in the lecture and other didactic teaching methods? In addition to justifying the ongoing value of the lecture format, Hopkins provides a rationale for why women's studies courses should be taught through distance education. She explores the obstacles she has faced in her (at that time) five years' experience teaching women's studies courses online, as well as a variety of techniques she has used to overcome these obstacles. Given the increasingly technological orientation and savvy of our students, not to mention the pressures on our institutions to provide distance education, women's studies programs and feminist teachers in all fields of study would do well to engage actively in exploring this teaching environment and the development of appropriate, and still feminist, pedagogies.

In all, the chapters in this section illustrate different approaches to teaching. The authors, as feminist scholars and pedagogues, explore the theoretical reasoning, context-specific challenges, and creative processes for using a variety of classroom-based and online teaching strategies. They also demonstrate how our teaching is so much a part of our evolving identity as feminists as we grapple with how to be true to our principles and effective in our classrooms despite complex intellectual, demographic, and material challenges.

Part III: Race Matters: Intersectional Analyses of Classroom Dynamics

The next part brings intersectional analysis of race to the center of focus. Authors in previous sections engaged theoretically with the need for intersectional awareness and, in particular, the ways postmodern and poststructural feminism can guide our inquiry and our teaching. Previous chapters also explored how identity politics functioned in specific classroom contexts and the ways these politics influenced course content and process. The authors in this section foreground the role of critical race theory, including how it has broadened, deepened, and sharpened feminist thought in recent years. It is a logical step, then, to consider how critical race consciousness has and can become integral to theorizing and practicing feminist teaching (see, e.g., LatCrit theory).

Lili Kim (2001) begins her chapter with a review of the major tenets of feminist pedagogy, including a conscious engagement of its critics. In doing so, she uses her course, "Women of Color and the American Experience," to illustrate the importance of focusing on racism, classism, homophobia, and other vectors of women's oppression in women's studies classes. She shares an overview of her course, an argument for why classes that focus on the experiences of women of color remain necessary in women's studies curricula, some of the specific assignments she has tried, and a critical analysis of student responses and classroom interactions. Particularly because of the dynamics created by the demographics of her students (largely African American women, working mothers, and first-generation students), and the reflexive engagement with her own identity as a novice Asian American professor, Kim's discussion of what happens in her class is captivating and revealing. She explores several challenges she has faced, such as resistance from self-proclaimed feminists who objected to discussing homophobia, surprise among African American women to learn that a course on race would be taught by an Asian American and include the experiences of Native American and Latina women, and the distinctive work of keeping white women from becoming alienated as discussion inevitably turned to race privilege.

The story of her chapter title and how she later incorporated it into an assignment in future classes is compelling and provides a wonderful example of how student voices inform our teaching, just as they inform Kim's theorizing about feminist pedagogy. Kim's chapter is well-grounded in "classical" feminist theory; she also incorporates important works by women of color feminists (most notably Margaret Anderson and Patricia Hill Collins' 1998 volume, as well as works by bell hooks, Audre Lorde, Chandra Mohanty, and Cherríe Moraga), which have continued to have an impact on feminist inquiry and teaching in profound ways.

In the same way that Kim's chapter reveals the powerful and transformative potential of feminist pedagogy for first-generation undergraduate students, Anne Donadey (2002) brings similar issues to the graduate feminist criticism course and invites us to consider how teaching about race issues is encountered in the formation of future feminist scholars and teachers. Her analysis is more focused on student resistance than empowerment (compared with Kim's). Of interest to NWSA members and readers of the *NWSA Journal*, she situates her discussion in relation to the recent struggles within NWSA over different visions of feminism and a growing critique of white supremacist ideology in the women's movement and professional organizations.

The tropes of "safe space" and "student voice" are invoked through a series of questions about the ways students are silenced in the classroom, the degree to which feminist notions of safe space apply to differently situated students, and the consequences of openly racist comments on students, feminist dialogue, and subsequent classroom conversations about the interlocking nature of oppression.

Donadey encounters much the same kinds of resistance as did Kim, though it is even more fervent, perhaps because the graduate students in a women's studies program/course have become more adept at and invested in gender-based analysis. She notes that, while the chapter represents her process of reflecting on a painful teaching experience and her analysis incorporates influences from conversations with students and antiracist colleagues, her analysis does not constitute a pedagogy, per se. However, we submit that it not only illustrates her pedagogy and the ways she endures to apply feminist and critical race theory in her classroom, but that her process exhibits a powerful feminist pedagogical praxis.

And so, in some ways, we have come full circle, back to the need to theorize. Not only do we witness, in Donadey, the struggles of future feminist teachers and scholars as they confront the complexities of feminism and pedagogy, but we are also reminded of the ways that many of the assumptions of feminist theory and movement are challenged by critical race theory and truly pluralistic analysis. Donadey points out the irony in radical feminism in that an uncritical trust in our ability to create safe space and promote free speech "replicate[s] the assumptions of the bourgeois concept of the public sphere" (p. 214). It is particularly urgent to note that the mostly white female students in her graduate seminar resisted engaging in analysis of multiple oppressions mainly in relation to race and colonialism. This, then, points to the road ahead.

Part IV: Bibliographies

The final section includes two bibliographies published by *NWSAJ*, which we include to fortify the practical value of this retrospective. While we refer to some of the foundational works on feminist pedagogy in the first section of this introductory chapter, we have in no way referenced all of the historically important writing on feminist pedagogy, let alone its precursors. We hope that these two bibliographies, along with the references provided by each author in the volume, will facilitate the ease with which readers can access additional resources. After all, reading our foremothers is critical to developing and reflecting upon our own pedagogy.

The first bibliography, by Lori Goetsch, was published in 1991 and includes work published between 1986 (the end date of Carolyn Shrewsbury's bibliography published in *Women's Studies Quarterly*, 1987a) and 1990. Goetsch provides a context for her selections, as well as short but useful annotations for each of the fifty-one citations.

With very little overlap, the second bibliography, compiled by Stephanie Riger, Carrie Brecke, and Eve Wiederhold (1995), is more comprehensive in terms of time and range of content. It includes citations from the early 1980s through 1995. This bibliography is organized helpfully, especially in assisting readers without training in exploring multiracial feminisms and critical race theory and in preparing for the kinds of experiences explored by many of the authors in this volume.

We hope that future bibliographies of feminist pedagogy published in *The NWSA Journal* will also include writings from transnational and postcolonial feminists. There are also works such as Jyl Lynn Felman's arresting *Never a Dull Moment* (2001). Such works may be easy to miss in literature reviews because they seem to be about performance rather than pedagogy. While many of our graduate training experiences did not include exploration of such wide-ranging theoretical streams, let alone consideration of the ways they might impact our thinking about feminism or teaching, we are all responsible for reading, listening, learning about, and practicing an increasingly inclusive, antioppressive, and transformative pedagogy.

In Closing

This retrospective illustrates the ways that the *NWSA Journal* has always been a place where feminist teachers and scholars look to publish scholarship on teaching and learning. It should not be surprising, then, that the journal is a place where NWSA members and other readers go to read about, reflect upon, and gather ideas for their own teaching. The articles on pedagogy published in *NWSAJ* represent the various streams of writing about feminist classrooms and teaching, and reveal much about how feminist pedagogy has evolved in the past twenty years. Earlier articles, not surprisingly, focus mainly on gender as an organizing principle and central concern for course content and for understanding teacher and student interaction. Later articles bring complex intersectional analysis of race, class, sexuality, and gender more into the center of theorizing and practicing feminist pedagogy.

Although the essays collectively explore the philosophical and theoretical dimensions of feminist pedagogy, they also illustrate how it is practiced. Specific teaching methods, thick description of particular teaching contexts and moments, and an attention to trial and error characterize the feminist teaching explored in these chapters. Tried-and-true teaching methods are problematized, as new approaches are attempted, sometimes successfully and often in unexpected ways. More empirical research on what feminist teachers actually do in their classrooms, as well as about the theories and assumptions that underlie practice, is needed. It would certainly be useful, for example, to update what we learned from Julia Brown's 1992 survey.

Tellingly, many of the essays are highly reflexive, which demonstrates teaching praxis while also being generative of theory. These essays narrate a feminist pedagogy in action, as expected and unexpected consequences emerge in relation to the variables presented by the students, the contexts where we teach, the climate of the larger society, and teachers' identities and gifts. These essays also reveal areas for future theorizing, empirical study, and reflexive practice.

Based on our informal tallies, about half of the authors who are publishing on the topic of feminist pedagogy (in *NWSAJ* and elsewhere) seem to be English professors with primary training and/or research interests in literary criticism. In addition, with the exception of a few women of color and white men, and even in the cases of writing about antiracist feminist pedagogies, most of the authors seem to be white women. These trends make us wonder: What are the stories of feminist pedagogy that are not collected in volumes about feminist pedagogy? A meta-analysis of all volumes on pedagogy should pay particular attention to these issues as well as who is being cited, and which discussions are taken up by which authors, in order to understand the changing demographics, theories, and practices of feminist pedagogy. It does seem that the more recent volumes on feminist pedagogy, like the more recent articles in this collection, are more likely to focus on intersectional analysis and *praxis*, and are more likely to be written or co-authored by self-identified lesbian or openly queer authors and ethnically/racially diverse authors.

In all, we hope this *NWSA Journal* retrospective continues the project of theorizing feminist pedagogy as multiple voices and perspectives are brought into the conversation. We also hope it will assist readers in their own attempts to develop theoretically grounded classroom practices informed by the advice and experience of others, and to reflect creatively on their own teaching.

Works Cited

Anderson, M. L., and Hill Collins, P., eds. (1998). *Race, Class, and Gender: An Anthology*. New York: Wadsworth.

Bauer, D. M. (1990). Authority. *NWSA Journal* 3, no. 1: 95–97.

Belenky, M. F., Clinchy, B. M., Goldberger, N. R., and Tarule, J. M. (1986). *Women's Ways of Knowing: The Development of Self, Voice, and Mind*. New York: Basic.

Brown, J. (1992). Theory or Practice: What Exactly is Feminist Pedagogy? *Journal of General Education* 41: 51–63.

Caughie, P. L., and Pearce, R. (1992). Resisting "the Dominance of the Professor": Gendered Teaching, Gendered Subjects. *NWSA Journal* 4, no. 2: 187–99.

Cohee, G. E., Daumer, E., Kemp, T. D., Krebs, P. M., Lafky, S., Runzo, S., eds. (1998). *The Feminist Teacher Anthology: Pedagogies and Classroom Strategies*. New York: Teachers College Press.

Crabtree, R., and Sapp, D. (2003). Theoretical, Political, and Pedagogical Challenges in the Feminist Classroom: Our Struggles to Walk the Walk. *College Teaching* 51, no. 4: 131–40.

Dewey, J. (1916). *Democracy and Education*. New York: Macmillan.

Donadey, A. (2002). Negotiating Tensions: Teaching about Race Issues in Graduate Feminist Classrooms. *NWSA Journal* 14, no. 1: 82–103.

Felman, J. L. (2001). *Never a Dull Moment: Teaching and the Art of Performance*. New York: Routledge.

Fonow, M. M., and Marty, D. (1991). The Shift from Identity Politics to the Politics of Identity: Lesbian Panels in the Women's Studies Classroom. *NWSA Journal* 3, no. 3: 402–13.

Freedman, E. B. (1990). Small Group Pedagogy: Consciousness Raising in Conservative Times. *NWSA Journal* 2, no. 4: 603–24.

Freire, P. (2000). *Pedagogy of the Oppressed*, trans. M. B. Ramos. New York: Continuum. (Originally published in English in 1970)

Gardner, S. (1993). Teaching about Domestic Violence: Strategies for Empowerment. *NWSA Journal* 5, no. 1: 94–102.

Gilligan, C. (1982). *In a Different Voice: Psychological Theory and Women's Development*. Cambridge, MA: Harvard University Press.

Giroux, H. A. (1997). *Pedagogy and the Politics of Hope: Theory, Culture, and Schooling*. Boulder: Westview Press.

Goetsch, L. A. (1991). Feminist Pedagogy: A Selective Annotated Bibliography. *NWSA Journal* 3, no. 3: 422–29.

Holland, J., and Blair, M., eds. (1995). *Debates and Issues in Feminist Research and Pedagogy*. Philadelphia: Multilingual Matters.

hooks, b. (1994). *Teaching to Transgress: Education and the Practice of Freedom*. New York: Routledge.

hooks, b. (1995). *Killing Rage: Ending Racism*. New York: An Owl Book.

hooks, b. (1996). Feminist Theory: A Radical Agenda. In *Multicultural Experiences, Multicultural Theories*, ed. M. F. Rogers, 56–61. New York: McGraw-Hill.

Hopkins, A. H. (1996). Women's Studies on Television? It's Time for Distance Learning. *NWSA Journal* 8, no. 2: 91–106.

Johnston, S. (1995). Not for Queers Only: Pedagogy and Postmodernism. *NWSA Journal* 7, no. 1: 109–22.

Kim, L. M. (2001). "I Was So Busy Fighting Racism That I Didn't Even Know I Was Being Oppressed as a Woman!" Challenges, Changes, and Empowerment in Teaching about Women of Color. *NWSA Journal* 13, no. 2: 98–111.

Laskey Aerni, A., and McGoldrick, K., eds. (1999). *Valuing Us All: Feminist Pedagogy and Economics.* Ann Arbor: University of Michigan Press.

Lather, P. (1991). *Getting Smart: Feminist Research and Pedagogy with/in the Postmodern.* New York: Routledge.

Lorde, A. (1984). *Sister Outsider: Essays and Speeches by Audre Lorde.* Freedom, CA: Crossing Press.

Luke, A., and Luke, C. (1994). Pedagogy. In *The Encyclopedia of Language and Linguistics,* ed. R.E. Asher and J.M. Simpson, 566–68. Tarrytown, NY: Elsevier Science/Pergamon.

Luke, C., ed. (1996). *Feminisms and Pedagogies of Everyday Life.* Albany: State University of New York Press.

Macdonald, A. A., and Sánchez-Casal, S., eds. (2002). *Twenty-First-Century Feminist Classrooms: Pedagogies of Identity and Difference.* New York: Palgrave Macmillan.

Maher, F. A., and Thompson Tetrault, M. K. (2001). *The Feminist Classroom: Dynamics of Gender, Race, and Privilege.* New York: Rowman & Littlefield.

Mayberry, M., and Rees, M. N. (1997). Feminist Pedagogy, Interdisciplinary Praxis, and Science Education. *NWSA Journal* 9, no.1: 57–75.

Mayberry, M., and Rose, E. C., eds. (1999). *Meeting the Challenge: Innovative Feminist Pedagogies in Action.* New York: Routledge.

McLaren, P. (2000). *Che Guevara, Paulo Freire, and the Pedagogy of Revolution.* Lanham, MA: Rowman & Littlefield.

Mohanty, C. T. (1991). Under Western Eyes. In *Third World Women and the Politics of Feminism,* ed. C. T. Mohanty, A. Russo, and L. Torres, 51–80. Bloomington: Indiana University Press.

Moraga, C. (1998). La Guerra. In *Race, Class, and Gender: An Anthology,* ed. M. L. Anderson, and P. Hill Collins, 26–33. New York: Wadsworth.

Munson Deats, S., and Tallent Lenker, L., eds. (1994). *Gender and Academe: Feminist Pedagogy and Politics.* New York: Rowman & Littlefield.

Novek, E. M. (1999). Service-Learning Is a Feminist Issue: Transforming Communication Pedagogy. *Women's Studies in Communication* 22, no. 2: 230–40.

Riger, S., Brecke, C., and Wiederhold, E. (1995). Dynamics of the Pluralistic Classroom: A Selected Bibliography. *NWSA Journal* 7, no. 2: 58–75.

Ropers-Huilman, B. (1999). Scholarship on the Other Side: Power and Caring in Feminist Education. *NWSA Journal* 11, no. 1: 118–35.

Rose, S. (1989). The Protest as a Teaching Technique for Promoting Feminist Activism. *NWSA Journal* 1, no. 3: 486–90.

Shor, I. (1996). *When Students Have Power: Negotiating Authority in a Critical Pedagogy.* Chicago: University of Chicago Press.

Shrewsbury, C. M. (1987a). Feminist Pedagogy: A Bibliography. *Women's Studies Quarterly* 15, nos. 3 and 4: 116–24.

Shrewsbury, C. M. (1987b). What Is Feminist Pedagogy? *Women's Studies Quarterly* 15, nos. 3 and 4: 6–14.

Storrs, D., and Mihelich, J. (1998). Beyond Essentialisms: Team Teaching Gender and Sexuality. *NWSA Journal* 10, no. 1: 98–118.

Wallace, M. L. (1999). Beyond Love and Battle: Practicing Feminist Pedagogy. *Feminist Teacher* 12, no. 3: 184–97.

Weiler, K. (1991). Freire and a Feminist Pedagogy of Difference. *Harvard Educational Review* 61: 449–74.

Wood, J. T. (1993). Bringing Different Voices into the Classroom. *NWSA Journal* 5, no. 1: 82–93.

PART I   **Feminist Pedagogical Theory and Praxis**

CHAPTER ONE

Authority

DALE M. BAUER

The authority of feminist criticism is a rhetorical one (which can, in certain cases, be used against feminism). "Authority is always a source [. . .] of struggle," and that struggle does not guarantee equitable "social effects."[1] We are accustomed to thinking of authority as an object—as in someone "invested with authority"—but we need to think of it, instead, as a rhetorical effect. Authority is the effect of successfully enforcing rhetoric; and, I would argue, a successful feminist rhetoric produces powerful and persuasive and sometimes dangerous effects. To that end, we have still more authority to claim for very specific political purposes.

Twelve years ago Arlin Diamond and Lee Edwards published *The Authority of Experience* (1977), giving testimony to women's experiences of oppression. Diamond and Edwards claimed an authority for feminist criticism as justified by experience. However, their authority—an imperative that the marginal voices from the canon and the academy be given voice—is not my notion of authority. How, in this political and social climate, do we define the authority feminist critics have attained?

First, why is "authority" such a hard word for feminists? Like the word "power," it suggests an identification with patriarchy. Kathleen Jones suggests "that authority currently is conceptualized so that female voices are excluded from it. . . . Authority, like judgment, is necessarily hierarchical and dispassionate" versus compassionate.[2] We can feel ambivalence about seeking authority—and power; we know its associations when we have been excluded from it. At the heart of defining authority is the understanding that institutions are embedded in historical and social contingencies and complexities; these institutions can never be "utopias of consensus." As such, authority within the institution will always involve further struggles. In the words of one critic, "authority is always imaginary, but the power of authority is always real."[3]

Early feminist criticism often argued against the idea of "authority."[4] But I appeal to Catherine Clément and Hélène Cixous's exchange in *The Newly Born Woman* as a counterargument: they state that authority is inevitable since "we are within the same cultural system" that thrives as male discourse.[5] Feminists have had trouble occupying this position of authority because of its association with domination. But for the nineties—even as we do so ambivalently—we need to accept the authority which the institutionalization of feminism has given us. What we do with that authority—an authority always in flux—is still in question.

Originally published in the Winter 1991 issue of the *NWSA Journal*.

But it is not an uncomplicated or unambivalent stance; rather than seek to reduce that ambivalence, we must use the tension that authority fosters to advance social change.

A recent experience suggested to me the consequences of claiming authority when in 1989, I delivered a talk on feminist authority in the classroom, claiming that feminism is not only a method (or a pedagogy) but also a subject, a discipline, for study. Some members of the audience responded in what I could only call rhetorical violence: that I was a cryptofascist in desiring this authority for feminism and suggesting that "I was cutting my own throat" for making the claims for authority before I had tenure. Immediately after the talk, one of the members of the audience announced what had happened that night at the University of Montreal.[6] The confluence of events—my talk on feminism in the classroom, the anger it evoked in the audience, and the very real violence in Montreal against feminists and their perceived authority—brought the lesson home about the dangers in claiming that authority.

Feminist rhetoric in the nineties could be seen as a provisional micronarrative devised, in this contemporary critical arena, to provide a body of political positions but not to establish a univocal voice. Feminist authority, therefore, is more pragmatic than true. It corresponds to our lived experience of feminism—as fractured, often contradictory—where our allegiances often pull us in several different directions. Authority is contingent on our recognitions of differences within feminism. Our own authority is provisional but no less powerful in its effects for being so.

As feminists, our authority comes with an understanding of how it has been used against us. We must sustain a sense of authority in flux— the very definition of the political (according to Daniel Cottom's *Text and Culture*). For me, authority and ambivalence go hand-in-hand. "The inability to reconcile authority with human agency," Kathleen B. Jones argues, "is the result, in part, of a conception of the self in isolation from others as opposed to a self in connection with others."[7] Reconciling authority with compassion and feminist politics is the task we now face.

In short, it is now necessary to historicize the notion of authority, just as it is necessary to historicize terms like "the body," "sisterhood," and all of the other feminist bywords. We cannot accept the fear of authority or power that we have seen linked with domination and eschew it in favor of some decentered classroom.[8] There is bound to be ambivalence in this model: the feminist claiming authority meets with all sorts of resistance, mostly based on the fact that we are not socialized to see women as authorities at all. Or, for that matter, to claim that authority comfortably.[9] A former colleague, Ann Ardis, put it this way about a graduate class in which she struggled with authority: "I'm glad . . . you teach your first graduate course only once in your life. . . . Were students resisting the feminist content of the course—or was it the feminist pedagogy that created dissonance in the class? And how much of what might be termed feminist pedagogy in this course was really feminist pedagogy and how much was just my female insecurity about my authority in the classroom?"[10]

How does who we are, as gendered bodies and as professors positioned in the academy, affect our relation to authority? Feminist rhetoric matters all the more in its deployment and in its political ends. In the struggle for authority, we cannot let our points of agreement be lost in the points of disagreement.

Why not think of *claiming* authority as an emancipatory strategy: authority, in this sense, involves what is called in critical pedagogy becoming a transformative intellectual. To think of claiming authority in such a way means being aware of the authority we assume in fighting forms of oppression and, most of all, enlisting colleagues and "treating students as if they ought to be concerned about the issues of social justice and political action."[11] To assume any less is to relinquish the only sort of authority that matters.

Notes

This essay is a slightly revised version of a presentation delivered at the Modern Language Association annual meeting on 28 December 1989 in Washington, D.C.

1. Daniel Cottom, *Text and Culture* (Minneapolis: University of Minnesota Press, 1989), 11.

2. Kathleen Jones, "On Authority: Or, Why Women Are Not Entitled to Speak," in *Feminism and Foucault*, ed. Irene Diamond and Lee Quinby (Boston: Northeastern University Press, 1988), 120–21.

3. Cottom, *Text and Culture*, 13, 40.

4. bell hooks, *Talking Back: Thinking Feminist, Thinking Black* (Boston: South End Press, 1989), 45.

5. Catherine Clément and Hélène Cixous, *The Newly Born Woman*, trans. Betsy Wing (Minneapolis: University of Minnesota Press, 1986), 137.

6. Marc Levine shot twenty-seven people, killing fourteen, shouting: "You're all a bunch of feminists and I hate feminists."

7. Jones, "On Authority," 128.

8. See Margo Culley, "Anger and Authority in the Introductory Women's Studies Classroom," in *Gendered Subjects*, ed. Margo Culley and Catherine Portuges (Boston: Routledge, 1985), 211.

9. See Susan Stanford Friedman, "Authority in the Feminist Classroom: A Contradiction in Terms?" in *Gendered Subjects*, 206.

10. Ann Ardis, "Feminist Pedagogy Seminar," Miami University of Ohio, Fall 1988.

11. Henry Giroux, *Schooling and the Struggle for Public Life* (Minneapolis: University of Minnesota Press, 1989), 139.

CHAPTER TWO

Resisting "the Dominance of the Professor":
Gendered Teaching, Gendered Subjects

PAMELA L. CAUGHIE AND RICHARD PEARCE

We write in sexual difference. That is the critical difference in feminist inquiry.

—Jane Gallop

The dialogue that follows was initially presented at a special session on feminist pedagogy at the 1989 Modern Language Association (MLA) Convention: "Teaching Woolf: Issues of Gender and Authority in the Classroom." The two of us met six months before the convention, discovered that we had mutual scholarly and pedagogical interests, and decided to explore the issues of gender and authority presented in teaching Woolf through an exchange of letters. We seemed ideal complements: Pamela Caughie is a younger woman teaching at a coed urban university, Loyola University Chicago; Richard Pearce is an older man teaching at Wheaton College, a small women's college that had just admitted men. In our correspondence, we wanted to explore the general pedagogical questions of this panel—what can teaching Woolf tell us about teaching?—in terms of a specific issue: what difference does our difference in gender make when it comes to feminist pedagogy? In editing our correspondence for the MLA presentation, we chose to focus on a recurring concern in our letters: the structure of authority, both in the classroom and in narrative. And by way of answering our question about gender difference, we chose to present our paper as a dialogue. The dialogue not only captured the dynamics of our exchange, the collaborative give and take, reflection and growth, logic and leaping that characterized our correspondence. It also enabled us to deal head-on with the potentially divisive issue of gender differences and the potentially hegemonic role of authority. We present this essay version in its original dialogue form, moving from a discussion of teaching Woolf to a discussion of gendered teaching, as a way of enacting the insights we gained from our ongoing discussion and as a way of playing out the implications of Woolf's own exercise in pedagogy, *A Room of One's Own*, which is forever displacing its own conclusions in the need to address something or someone else.

Pamela: Our title, "Resisting 'the Dominance of the Professor,'" comes from Virginia Woolf's celebrated essay, *A Room of One's Own*, which is

Originally published in the Summer 1992 issue of the *NWSA Journal*.

based on two lectures Woolf gave at Newnham and Girton Colleges in October 1928, and which both promotes and enacts a feminist pedagogy. In chapter 2, Woolf writes: "The most transient visitor to this planet . . . could not fail to be aware . . . that England is under the rule of a patriarchy. Nobody in their senses could fail to detect the dominance of the professor" (33). Specifically, Woolf refers to those (male) professors who write books about the mental, moral, and physical inferiority of women. More generally, Woolf uses the professor as the embodiment of those institutionalized patriarchal power relations where the superiority of one social group presupposes the inferiority of another. For Woolf, the dominance of the professor depends on the polarity of gender differences, what she calls "this pitting of sex against sex, of quality against quality" (Room, 110). It is this polarity that our six-month epistolary exchange focused on.

Dick: I'd been teaching at a woman's college for twenty-four years and—though angry when the college became coed—I was looking forward to teaching young men what I had learned about gender. I had an ideal opportunity when we came to A Room of One's Own. But it turned out to be complicated—when one of the few male students said, "I like Virginia Woolf: she had a lot of balls." For suddenly I had to focus not only on the problem of discourse, but on a male student testing his power. And our contest could easily displace the woman he admired with such manly grace—and turn the women in the class from participants to spectators.

Pamela: Such power is, of course, precisely what's at issue in Woolf's essay as well as in the pedagogical practice it enacts. A Room of One's Own provides a model for approaching any issue as difficult and divisive as the relation between gender and writing or gender and teaching, and one that may prove useful when responding to strong male students; for its flexible method of investigation changes with the problems she takes up, the contexts she enters into, and the audience she addresses. Despite the avowed topic of her essay, the relation between women and fiction, Woolf never does tell us the "true nature of woman" or the "true nature of fiction" (Room, 4) because she investigates ever-shifting relations and because she foregrounds her own methods of investigation. In each chapter, she draws stark contrasts between women and men, emphasizing the difference in their prosperity, their values, their sentences; then in the last chapter she decides that the first sentence of her lecture on "Women and Fiction" would be. "It is fatal for anyone who writes to think of their sex" (Room, 108). And yet it seems Woolf has thought of little else.

If we take this sentence at face value, we may conclude that for Woolf, awareness of gender differences has nothing to do with writing, or with teaching. But the method of her essay shows that gender differences certainly matter to Woolf. The problem is thinking of gender differences in terms of stable oppositions (pitting sex against sex, quality against quality). When the narrator considers the "comparative values" of women and men, charwoman and barrister, she cannot draw a conclusion because the measuring rods, as she calls them, change, just as they change in the course of Woolf's essay (*Room*, 40, 89). Gender differences have everything to do with writing and teaching, but Woolf wanted to find a way out of the polarity, the opposition between genders.

Dick: I agree that Woolf wanted to find a way out of the opposition between genders, and, as you argue so well, that she does. She also replaced duality with multiplicity, and traditional goal-oriented and hierarchical story lines with fields of changing relationships. And she rejected the male sentence, disrupted and decentered the totalizing story line, developed a new authorial voice, and valorized a variety of women and women's experiences. But her discourse, her way out, exists within a larger field that is dominated by male authority.

For in her major novels the men have at least virtually the last—unifying—word. Peter Walsh has the climactic vision of *Mrs. Dalloway.* Lily Briscoe must complete the story of the father and son landing at the lighthouse before she can complete her own painting. And Bernard tells the story of the lady writing, "sums up" a fragmentary and heterogeneous novel, and ends by riding against death "with my spear couched and my hair flying back like a young man's, like Percival's when he galloped in India" (*The Waves*, 297).

Take *The Waves*, Woolf's most successful achievement of multiplicity and shifting interrelationships. Notice how the male characters have the narrative power. For example, everyone as far as I know accepts Louis's story about his devastating encounter with Jinny. Feeling alienated by his nationality and class, he stands alone by the wall, watching "Bernard, Neville, Jinny and Susan (but not Rhoda) skim the flower-beds with their nets." He wants to be unseen and stands "rooted to the middle of the earth," peering through an eyehole in the hedge. But now Jinny's eyebeam slides through the chink. "She has found me. I am struck on the nape of the neck. She has kissed me. All is shattered" (12–13).

But Jinny tells a different story, which no one seems to have noticed. She sees the leaves moving in the hedge and thinks it is a bird in its nest. But there is no bird in the nest, and the leaves go on moving, and she is frightened. "I ran past Susan, past Rhoda, and Neville and Bernard in the tool-house talking" (13). Note that in her story Rhoda is with the children, who are not skimming the flower beds with their nets, as Louis reported, but in and around the toolhouse. Once we recognize that Louis and Jinny are telling different stories, we can begin to understand the struggle for narrative control, and we may see Jinny's reaction in a different light. "I cried as I ran, faster and faster. What moved the leaves? What moves my heart, my legs? And I dashed in here, seeing you green as a bush, like a branch, very still, Louis, with your eyes fixed. 'Is he dead?' I thought, and kissed you, with my heart jumping under my pink frock like the leaves" (13). Jinny's "speech" is in the second person; she is speaking directly to Louis. And why does she kiss him? Because of her sensuality, which, especially considering her later thoughts and actions, has been labeled as aggressive and narcissistic. But perhaps we have not been alert to the story she is trying to tell. And recent changes in psychological theory, lead us to understand how we have been caught up in the male paradigm, and what Jinny's story might entail.

Irene Stiver (director of psychology at McClean Hospital in Massachusetts) tells of a young woman who developed a psychotic condition after her stepfather had a stroke. She talked of wanting to sleep with him. Not content to draw a Freudian conclusion, Stiver questioned her more closely. She found out that the stepfather had been a powerful businessman, contemptuous of weak people like her mother, but very kind to her as a child. After his stroke, he became terrified: he was afraid to close his eyes for fear he would die. The young woman was not motivated by incestuous desire, as male-stream psychology would have it. She simply could not bear to see this powerful man become so vulnerable. "I thought . . . if I slept with him, if I put my arms around him, comforted him, he would be less afraid, that he would sleep, and he would stay alive" (Stiver 1986, 26).

Stiver provides another frame of reference in which to see Jinny. She is a physical person and will develop into a woman who "can imagine nothing beyond the circle cast by my body" (128–29). But her instinct toward Louis is neither sexual nor aggressive. It is simply caring. She is sensitive to Louis's devastating feeling of isolation and inadequacy, which is like death. And her instinct is to nurture him, to make him feel warm and wanted, to physically revive him. Moreover, her later refusal to be "attached to one person only . . . to be fixed, to be pinioned" (55), may now be seen, not as narcissistic but as a need to connect with everyone. This need, as Jean Baker Miller and Carol Gilligan point out, is devalued in a culture dominated by male values of independence—and is continually misinterpreted and therefore frustrated by the men Jinny meets.

Jinny's kiss initiates both Louis and Jinny into the threatening world of sexuality—or gender and power. Jinny intrudes into Louis's haven when, due to his colonized status and class, he is feeling powerless. But, his gender gives him power and privileges his story over hers. Susan and Bernard reinforce Louis's reaction to Jinny and, therefore, his version of the story; indeed, they form the social mirror through which Jinny begins to define herself. But, more important, they also form a narrative power structure that suppresses Jinny's story and begins to shape our view of her.[1]

Pamela: To read Jinny's story in terms of female nurturing and to valorize such nurturing as a feminine alternative to masculine autonomy may be to support unwittingly the very gender polarity that has served patriarchal domination. As Jessica Benjamin argues in *The Bonds of Love,* domination stems from the failure to recognize the other's independence and from the identification of nurturance and intersubjectivity with women alone. After all, however much you show us, Dick, that our responses to Jinny's sexuality have been shaped largely by male values, as a woman, I still may want to interpret her kiss as an aggressive act, to read Jinny as narcissistic, as a woman who isn't afraid to live out her sexual desires and to put her own desires above a man's needs. And I may choose this reading in order to expose Louis's fear of female sexuality and the threat independent women pose to his own autonomy as a man.

I agree with you that Woolf's writing, like feminist teaching, takes place within a larger "field" defined by male authority. What I want to resist, however, is the desire to offer an alternative model that might compete with the dominant one, to talk about female nurturing versus male authority or female forms of narrative versus male forms, as if we were talking about stable oppositions or clearly defined contrasts. *The Waves* may be dominated by male narrators, as you argue, but Bernard as a narrator differs from Louis and Neville in that novel, and even more from Mr. A in *A Room of One's Own* whose bar-like "I" shadows the page so that his writing subjects the reader to one point of view only (103–4).

For me, what makes your reading of *The Waves* so valuable is not that you demonstrate the superiority of female modes of narrating, but that you demonstrate the priority of narrative and the diversity of narrative forms. Instead of beginning with differences in gender and looking for their different forms of narrative authority, we might begin with the point and the context of the narrative structure and note the kinds of authority it gives rise to or allows for.

Let me take *To the Lighthouse* as an example. This is Woolf's most famous novel precisely because it was early canonized as a representative modernist narrative, as Erich Auerbach describes it in his highly influential essay, "The Brown Stocking." Critical attention focused on the ways in which Woolf and her fictional surrogate, Lily Briscoe, achieved unity, harmony, and vision in their artworks. Recently, feminist critics have challenged such modernist readings by identifying the specifically female narrative strategies in this novel. Marianne Hirsch, for example, singles out contradiction, oscillation, and irresolution—strategies produced by the artist's focus on the mother-daughter plot—as the "mark of female difference" in this modernist narrative (108–18). The female artist, Hirsch argues, remains suspended between equally untenable options, which she neither chooses between nor reconciles: on the one hand, the desire to merge with the mother, which would mean intimacy but also annihilation, and, on the other hand, the desire to follow the traditional male developmental plot and the narrative aesthetic associated with it, one that resolves contradictions and moves toward some kind of closure. Woolf's "modernist" style, with its abrupt shifts in perspective and its discontinuities, both expresses and maintains the tension between two alternatives.

Yet however different Lily's, and Woolf's, artworks may be from the prevailing masculine art of their time, the traits Hirsch values in this narrative are not the *properties* of novels produced by women who think back to their mothers; rather, they are the *effects* produced by a change in critical emphasis, from formal relations (the concern of modernist critics and of Lily in Part I) to narrative relations (the concern of feminist-psychoanalytic critics, and of Lily in Part III). That is, focusing on narrative motives and desires, rather than distinguishing between two types of narratives, enables differences to emerge without having to specify those differences in advance, as if the writer were unambiguously gendered from the beginning.

For another example, let me turn to the opposite end of the canonical scale and take what has been, until recently, Woolf's least-discussed novel, *Between the Acts*. Woolf's last novel was long neglected in part because its fragmented structure suggested to critics that the novel, unrevised at Woolf's death, was incomplete. The action of the novel consists largely of the preparations for, the staging of, and the audience responses to a play produced by Miss La Trobe. The play, part of an annual village pageant, is a parodic reenactment of British literary history staged in June of 1939. Performed outdoors by local talent, the play is continually interrupted, by a rain shower, by airplanes flying overhead, by the village idiot who bursts onto the stage (perhaps part of the play, perhaps not), by the required intermission for tea. The discontinuous structure of Miss La Trobe's play, as well as Woolf's novel, has been read by critics in seemingly opposing ways. The discontinuity is interpreted either as Woolf's despair of the unifying power of art in the face of World War II or as Woolf's faith in the unifying power of art despite the threat of global destruction. If we consider the artist's gender as primary, these readings may put us in an uncomfortable position. We run the risk of concluding either that the woman artist (or the lesbian or the foreigner, since La Trobe is all of these) is unable to unify society—indeed, may even be responsible for its loss of unity—or that the woman artist (or the "other") is the one capable of saving us.

ʾ What if we begin instead not with the gender, sexuality, or ethnicity of the artist but with the status of the narrative? How can this highly self-reflexive, indeterminate, parodic narrative enable us to respond differently to differences, particularly in gender? We could read those interruptions in Miss La Trobe's play as revealing how much any creation (an outdoor pageant, a novel, a feminist classroom) depends on certain contingencies, in this case, bad weather, limited budgets, tea time, world war, and, most importantly for our pedagogical interests, audience expectations, the assumptions people bring to the performance. Critics who try to sum up this novel as despair or affirmation bring to it the same expectations that La Trobe's audience brings to her play (and our students bring to our classrooms): the audience "liked to leave a theatre knowing exactly what was meant" (*Between the Acts*, 164). If, however, we accept the contingency of narrative, if we do not conceive the novel as a separate order providing stability in a world of change, if we do not consider teaching as imparting knowledge and building consensus but instead accept the implication of each in the larger cultural economy, then we may come to see discontinuity and indeterminacy not as problems to be overcome or as features of a new, highly valued narrative form (e.g., female or feminist), but as *functions* of the very circumstances (social, historical, institutional) in which the narrative is produced, which include cultural constructions of gender differences.[2] ˒

While it *is* significant that La Trobe is a woman, a lesbian, and a foreigner, her "otherness" can serve to remind us that confronting such differences as those of gender and sexuality requires a new way of conceiving social, literary, and personal authority. Woolf's novel, like La Trobe's play, seeks to change our expectations of narrative, to acknowledge the importance of the audience (or students) in any production. The question of authority is very much at issue in this prewar novel, yet authority does not lie where critics look for it, in the author or the text, but in the relations between writer and reader, just as the authority in the classroom lies in the interactions between teacher and students. Whom to thank? the audience asks as they leave the village pageant; whom do we make responsible? (*Between the Acts* 195). The audience must learn to accept their implication in this production, and in the production of narrative authority.

Dick: So what are the consequences for teaching Woolf? Not simply to tell Jinny's story or describe the structure of *Between the Acts* but to expose the contending narrative forces. Nor can we simply tell this to our students, that is, lecture to them from our traditional positions of authority. We must change the structure of the classroom to insure the multiplicity of voices, or to prevent male hegemony like that in *The*

Waves. Indeed, what's been becoming more and more clear in our dialogue is the relationship between narrative authority and authority in the classroom. And perhaps we need to make this relationship more explicit, especially as we teach novels that are attempting to resist traditional authority.

Faculty often don't recognize the ways that men attract attention and tend to dominate discussion until they see videos of their classes. According to Catherine Krupnick, who has watched thousands of hours of videoed classes, men speak proportionately more than women, much longer, and are far more likely to set the agenda. We must also change the relation of faculty to students, or the learning transaction—which Walter Ong terms "agonistic," deriving from the tradition where boys were taken away from their families to a school where they were taught forms of ceremonial combat in the classrooms as well as the playing fields. I think all this is what Woolf was getting at in *Three Guineas.*

Feminist pedagogy and collaborative learning offer good alternative models. But they are hard to develop because of the conservative pedagogical bias of most faculty, because they don't lead to prestigious publication, but most of all because they exist within a field where the dominant model is dualistic, individualistic, and competitive. And when you put a cooperative model together with a competitive model—or Jinny's story next to Louis's—guess who wins? The politics of the classroom, like the politics of narration, lead from heterogeneity to polarization, from multiplicity to dualism, from the carnival to the agon.

Pamela: Yes, I agree that we must change our classroom structures "to insure the multiplicity of voices." Yet this need for a collaborative pedagogy cannot be effected by changes in our classroom practices alone. A change in our pedagogy will require, as you point out, a change in the larger institutional "field" defined by male authority. I also agree that the politics of the classroom can lead to polarization; for however much I want to resist the female versus male arguments when it comes to discussing *narrative* methods, I have tended to fall back into such oppositions in our discussion of *teaching* methods. Diana Fuss warns that in a feminist classroom (or a Woolf seminar, I might add) gender is likely to be privileged over other kinds of differences, reducing women and men to their femaleness and maleness respectively and leading us to predict certain kinds of responses from students or professors based on their gender alone (Fuss 1989, 116).

In acknowledging this tendency, and in emphasizing the importance of the classroom context, I want to suggest that a feminist pedagogy based on gynocentric models, such as those provided by Elaine Showalter and Carol Gilligan, might work better for men than for women, especially in a coed classroom. You can offer a reading that promotes female experiences without running the risk of appearing biased or (what's worse in the academy) subjective. As a woman, I can be accused of reading myself into the text if I offer a similar reading. Where you can sound tolerant and open-minded, I might sound biased and defensive; where you can be praised as one of those enlightened men who join women in exposing the sexism of our culture, I might be dismissed, by male students especially, as one of those tiresome women or "interested" critics who see sexism everywhere.

A feminist pedagogy that would encourage us to relinquish an authority derived from concepts of autonomy and independence because such concepts are masculinist, may be easier for male professors to enact than female. After all, male professors who have been traditionally invested with institutional authority can relinquish such a position more easily than women whose status as an authority has not been firmly established in the academy. As Susan Stanford Friedman has argued in her essay in *Gendered Subjects*, the assumption that as a woman she has to undermine her authority in the classroom may lead to the denial of authority to women (Culley and Portuges, 207). This is the paradoxical position a female feminist teacher finds herself in whenever she addresses issues of authority: in protesting women's lack of authority, as you do in your reading of Jinny's story, she runs the risk of calling into question her own authority to make such a claim; and if she does assert her authority in the classroom, she ends up protesting women's lack of authority from a position of authority.

This paradoxical position may be one reason male students tend to accept feminist ideas more readily from male professors than from female ones: they have come to accept that authority is male. I'm not suggesting that we find a way out of this paradox but that we recognize it and thus find ways of *using* it to critique the institutional and cultural contexts in which our authority is shaped, to ask how and why authority came to be gendered in the first place. In *Gendered Subjects*, Nancy K. Miller presents a different response to the question of authority. "It is crucial," she writes, "for women and feminist scholarship to have a less mystified relation to mastery . . . a more ambiguous and less predictable pedagogy," which entails the risk of losing her "own identity as the teacher" (Culley and Portuges, 198).

Dick: Your view of yourself as a female feminist teacher is even more complicated than you describe. *(Oh, Oh, I realized at this point in our presentation, as did everyone else as we all started laughing: here I was a male feminist telling a female feminist what to think of her situation. As I gesticulated helplessly, hoping somehow to draw myself out of the abyss, someone called out, "Dick, stop shaking your fist at her." Whereupon I put my hand in my pocket—only to realize that there was no escape from the authority of a male constructed body.)* For, while you may lack authority as a female, you are an authority as a teacher. Moreover, no matter how you see yourself or what you do with your material or your students, you cannot abdicate this authority—any more than I can. And this complicates the problem of a male feminist who hates authority trying to expose sexism and institutionalized forms of power and open students' minds to multiple alternatives. We are many selves and speak with many voices, but the authorial voices (of the teacher as well as the narrator) has a dominating resonance. This resonance, or power, derives from the pedagogical tradition—the ways of teaching, learning, reading, and writing established by the class whose authority the authorial voice reflects and perpetuates. It reduces the multiplicity of voices, or positions, to two: those that enhance its power, either deliberately or by co-optation, and those that oppose it. And it does so not only because that's the nature of hegemonic relations, but because aggression, competition, and dualism are so ingrained, or, as Walter Ong points out, the tradition is agonistic.

As you say, you can't resist "falling back into the kind of men versus women [you] want to resist," and you are caught in a dualistic paradox when you think about giving up authority that as a woman you've never had. The male paradox is just the reverse. For, while a man may say to himself, "I'm giving up my authoritative stance," he can't do it. I know I'm treading dangerous ground by focusing on the problems of men in power, even when they consider themselves to be feminists and hate authority, but it's a topic that has come up very often in my twenty-four years of teaching at a women's college and in being the father of two daughters. For authority is inscribed in roles as teachers and as fathers. I've never outgrown my adolescent urge to resist authority and never felt adult enough to see myself as a father figure. But my eyes were opened two years ago when my daughters gave me a book called *Fathers.* As a variety of women authors reflected on their fathers, I began to see how my daughters had to see me, no matter how I saw myself. And I began to realize how authority was inscribed not only in my role but in my physiognomy and voice, in the way I stood and talked, in the noise I made when I walked, in the sound and rhythm of my speech. My anger had a different impact than my wife's. My expectations had more urgency. Moreover, expectations of my wife and daughters, despite their feminist consciousness, often forced me into male postures. So if women accept feminist ideas more from male than female teachers—and this hasn't been my experience at Wheaton—they may be accepting them for the wrong reasons.

Pamela: (At this stage of our exchange, I was suddenly struck by the numerous personal examples Dick used in his inquiry into gender and authority and by the absence of personal examples in my own remarks. Does this difference reflect different theoretical orientations or prose styles? Or is it a symptom of the very disposition of power relations that we are exploring here? Am I less willing to risk the personal because I'm a woman, because I'm untenured, because I'm younger than Dick? I would like to think my avoidance of personal examples is a conscious choice, a rigorous adherence to a poststructuralist theory that resists treating gender differences literally, as empirical or psychological differences, and instead treats them as a trope for structures of authority, I would like to think this.) Ah, but I didn't say that *women* accept feminist ideas from male teachers more easily than from female, but that *men* do. This is a good example of how the make-up of our classes affects the ways we conceive of teacher-student relationships: your classes have long been composed of women; mine have often been dominated by men, especially at the University of Virginia where I taught as a graduate student. At least our dialogue has brought to my attention a limitation of much pedagogical theory: its tendency to generalize about *the* teacher and *the* student, not only apart from such variables as gender, race, and class, but also apart from particular classroom and institutional contexts.

Dick: Our dialogue has helped me clarify a point I hadn't fully understood while writing *The Politics of Narration* (from which my reading of Jinny comes) and I'm glad I have time to revise my conclusion. The politics of narration and the politics of teaching are polarizing. And, in our desire for openness and multiplicity, we can't ignore the power of the authorial voice—without it taking over.

Pamela: Yes, you seem to be raising "*the* feminist question par excellence" as Barbara Johnson puts it in her essay, "Teaching Ignorance": "to what structure of authority does the critique of authority belong?" (79). But I sense a note of despair in your voice, as if you regretted the agonistic, as if multiplicity were the more highly valued alternative to competition, if only we could get everyone to see that. But getting everyone to see that or to accept any one value system is to risk hegemonic authority. The problem with posing an alternative pedagogy is that it could consolidate into a new norm. What we need is a pedagogy that enables us to displace the authority of any one model, including its own, as I believe our dialogue has enabled us to do.

What, then, if we begin not by defining the traits of a feminist classroom (multiplicity, collaboration, irresolution) beforehand, but with assessing the implications for feminism of a certain pedagogical practice in the very process of enacting it? For our dialogue has made clear to me that any pedagogy, like any narrative, must take into account the audience for or with whom it is produced. For whatever our theory of teaching, in practice we must contend with the student who describes Woolf's audacity by the language of male anatomy: Virginia Woolf had a lot of balls.

Dick: Yes, but remember that the student is male, and that one of his goals is to contest my authority. So when I contend with him, I become complicit in shifting the class's attention from a powerful woman writer to a male power struggle.

Pamela: Perhaps one way to resist the dominance of the professor and to subvert gender polarities would be to make our authority in the classroom self-reflexive by making our pedagogy a part of the class, a subject of investigation and critique along with the subject matter of the course, as Woolf does in *A Room of One's Own.* Once again, I return to that text as a model for a feminist pedagogy. All that we normally downplay when we present our conclusions to our students—our methods and our motivations, our doubts and our disappointments—is laid bare in Woolf's essay. By laying bare our pedagogy, we may help the students to see the ways in which they play the power game through their own desire for recognition and approbation by receiving, as Woolf says, "from the hands of the Headmaster a highly ornamental pot" (*Room*, 110). So when I consider how a feminist professor in a still largely male-identified institution can resist the dominance of the professor, I think of Woolf's essay, how she implicates the "other," the reader or student, in her inquiry, and how her resistance to authority takes many forms, never finally settling into one method. For such resistance must be enacted over and over again, just as such dialogues as ours must never conclude.

Notes

1. These points are developed in Pearce's *Politics of Narration.*

2. These readings of *To the Lighthouse* and *Between the Acts* are developed further in Caughie's *Virginia Woolf and Postmodernism.*

Works Cited

Auerbach, Erich. *Mimesis: The Representation of Reality in Western Literature.* trans. Willard R. Trask. Princeton: Princeton University Press, 1953.
Benjamin, Jessica. *The Bonds of Love: Psychoanalysis, Feminism, and the Problem of Domination.* New York: Pantheon, 1988.

Caughie, Pamela L. *Viriginia Woolf and Postmodernism: Literature in Quest and Question of Itself.* Urbana and Chicago: University of Illinois Press, 1991.

Culley, Margo, and Catherine Portuges, eds. *Gendered Subjects: The Dynamics of Feminist Teaching.* New York: Routledge and Kegan Paul, 1985.

Friedman, Susan Stanford. "Authority in the Feminist Classroom: A Contradiction in Terms?" In Culley and Portuges, 203–08.

Fuss, Diana. *Essentially Speaking: Feminism, Nature and Difference.* New York: Routledge, 1989.

Gallop, Jane. "Critical Response—Writing and Sexual Difference: The Difference Within." *Writing and Sexual Difference.* ed. Elizabeth Abel. Chicago: University of Chicago Press, 1982: 283–90.

Gilligan, Carol. *In a Different Voice.* Cambridge, MA: Harvard University Press, 1982.

Hirsch, Marianne. *The Mother/Daughter Plot: Narrative, Psychoanalysis, Feminism.* Bloomington: Indiana University Press, 1989.

Johnson, Barbara. "Teaching Ignorance." In *A World of Difference.* Baltimore: Johns Hopkins University Press, 1987.

Krupnick, Catherine. "Women and Men in the Classroom: Inequality and Its Remedies." *On Teaching and Learning.* ed. Margaret M. Gullette. *Journal of the Harvard-Danforth Center for Teaching and Learning* (May 1985): 18–25.

Miller, Jean Baker. *Toward A New Psychology of Women.* Boston: Beacon Press, 1976.

Miller, Nancy K. "Mastery, Identity and the Politics of Work: A Feminist Teacher in the Graduate Classroom." In Culley and Portuges, 195–99.

Pearce, Richard. *The Politics of Narration: James Joyce, William Faulkner and Virginia Woolf.* New Brunswick: Rutgers University Press, 1991.

Ong, Walter. "Agonistic Structures in Academia: Past to Present." *Daedalus* 103 (Fall 1974): 229–38.

Showalter, Elaine. "Feminist Criticism in the Wilderness." *The New Feminist Criticism.* ed. Showalter. New York: Pantheon, 1985.

Stiver, Irene. "Beyond the Oedipus Complex: Mothers and Daughters." *Work in Progress.* A publication of the Stone Center for Developmental Services and Studies, Wellesley College, Wellesley, MA, no. 26, 1986.

Woolf, Virginia. *Between the Acts.* New York: Harcourt Brace Jovanovich, 1941.

———. *Mrs. Dalloway.* Harcourt, Brace and World, 1925.

———. *A Room of One's Own.* New York: Harcourt, Brace and World, 1929.

———. *Three Guineas.* London: The Hogarth Press, 1938.

———. *To the Lighthouse.* New York: Harcourt, Brace and World, 1927.

———. *The Waves.* New York: Harcourt, Brace and World, 1931.

CHAPTER THREE

Scholarship on the Other Side: Power and Caring in Feminist Education

REBECCA ROPERS-HUILMAN

Time is the space between you and me.

—"Prayer for the Dying," Seal

Feminist teaching is a practice that has been well documented, problematized, and critiqued. Examinations of the intersections between feminism and higher education have produced considerable scholarship on feminist research, service, and pedagogy, all with the underlying quest to understand what it means to engage in feminist teaching and learning (Brown 1992; Bunch and Pollack 1983; Culley and Portuges 1985; Frye 1980; Gore 1993; Heald 1989; Lather 1991; Maher and Tetrault 1994).

Two interwoven threads frequently emerge in conversations about feminist teaching. These threads, often represented by the terms *power* and *caring,* seem to be crucial—but not easy—concepts for feminist educators to grapple with and enact. For example, Roberta Bennett (1991) suggested that feminist teaching generally supports attempts to create nonhierarchical, egalitarian classrooms where teachers and students value each others' interpretations of their lives. Yet others wonder if a nonhierarchical class is possible or if all experiences should be (or could be) valued in the same ways (Ellsworth 1989; Luke 1996; Ropers-Huilman 1998). Jennifer Gore (1993) suggested that discussions about feminist pedagogy have often emphasized the importance of student experience and voice, along with a simultaneous empowerment for social change. Yet several scholars wonder whether empowerment is desirable or possible within the social and institutional constraints that feminist educators are generally operating (Gore 1990; Orner 1992). Carmen Luke (1996, 296) asserts, "Feminism is still fundamentally about transformation and enlightenment and, therefore, feminist educators still attempt in their teaching to give students access to 'better,' more inclusive, socially just, and nonexploitative knowledges." In this vein, feminist education continues to question how teachers can use their power to enact care for students.

Still, feminist teaching is not a "pure" practice. It is affected not only by participants but also by the institutions in which it takes place. While many scholars have suggested the potential benefits of feminist ap-

Originally published in the Spring 1999 issue of the *NWSA Journal.*

proaches to teaching and learning, others have recognized the limitations of feminist teaching when it remains situated within educational institutions (Gore 1990; Middleton 1995). Magda Gere Lewis (1993, 145) reminds us, "Universities are both the site where reactionary and repressive ideologies and practices are entrenched and, at the same time, the site where progressive, transformative possibilities are born." Within those contexts, then, feminist educators have realized that certain guidelines and expectations—both implicit and explicit—affect the ways they can operate within higher education settings. Norms and expectations are interpreted in multiple ways by all who choose to participate, yet no one fully escapes the pressures and effects of standards and structures embedded in institutional climates (Damrosch 1995). While each institution undoubtedly has its own unique characteristics, feminism has been characterized as "subversive" to the commonly accepted traditions of academe (Bezucha 1985). Feminist education can be cloaked with institutional trappings yet continue to seek "progressive and transformative possibilities."

I propose that one way feminism has subverted traditional roles of educational participants in academic climates is by reconsidering the proper or most useful roles and interactions of teachers and students, especially as they relate to power and caring. Who can or should care for whom? Nel Noddings (1992, 14) poses the questions: "What does it mean to care?" and "Can we make caring the center of our educational efforts?" These questions urge a consideration of the deliberate ways in which we, as educators, can use our positions to improve educational practices through an intense and respectful engagement with students. Yet complicating these considerations are poststructural questions about the instability of power within any position. Who really has "the power" in classrooms? How would one know? What are the ways the use of power helps and hinders learning? The student-teacher dichotomy whereby all educational participants are essentialized by their place on a designated side of the divide pervades educational literature and thought (Mayberry and Rees 1997). I suggest that feminism offers new ways of thinking about the usefulness of strict enforcement of that dichotomy and considers the complexities of moving from "one side" to the other—from student to teacher and back again.

Underlying much of the literature on feminist educational experiences is a concentrated and deliberate examination of the uses of power and caring in our teaching and learning settings. In this chapter, I examine the various relationships that feminists, as both students and teachers, experience in formal teaching and learning settings in higher education. Further, I consider the complexities of expanding those relationships within the structures that define higher education. Undergirding this analysis is my belief that power and caring are not dichotomous concepts.

I do not try to get my power as a teacher "out of the way" so that I can care for the students with whom I work. Simultaneously, I do not try to care about students by ensuring either that they have power over others or that we exist in a powerless classroom. Contrary to common understandings, I propose to examine power and caring not as dichotomous terms, but rather as terms whose enactment lends strength each to the other. Further, I hope to explore how power and caring intersect and, often, have unintended effects.

Philosophical Framework

The use of poststructural theories and approaches in feminist work has been oft considered in recent years. For various reasons, many feminist thinkers have claimed that poststructuralism could be useful for feminist purposes at this particular time in history (Gore 1991; Lather 1991; Sawicki 1991; Scott 1990). Others, though, have pointed out the potential dangers of a wholesale adoption of poststructuralism and have suggested that feminists should consider what it could offer cautiously, if at all (Alcoff 1988; Nicholson 1995). As someone who is quite optimistic about what a feminist poststructuralism might offer intellectually, politically, and strategically to my life's work in and outside of academic settings, I have followed these discussions with great interest.

Feminist poststructuralism, as a theory that recognizes fluctuating power relations and situational meanings, yet acknowledges our own place as gendered actors in those relations, can be useful in understanding classroom and educational interactions. Still, one of the primary criticisms of poststructuralism has been its lack of applicability to "real world" settings (Alcoff 1988; Lather 1991). Within higher education, one scholar has suggested that the ramifications of poststructural theorizing have been decidedly absent from our professional conversations (Bloland 1995). While several pieces of feminist poststructural work deftly examined poststructural tenets in varied higher education settings (Ellsworth 1989; Gore 1993; Luke 1996; Orner 1992), those of us who are attempting to embrace and problematize poststructural and feminist offerings in our higher education settings continue to encounter much ambiguity.

One of the greatest uncertainties at this point is the use of power and caring in teaching and learning settings. If power is fluid and shifting (Foucault 1978), how can teachers and students enact it? Where can educational participants carve out places for action for themselves and others? How can teachers and students use or direct power in caring ways? Carmen Luke (1996) has pointed out the absence in the literature of discussions of those "decidedly visceral moments" when women teachers begin to feel their power and authority in educational settings (286). My task herein is to detail the visceral moments of my transition from feminist student to teacher and to begin a response to the question: how can feminist educational participants enact power to care about each other? I intend to do this while examining the usefulness of the power versus caring dichotomy that is frequently found in feminist teaching literature (Luke 1996) and the deconstruction of which is proposed by the theoretical approaches of feminist poststructuralism.

Feminist poststructuralism has much to offer a discussion on education as well as on teaching and learning processes (Ellsworth 1989; Gore 1993; Heald 1989; Lather 1991; Orner 1992). Not only does it problematize our understandings of knowledge and how those understandings have shifted over time, it also can aid in our understandings of power relations within our educational systems. As Chris Weedon (1987, 139) stated:

> From a feminist poststructural perspective the process of criticism is infinite and constantly changing. At any particular historical moment, however, there is a finite number of discourses in circulation, discourses which are in competition for meaning. It is the conflict between these discourses which creates the possibility of new ways of thinking and new forms of subjectivity.

Criticism that acknowledges and problematizes power relations in social interactions is particularly useful in considering the ways in which power is related to, and supportive of, caring practices in education.

A feminist poststructural approach to education would involve a conscious effort to recognize and utilize the positions that one embodies as a participant in feminist education, with the caveat that we cannot always know the effects of the actions that we choose. Further, since feminist education has often advanced examinations of participants as they relate to power and caring, our chosen actions should be evaluated with these concepts in mind. In this analysis, drawing on feminist poststructural philosophy led me to look closely at the ways in which power relations were enacted as I, or other teachers and students, attempted to care about others within several educational settings. I look at ways that I perceived feminism and higher education to disrupt each other, especially as these disruptions affected my attempts to engage within feminist learning environments.

Power and Caring as Student and Teacher

In August 1996, I took my first postgraduate teaching position at Louisiana State University. Having completed my doctorate at the University of Wisconsin–Madison just months before assuming my new responsibilities, I found the summer of 1996 to be filled with tension, challenges, and excitement. What would I be able to teach the graduate students with whom I was going to work? That I would learn from them was unquestioned in my mind. What if none of the students thought that I was worth listening to or working with? Why was I, who at the time identified much more with the "student" position, thought to possess certain skills that had magically changed my status from student to teacher? The barriers that I perceived between those two roles had seemed nearly insurmountable. As the fall approached, I wondered at the impermanence of those barriers through which I apparently had passed.

The approaching professorship was unsettling. I had experienced a wide range of interactions with professors in graduate school and was looking forward to the time when I determined my own path of study and developed my own timeline for following that path. In much of my previous education, I felt that my learning was determined by others in ways that were sometimes uncomfortable, offensive, and even boring. I felt that my "best interests" or educational needs were not always being respected, or cared for. How was I to ensure that my attempts to provide a structure for others' learning would not make them feel as I occasionally did? As I prepared for the new position, I realized that the institutionally sanctioned power that others used to determine the structures of my learning would now be granted to me. The gravity of this responsibility was both exhilarating and overwhelming.

My concerns were elevated by my conscious desire to hold fast to certain principles that I admired (or sorely missed) in other teachers' practices. I had recently completed my dissertation on feminist teaching and had encountered many issues in my research participants' work that seemed unresolvable (Ropers-Huilman 1996a). For example, was empowerment useful, harmful, or both when talking about what teachers should do to or for students in their relationships? To what degree should we strive to nurture community and/or difference in our classrooms? When should teachers consciously try to use their power to encourage "desirable" or stifle "undesirable" student behaviors, in order to balance group dynamics in the class or individual class members? Regardless of my uncertainties, I wanted to identify as a feminist educator and, therefore, knew that I would have a bumpy road ahead of me (Middleton 1993; Frye 1980; Lewis 1993; Ropers-Huilman 1997; Weiler 1988).

Many of these unresolved concerns related to the concepts of power and caring. Primarily, I was interested in how power circulates in feminist educational environments and where and how the openings for both student and teacher agency were located and crafted. My belief is that feminist educators can be powerful, in both deliberate and spontaneous ways, while simultaneously caring for the overall purposes of the class as they relate to individual students. In this exploration, I focus on my experiences as a feminist in transition from student to teacher and consider the factors that shape my responses to these concerns and my subsequent practices. Through three teaching and learning "scenes," I examine the contradictions I encountered in attempting to enact power and caring on both sides of the student-teacher dichotomy.

Scene One: Peeking Out from under the Cloak of Power

As a student, I saw power as ubiquitous among the faculty. Regardless of faculty members' practices, they still had an authority over students' lives in meaningful ways. Yet that authority, while apparently omnipresent in the academic area of my life, seemed entirely absent from the personal area. I was being conditioned toward individuality, separateness, and hierarchy during graduate school, the time when "habits of mind are learned and reinforced [and] . . . choices made by the profession begin to seem natural" (Damrosch 1995, 140). Yet "natural" would never have been my chosen word to describe a learning where personal lives and school lives were in conflict, where "school learning" was divorced from "real learning." I was more convinced than ever that "Who we are, to whom we are related, how we are situated all matter in what we learn, what we value, and how we approach intellectual and moral life" (Noddings 1992, xiii).

As a graduate student, I felt powerless in many arenas for the first several years of my experience. Later, I learned that my previous analysis was quite simplistic. Foucault (1978) reminds us that power is not stable or consistent. While it can be situated in certain ways within discourses, it is fluid and, therefore, always moving. Faculty and students were engaged in a dance of power that was shaped by each person's talents, hesitancies, limitations, and desires. Still, the norms of our graduate school context that dictated "proper" relations between teacher, student, and knowledge (Damrosch 1995) circumscribed the variety of dances that might have taken place.

Considering my relation to power made me nervous. I felt sure that if I voiced my beliefs, they wouldn't make sense to anyone else and, in worrying about such an event, I was often unable to think of anything to say at all. I thought that people would hear my words, pause briefly, and then go on as if I hadn't said anything. This happens all too often to certain students (hooks 1994) and has happened to me many times. I worried that someone in a seminar, either the professor or other students would interrupt me, and I would feel obligated to stop my thoughts in midstream, acknowledging that my thoughts were not going to shape the ensuing discussion. I recognized my lack of power in this setting and resonated with Magda Gere Lewis's (1993, 49) words: "The potential power of a pedagogical practice, whether in the realm of the personal or that of the political, whether inside the academy or out, is its ability to bring people to a point where they care to listen." It seemed there was only a finite amount of power available—represented, in part, in speaking prominence—and faculty members and a very few students held the pot in which it was kept tightly against their bodies. Students and teachers cared to listen differently to different participants.

Caring was an elusive concept for me when I was a student. I was socialized to think I was caring about someone when I allowed them to speak over me, when their problems and concerns received prominence, and when I succumbed to their wishes without burdening them with mine. In classrooms, then, caring was a bit problematic. How was I to learn to be a critical thinker if my thoughts were subsumed by others? How was I to be a participant in active learning—a hallmark, in my mind, of feminist education? I felt rude and uncaring if I interrupted others, even if it was the only way to make my voice heard. I did not expect the teachers who led my classes to "care" about me. I believed that they had better things to do and many students with much grander ambitions with whom they could work. Of course, caring is no more simple a concept than power. How could faculty members have demonstrated their care for me in a way that I would have noticed or accepted it? Nel Noddings (1992) asserts that caring is only realized when both the "carer" and "cared-for" are willing and able to enter into such a relationship. If students are resistant to such interactions with faculty members, or, in other words, are not trained or willing to see their teachers in caring roles, is there anything a teacher can do to break down students' preconceptions?

How can teachers and students broaden educational discourses to reconceptualize the intersections of power and caring in their relationships? Here we circle back to the difficulty of the relationships between care and power. Who can interrupt hierarchical and distant teacher-student interactions? In what discourses is this possible? What are the strategies through which power and caring can be disrupted and reshaped in learning and teaching relationships? More important, what are the assumptions underlying a desire for certain shaping? And whose desires ultimately get played out in which classrooms?

Potential responses to these questions are constantly spinning as we draw lines in the sand between and among teachers and students. Below, I describe an experience at the end of my graduate years that stands out prominently as shifting the sands of power and caring that demarcated those lines within a classroom. Through this example, I hope to show how the middle position—somewhere between student and teacher—taught me about my desires to engage in both powerful and careful educational practices.

During my last semester at the University of Wisconsin, I audited a seminar course in my major area. From the beginning, there was something different about this course for me. While I am still uncertain about the complex changes that occurred within that context, some relevant variables come to mind. First, I had worked for almost four years establishing a relationship with the teacher that existed both within and outside of the classroom. We had been in several classes together, and I felt that I knew his style fairly well. Because of the associated power linked to that knowledge, I felt comfortable attempting to care about and attend to class dynamics when I felt that the current line of conversation was not working for me or for other students in the class. Second, the professor and I had taken the time to talk about student-teacher relationships both in general and as they applied specifically to our interactions. We had learned a bit about each other's fallibility and knew that beyond being teacher and student, we were also people with strengths, weaknesses, aspirations, and disappointments. In various ways, I had the sense that I was both cared for, and worthy of expressing care, in this relationship. Third, the class was small, met in a comfortable place off-campus, and regularly encompassed a meal or snack together. In this way, we cared for our physical needs for comfort and interaction, while in some ways crossing the boundaries that are typically enforced by the traditional positioning of students sitting in rows facing a teacher behind a podium or desk. Fourth, I felt confident about my own work in a role outside that of a student. I successfully completed my dissertation during that semester and had received positive feedback from a variety of sources, both within and outside academe. I had learned a lot on my own volition and felt very "in charge" of my own learning experiences. Fifth, I was not being graded—or degraded, as Page Smith (1990) suggests.

While I completed the majority of the assigned work for the class (and additional work that I thought would add to class discussion), I regarded the teacher's feedback on my participation as *one* perspective, rather than *the* perspective. My valuing of people in this class was based on much more than student or teacher status. In my mind, I was able to more clearly see how each member of our discussion group could both contribute to and learn from our interactions. We were all powerful and, therefore, had the responsibility to care for each other.

Although undoubtedly other factors played a part in making this experience different from previous ones, I believe that those listed here serve a useful purpose in exploring my transforming definitions of power and caring as I moved from student to teacher. I learned that I enjoyed power, to some extent. As a teacher/student, I experienced a power that gave me the opportunity to care for myself and others. I read additional material and developed unassigned summaries and critiques of texts. I brought copies of additional readings that I thought would further the class members' learning about a given issue. I liked being in control of my learning, while attempting to contribute to others'. For various reasons, power seemed to be circulating through me this time, and was finally palpable. Power was indeed alive, and I was invigorated by it.

My role as a student/teacher was complicated by various other identities, attitudes, and experiences and was situated within a unique context. I was more than a student, just as teachers are more than teachers. As feminist teachers and students who value inclusive classrooms wherein power is used to care about, for, and with others, we have choices, opportunities, and responsibilities to recognize the strengths and challenges of our own multiple positions and those of others. It is only then that educational participants can shape practices aimed at creating an inclusive society that discovers and utilizes the potential of its actors. This goal, though, is not as simple as it seems. I turn now to the other side and to my attempts to enact these emerging feminist beliefs from the standpoint of a teacher.

Scene Two: Finding the Ruptures in Power and Caring

It seemed I had come too late to my realizations about the various forms teaching and learning interactions could take. After more than two decades of schooling, I had finally got it. I thought I had some substantial control over my own learning. While this control was admittedly a comforting feeling, I recognized the instability of that feeling and its illusory qualities. The time had come to move on.

When I arrived at Louisiana State University to take an assistant professor position, power issues related to my newly acquired "teacher" status were immediately apparent. I remember very clearly the first time a student, who was an African American woman, walked into my office. While I was dressed quite informally and was in the middle of doing manual labor (moving boxes into my office), the student seemed to immediately acknowledge my position as a professor. I remember the unnerving feeling, more than the details, of this situation. The student asked about an upcoming class I was teaching and about my work. I wondered why she was acting so strangely, why she cared. Why was I immediately given a respect that I had to fight for with many professors as a graduate student? Was this related to the South? Our races? Our positions as teacher and student? Through her questions and interest in my work, this person cared for me as an intellectual, perhaps in an effort to get me to use a presumed power to care for her progress in her academic program. I knew at that moment, as I went to work trying to convince her that I was a "normal"[1] person, that I had, in this situation, crossed to the other side.

In the first few weeks of my graduate level class that fall, I had similar deliberations about enacting power and caring as I attempted to stretch my role to include active educational participation. After the first day of class, I wrote the following in my teaching journal:

> I realized that most people looked at me when they were introducing them-selves, rather than at their other colleagues. The people in the class are so experienced and have so much to offer. . . . Should we always push as far as we can? Or should we place barriers in front of ourselves to limit our experiences if we don't think we can contribute? . . . In some sense, if I don't speak out and take an active part in this discourse, I will live and die without being heard—without making a difference. (1996b)

I started this entry concerned that students were talking primarily to me instead of to their other class colleagues. I wanted to immediately refute the idea that all students would need to respond to and craft their "answers" for me. This concern, though, quickly turned to a concern about my need or desire to participate. I wanted to enact power to care for oth-ers, but I also wanted to use that power to insist my contributions be at-tended to—and cared for—as well. While I didn't want to leave anyone out, my gendered role of being a nurturer, while useful and expected in some ways, threatened to push my contribution out of the conversations.

I soon learned that even if I had wanted to remain silent, students' strong expectations for teacher direction would have made that very dif-ficult. Power and caring were both part of my responsibility as a feminist educator. I had to discover how to enact them in a way that was useful, both for students and for myself.

On the second night of this class, I reflected again on the ways in which power and caring can be manifested in educational environments:

> I hope that people are soon able to find more of a voice in arguing with each other. I hope I continue to keep learning how to do that better. . . . We do have some caretakers in the class. I'm one of them. We want there to be disruption, but we want others to disrupt each other within the bounds of our own nor-malcy. What a fiasco we've got going on here. What does the phrase, "Be nice" really mean? There's been some discussion that it means different things in different cultures (Moffatt 1989; hooks 1994). Doesn't it relate to what we think our end goal for somebody should be? If we love or care for someone, shouldn't we want an *outcome* to be the best possible for them? Therefore, maybe it's not the process, but the end that would be most important. I guess I really don't subscribe to that view, though. How could I when we're always in process? Therefore, what we're doing right now needs to be important. It can't be put off until we know more or until we feel more competent. We need to engage with Each Other, Each Time in caring ways that reflect our constructed hopes and desires. We're always operating with a working definition. (1996b)

Again, this entry demonstrated my struggles to move from being a feminist student who was concerned primarily with my own interactions in the classroom, to a feminist teacher who used my power to ensure caring interactions of all involved. That change of focus, though, does not lead to clear and distinct ways of behaving in relation to power and caring. In an effort to care, can and should we enact power over others? When and how? To what degree is it our choice to do that? I was beginning to learn that power was a fluid and reciprocal relationship in educational interactions. In other words, the power to care about students was only possible when students enacted power to care about what I could offer them.

In the final example I present here, I struggled with opening class discussion so much that I minimized what I could contribute to the interchange. After the third meeting of this class, I wrote:

> In class we talked about feminism—and brainstormed words that students associated with feminism. We put them all on the board—I felt somewhat radical writing "lesbians" and "bitchy" on the board. I didn't share what I knew about feminism with students, though. In fact, I really didn't include any of my adjectives or "thought words" on the board. I feel like I may have missed an opportunity to let them question me in terms of my experience thinking about and working within feminism. I also feel like I didn't provide any sort of "closure" whatsoever. Now, I know that's OK according to my own epistemologies and pedagogical preferences, but it sure felt uneasy—like they wanted the answer and I didn't give it to them. Maybe in class next week I'll give them an opportunity to ask me about feminism and my thoughts if they're interested. (1996b)

While I have consistently received very positive feedback on this particular class session from a variety of students, I wonder whether this was the most useful approach to our learning. The environment I helped to craft did a few things well, I think. First, it opened up the discussion in a safe way, so that even though students knew I supported feminism, they voiced both positive and derogatory views of the feminisms that they had encountered in their lived experiences. I cared about students and their perspectives on one of my primary political commitments. Second, the class provided students with an opportunity to contribute and have every contribution valued, regardless of their contradictions. Third, it provided a forum through which students could share their perspectives with each other and, in doing so, could learn from each other's experiences. On the other hand, I struggled with my participation. While admittedly I enacted power in initiating this discussion in class, my beliefs were only implicitly stated during this meeting. In trying to care about students and respect their views, I chose not to enact the "teacher role" who "taught" them historical and political information about feminist movement. In crafting an "open" space, I relinquished my power to care about the knowledge that I might have been able to share.

Scene Three: Reconsidering Power Ruptures in Classroom Practices

As evidenced in the discussion above, I have spent much time deliberating over the desired roles of teachers and students in feminist education, or rather what I desired. Literature on feminist pedagogy, while helpful in a variety of ways, does not provide me with easy or certain answers about the enactment of various feminist principles in my classrooms. It would violate its own assertions if it attempted to do so, since an acknowledgment of the personal as political necessitates an examination of relationships as uniquely embedded in particular contexts. The challenge of engaging with/in personally and locally defined teaching and learning practices has been appealing to me as I struggle with the issues raised in and outside of various classrooms.

Recently, I inadvertently initiated an incident that provoked the many complexities of trying to utilize my power in caring ways as a teacher. In a class session focusing on teaching and learning relationships, I proposed a change in the syllabus. While I believed that I was contributing to students' learning of class material, the discussion that unfolded taught me about the effects of power and caring in educational discourse as well.

As is customary in the classes I teach, I address administrative issues at the beginning of class so that we can move onto an unencumbered dialogue about the class texts for the rest of the time. That day, I proposed to revise the syllabus by omitting several readings and replacing them with a writing assignment (with a maximum of five pages) reflecting on the readings that we had already covered. After I handed out my proposal, everyone was silent as they reviewed the terms. While no one immediately objected, the rousing appreciation that I expected for my flexibility did not occur. What I perceived to be an act of care on my part was apparently not being welcomed by others in the room. Instead, people started asking clarifying questions. Eventually, one student expressed her discomfort with the change and her reluctance to support it.

In my efforts to understand her hesitancy and other students' less than enthusiastic responses, I asked them if they thought the writing would take more time than their readings would have. I said that I needed to reflect, not just race through additional readings, and asked, "Aren't you feeling that, too?" I wondered why they weren't unquestioningly embracing this teacher-supported break to reflect on what they were learning through our class this semester. I told them that I wouldn't be grading their papers except to indicate that they had turned them in. I merely wanted to see the writing so that I could dialogue with each student as an individual. Without extensive discussion, we came to an "agreement" that we would have these reflection papers due in two weeks instead of one. We then moved to our readings for the day, one of which (ironically) was Elizabeth Ellsworth's (1989) piece entitled, "Why doesn't this feel empowering?: Working through the repressive myths of liberatory pedagogy."

Given these events and the complexity of the issues that Ellsworth proposes in her work, I might have anticipated that we had not yet finished the discussion about the changed syllabus. By the end of the class, students had told me in many ways that my actions in proposing this change were both useful and problematic. They often invoked themes found in Ellsworth's work to support their concern. While some students thought it would be helpful to have time to reflect without having the responsibility of additional readings, others reminded me that they had not expressed the need to reflect. I was the one who had made that determination. I was presuming to know what was best. And as Jennifer Gore (1990, 63) suggested:

> In attempts to empower others we need to acknowledge that our agency has limits, that we might "get it wrong" in assuming we know what would be empowering for others, and that no matter what our aims or how we go about "empowering," our efforts will be partial and inconsistent.

Some students believed that it might be helpful for them to have my feedback on their work as a way to improve their writing skills, especially before the final paper was to be handed in and graded. Others indicated that they felt an incredible pressure to "produce" "good" writing if I was to read it and that it was this pressure that they were resisting. Finally, as I was trying to reassure them that this exercise was not about me grading them but was instead about their learning and reflection, one student told me, "We don't trust you that much." My immediate response was, "You shouldn't." With Ellsworth's caution that we can never be divested of the complexities of our identities in teaching and learning settings, I recognized the instability of my guarantees, the flexibility of my assurances, and the sound "rationale" that students were using when they distrusted my attempts to enact power and care.

While this statement will probably be eternally problematic in my mind, my initial reaction was one mired in compassion, intellectual stimulation, and respect for the classroom discourse that we had created, because it had evoked such a "risky" statement. I felt trusted because this student had the courage to tell me that his trust for me only went so far. I was reminded of Patricia Hill Collins' (1991) insistence on the importance of the discussions we have about the relationship between trust and truth: "Epistemological choices about who to trust, what to believe, and why something is true are not benign academic issues. Instead, these concerns tap the fundamental question of which versions of truth will prevail and shape thought and action" (202–3). The relationship between trust and classroom interaction was emphasized as others began to voice their agreement with the student who expressed some initial hesitancy in embracing my proposed changes. They said that they had been feeling similarly but did not feel comfortable to speak their thoughts because they did not know me well enough. The limits of our relationships were educating all of us about the complexities of feminist teaching and learning.

Throughout this discussion, I felt honored by students' forthrightness with me about their perceptions of the classroom discourses that we were struggling within. Yet, I also felt trapped by the constraints of pedagogy that attempts to enact power in efforts to empower and care in efforts to ensure comfort, ease, and positive outcomes in learning. I attempted to "care" about others through my "flexibility" in the use of my teacher-power. But I realized that my caring had different effects for individual students and was not desired or requested by all students. As I tried to change the relationships I had with students by providing "better learning opportunities" for them, I came to see that with various power sources that I claim, *I do not know the effects that my caring will have.* Further, if I proclaim to enact care in classrooms, while simultaneously trying to reposition teacher-student dichotomies through the lenses of liberatory ideals, my caring becomes suspect. If I can never omit power from our classrooms, then my assertions that any part of our relationship can be free from that dynamic come dangerously close to lying.

Final Thoughts

What then are we dealing with when researchers and teachers are made to rehearse the method for so long that they forget the purpose of the rehearsal and they all begin to do the two-step and try to eliminate from the dance floor those who would do the wild interpretive dance? Is method a need to define? To critique? To remove?

—Leck 1994, 93.

I learned many things about power and caring in feminist education through these classroom interactions. First, I learned that regardless of the seemingly clear lines between teachers and students in classroom contexts, all educational participants have the ability to enact the power to care. Power and caring are interwoven to form the wire on which we perch our performances: wild and interpretive, or otherwise. The embodiment of multiple educational positions, though, dictates a balancing act that is always being modified. Learning and teaching in feminist classrooms depend on continual attention to the ways in which our power is taking effect, and the ways that our caring practices are being perceived.

Second, I relearned the importance of actively recognizing and embodying both teacher and learner positions when I interact with others in educational environments. Even when positioned as an institutionally sanctioned "teacher," I find that what has been conceptualized as the "other side" of the teacher-student dichotomy has qualities that are far too appealing to me to give up. Learning is embedded in teaching; to tear one from the other would greatly diminish the possibilities for either. For students, though, it is risky for teachers to desire the "student side" and claim that crossing over is entirely possible and educationally useful. As students reminded me in the incident described above, our pleasure, power, and ability to care is marked and modified always by our multiple identity positions—one of which places us on one side or another of the teacher-student dichotomy—regardless of the pleasure class participants were deriving from our experiences. Carmen Luke warns, "Pedagogy without a locus of authority thus risks deceit: embodied difference and differential power access camouflaged under false pretense of allegedly equal subject positions" (1996, 297). It would be disingenuous and dangerous for me to ever mislead students to believe that we are in all ways equal; I can always retreat back to my side, a side which would not currently welcome them. It is dangerous for students if teachers forget their axes of privilege. In my current transition from student to teacher, it is most likely easier for me to remember multiple positions now than it will be after many years. I am learning that the assumptions and practices of an academy that positions us on one side or the other of a teacher-student dichotomy have already begun to restructure my thinking.

Third, our very modes of learning are deeply embedded in assumptions of which we are not always aware. For example, in the third scene above, I thought I was using my power to care by giving students the "opportunity" to "reflect." My "caring," though, had strict parameters. Students had to reflect on paper, to be handed in to a teacher, who at the end of the term assigns a grade. I would imagine that no student in the class felt free to say during this assignment, "I've already been reflecting, teacher, so I don't need to do this assignment, but thanks for the opportunity." Reflect. Present an image back. If students are reflecting for themselves, why is it necessary for a teacher to be involved with the process? At the same time, could it be helpful for a teacher to be involved? This tension, I believe, will be important to consider in future interactions.

Finally, I came to believe that it is imperative that we, as feminist educators, consciously model what we value and how we think values should take shape in educational environments. As Jo Anne Pagano believes, "To act is to theorize" (1991, 194). Our actions become statements of our beliefs, of the theories that guide us as educators. Decisions about how to interact with others are not easy, though, and require a willingness to continue movement around prescribed dichotomies in order to view situations from other locations. We need to realize the ways in which who we are as teachers is defined by the students with whom we are interacting. Further, the ways in which teachers and students can be powerful is related to the ways in which we have constructed caring relationships within our classrooms. Understandably, the struggles and choices we encounter in educational settings are not clear or predictable in their effects. Yet we have an obligation as the ones who are vested with an assumed power, even if that power is easily and regularly disrupted, to assess and address the effects that it is having on our classrooms.

The choices we make in our classrooms as we interact with students are vestiges of our beliefs about what educational experiences are supposed to be like. We need to share our struggles with students as we negotiate relationships supported and disrupted by power and caring practices. By our modeling, we teach students what we think it means to be feminist educational participants. Simultaneously, though, feminist teachers and students can model to each other the complexities of using our power to care about each other and the educational environments that we create.

Note

1. I wonder as I write this: What is "normal?" Is my student status normal? Is my teacher status normal? It is troubling to me that I want again to "care" for others by diminishing the unconditional/unproven respect that my voice accords. I want to "reduce" my "power" because I have experienced the hurtful place of being on the opposite sides of those who have seemed to hoard it. Poststructural conceptions of power, then, are difficult for me here. If power supposedly circulates and acts through each of us, why do some persons feel like they are unable to find or enact their power? For example, while Sue Middleton (1993) proposes that women's silence can be a form of resistance, I struggle with knowing that my silence, my "resistance," limited my options for participation in educational environments. My shaping of my own and others' knowing was sadly lacking. I wondered about myself and others who chose silence, "What knowledge . . . do students have of college classrooms that makes the decision not to talk a 'realistic' decision?"

(Karp and Yoels 1976/1994, 457). To what degree is silence a decision to resist or disengage with the acting out of power and care in classrooms?

Works Cited

Alcoff, Linda. 1988. "Cultural Feminism versus Poststructuralism: The Identity Crisis in Feminist Theory." In *Reconstructing the Academy: Women's Education and Women's Studies,* ed. Elizabeth Minnich, Jean O'Barr, and Rachel Rosenfeld, 257–288. Chicago: University of Chicago Press.

Bennett, Roberta S. 1991. "Empowerment = Work over Time: Can There Be Feminist Pedagogy in the Sport Sciences?" *Journal of Physical Education, Recreation, and Dance* 62:62–67, 75.

Bezucha, Robert J. 1985. "Feminist Pedagogy as a Subversive Activity." In *Gendered Subjects: The Dynamics of Feminist Teaching,* ed. Margo Culley and Catherine Portuges, 81–95. Boston: Routledge & Kegan Paul.

Bloland, Harland G. 1995. "Postmodernism and Higher Education." *Journal of Higher Education* 66(5):521–559.

Brown, Julie. 1992. "Theory or Practice—What Exactly Is Feminist Pedagogy?" *Journal of General Education* 41:51–63.

Bunch, Charlotte, and Sandra Pollack, eds. 1983. *Learning Our Way: Essays in Feminist Education.* Trumansburg, NY: Crossing.

Collins, Patricia Hill. 1991. *Black Feminist Thought: Knowledge, Consciousness, and the Politics of Empowerment.* New York: Routledge.

Culley, Margo, and Catherine Portuges, eds. 1985. *Gendered Subjects: The Dynamics of Feminist Teaching.* Boston: Routledge and Kegan Paul.

Damrosch, David. 1995. *We Scholars: Changing the Culture of the University.* Cambridge, MA: Harvard.

Ellsworth, Elizabeth. 1989. "Why Doesn't This Feel Empowering? Working Through the Repressive Myths of Critical Pedagogy." *Harvard Educational Review* 59(3): 297–324.

Foucault, Michel. 1978. *The History of Sexuality: An Introduction.* Vol. 1. New York: Random House.

Frye, Marilyn. 1980. "On Second Thought. . . ." *Radical Teacher* 17:37–38.

Gore, Jennifer. 1990. "What We Can Do for You! What *Can* 'We' Do for 'You'? Struggling over Empowerment in Critical and Feminist Pedagogy." *Educational Foundations* 4(3): 5–26.

Gore, Jennifer. 1993. *The Struggle for Pedagogies: Critical and Feminist Discourses as Regimes of Truth.* New York: Routledge.

Heald, Susan. 1989. "The Madwoman out of the Attic: Feminist Teaching in the Margins." *Resources for Feminist Research* 18:22–26.

hooks, bell. 1994. *Teaching to Transgress: Education as the Practice of Freedom.* New York: Routledge.

Karp, David A., and William C. Yoels. [1976] 1994. "The College Classroom: Some Observations on the Meanings of Student Participation." In *Teaching and Learning in the College Classroom,* eds. Kenneth A. Feldman and Michael B. Paulsen, 451–464. Needham Heights, MA: Ginn.

Lather, Patti. 1991. *Getting Smart: Feminist Research and Pedagogy With/in the Postmodern.* New York: Routledge.

Leck, Glorianne M. 1994. "Queer Relations with Educational Research." In *Power and Method: Political Activism and Educational Research,* ed. Andrew Gitlin, 77–96. New York: Routledge.

Lewis, Magda Gere. 1993. *Without a Word: Teaching Beyond Women's Silence.* New York: Routledge.

Luke, Carmen. 1996. "Feminist Pedagogy Theory: Reflections on Power and Authority." *Educational Theory* 46(3):283–302.

Maher, Frances A., and Mary Kay Thompson Tetreault. 1994. *The Feminist Classroom.* New York: Basic Books.

Mayberry, Maralee, and Margaret N. Rees. 1997. "Feminist Pedagogy, Interdisciplinary Praxis, and Science Education." *National Women's Studies Association Journal* 9(1):57–75.

Middleton, Sue. 1993. *Educating Feminists: Life Histories and Pedagogy.* New York: Teachers College.

———. 1995. "Doing Feminist Educational Theory: A Post-modernist Perspective." *Gender and Education* 7(1):87–100.

Moffatt, Michael. 1989. *Coming of Age in New Jersey: College and American Culture.* New Brunswick, NJ: Rutgers University.

Nicholson, Carol. 1995. "Postmodern Feminisms." In *Education and the Postmodern Condition,* ed. Michael Peters, 75–85. Westport, CT: Bergin & Garvey.

Noddings, Nel. 1992. *The Challenge to Care in Schools: An Alternative Approach to Education.* New York: Teachers College.

Orner, Mimi. 1992. "Interrupting the Calls for Student Voice in 'Liberatory' Education: A Feminist Poststructuralist Perspective." In *Feminism and Critical Pedagogy,* eds. Carmen Luke and Jennifer Gore, 74–89. New York: Routledge.

Pagano, Jo Anne. 1991. "Moral Fictions: The Dilemma of Theory and Practice." In *Stories Lives Tell: Narrative and Dialogue in Education,* eds. Carol Witherell and Nel Noddings, 193–206. Teachers College: New York.

Ropers-Huilman, Becky. 1996a. "Shaping an Island of Power and Change: Creating a Feminist Poststructural Teaching Discourse." Unpublished doctoral dissertation, University of Wisconsin-Madison.

———. 1996b. Teaching Journal. Unpublished.

———. 1997. "Constructing Feminist Teachers: Complexities of Identity." *Gender and Education* 9(3):327–343.

———. 1998. *Feminist Teaching in Theory and Practice: Situating Power and Knowledge in Poststructural Classrooms.* New York: Teachers College.

Sawicki, Jana. 1991. *Disciplining Foucault: Feminism, Power, and the Body.* New York: Routledge.

Scott, Joan Wallach. 1990. "Deconstructing Equality-versus-difference: Or, the Uses of Poststructuralist Theory for Feminism." In *Conflicts in Feminism,* eds. Marianne Hirsch and Evelyn Fox Keller, 134–148. New York: Routledge.

Seal. 1994. "Prayer for the Dying." *Seal* [compact disc]. Burbank, CA: Wea/Warner.

Smith, Page. 1990. *Killing the Spirit: Higher Education in America.* New York: Viking.

Weedon, Chris. 1987. *Feminist Practice and Poststructuralist Theory.* Oxford: Basil Blackwell.

Weiler, Kathleen. 1988. *Women Teaching for Change: Gender, Class and Power.* New York: Bergin & Garvey.

CHAPTER FOUR

Beyond Essentialisms: Team Teaching Gender and Sexuality

DEBBIE STORRS AND JOHN MIHELICH

The last decade has witnessed reform in higher education in terms of both curriculum and pedagogical practice. One important direction of curriculum reform has been toward a race, class, and gender integrated multicultural curriculum. Women's studies has played a key role in providing such courses. In addition to advocating for a multicultural and gender-inclusive curriculum, many feminist scholars have pushed for pedagogical reform, arguing that we must attend to *how* we teach as well as *what* we teach. Part of how we teach includes *who* teaches what we teach.

These questions informed our development of a team-taught course on gender and sexuality. The focus of the course is rooted in our shared professional interests in the critique of and challenge to essentialist socio-cultural constructions of gender and also on the intersection of class and race with those constructions. In both the course and in the present chapter we confront essentialist-gendered constructions on two fronts. First, we employ an inclusive curriculum, including a historical and cross-cultural comparative approach, to problematize contemporary American gender constructions and assumptions. We move beyond a static notion of femininity and female experience, to the processual dichotomous construction of femininity in relation to masculinity, to ultimately a more fluid understanding of genders and sexualities. Secondly, our mixed-gender, cross-discipline teaching team, through methods and example, explicitly and implicitly defies the essentialist notions and expectations produced by American gender constructions, including assumptions about who should teach what to whom.

This essay reflects our attempts to promote educational reform toward liberatory education, which is really about broadening what is taught, how it is taught, and preparing students to be part of the solution in working toward nonoppressive gender relations. We first review the larger debates concerning reform in higher education, then we situate our position within these debates, and finally we discuss our approach to the reform questions of who should teach what to whom.

Originally published in the Spring 1998 issue of the *NWSA Journal*.

What Is Taught

Curriculum integration involves attempts to broaden general education by including a wider range of experience, perspectives, and knowledge. Many universities have implemented mandatory courses on race/gender/ethnic relations of one form or another as part of the undergraduate curriculum.[1] Women's studies courses increasingly fulfill many universities' diversity requirements. The growing institutionalization and "mainstreaming" of women's studies at many universities make women's studies a potentially important player in successfully transforming the curriculum.

While historically women's studies has concentrated on white U.S. women's experiences, programs are increasingly attentive to issues of diversity. The focus on diversity expands women's studies curriculum in two ways. First, the vast majority of women's studies scholars and teachers recognize how women's differing social locations, particularly in terms of race, social class, and sexuality, within the United States significantly shape their experiences (Butler 1991; Bulkin 1980; Gardner, Dean, and Mckaig 1989). The experiences and contributions of women of color, working-class women, and lesbian and bisexual women are increasingly addressed, although techniques to illustrate the intersections of race, gender, and class in the experiences of women take different forms. Secondly, curriculum reform within women's studies encourages a globalization of women's studies. Teachers and scholars have broadened their analysis beyond their national borders, examining, for example, the relationship between industrialized and underprivileged nations on women's experiences and status (De Danaan 1990).

The debate over how to best incorporate feminist principles in ways that reflect the diversity of women's experiences reveals the range of feminist pedagogical practices that characterize women's studies as well as more mainstream academic departments. Chow (1985) delineates three teaching strategies that have been employed in sociology to incorporate the perspectives of women of color. These strategies are also used by feminist educators in women's studies and gender studies as they grapple with the complexity of women's issues and experiences.

The first approach used by scholars to integrate diversity in the study of women is the "comparison strategy." This is a typical strategy used in gender studies courses where men's and women's experiences are compared or in women's studies where white women and women of color are compared. The advantage of this technique is that it leads to a broader exposure of materials, and students begin to explore the diversity within the groups of women and men. The disadvantage of this approach is that all too often women of color or women in general become viewed by students as an appendage to the real focus of the course. In short, women of color in women's studies courses or women in gender studies can become tokenized (regardless of teacher intent). This strategy fails to question the paradigm that assumes white women and men are central categories of analysis to which other groups are compared (Chow 1985, 303–4).

The second approach identified by Chow is the "special treatment" technique in which women of color, lesbian women, or international women are bracketed and discussed in independent courses. The advantage of such a course is that students are given more time to explore in-depth issues and experiences of subgroups of women. The problem with this approach is that typically the independent courses are not institutionalized; they are not a part of the regular curriculum. The institutional marginality of these courses can convey a subtle message about the relevancy and importance of such topics. The same holds true within gender studies where courses focused on male experiences are offered independently of those that focus on female experiences. The division of independent female and male courses also runs the risk of neglecting the relationship between femininity and masculinity as they are constructed in the United States and elsewhere. Many women's studies programs and courses resist incorporating a gendered analysis that also includes men's experiences. This resistance is based on the historical, political, and philosophical motivation of women's studies to position women and women's experiences at the center of analysis and curriculum, unlike traditional and mainstream curriculum. While we support the important project to center women's experiences in women's studies, we feel that an effective gendered analysis should incorporate men's experiences at some point. Gender studies and more mainstream disciplines such as sociology and anthropology perhaps can provide a gendered analysis that incorporates both women's and men's experiences without diluting the practical and philosophical basis of women's studies (Chow 1985, 304–5).

The third strategy to incorporate diversity into education is a "mainstreaming" approach in which women of color are incorporated into courses about women, and diverse groups of men and women are incorporated into classes on gender and sexuality as part of the existing curriculum (Chow 1985, 305–6). This approach offers the advantage of shifting the paradigm and student's thinking in more inclusive ways. It is most useful in teaching about sex and gender because the approach posits sexualities and genders as the focus of inquiry and then uses cross-cultural examples to illustrate both the variation and similarities within and across cultures. The major limitation of this approach is the abundance of material on the topic, which often makes it difficult to incorporate it all into one course. Teachers face the task of limiting the scope of classes in order to make them manageable but still broad enough to reveal the variation, change, and fluidity of gender and sexuality systems. We continually grapple with this problem in our course but attempt to reach a reasonable balance between breadth and manageability.

How It Is Taught

Many feminist scholars, while generally agreeing on the necessity of race and gender inclusive curriculum, argue that pedagogy is a key site in the transformation of our educational system (Carby 1992, Schniedewind 1993). For example, Flintoff (1993) argues that we cannot focus simply on "what is taught and learned [but we need to focus on] how it is taught in the sense of the broadest social relations within which learning takes place" (p. 74).

Women's studies programs have a long history of challenging the social relations of learning. Several characteristics differentiate a feminist approach to education from a traditional one. One of the fundamental goals of a feminist approach to education is the replacement of hierarchical relations with egalitarian and cooperative relations. Schniedewind (1993) provides concrete examples of how this goal can be met through cooperative learning and evaluation methods including student task groups, the well-known jigsaw format, group outcome grades, and contract grading. A second goal, correlated with the first, more specifically addresses the visibility and vocality of both students and instructors. Feminist teachers encourage students to express themselves and help make the link between their own personal experiences to larger political, social, cultural, and economic structures that shape their lives. Rejecting hegemonic views of society, feminist educators attempt to provide students with opportunities to counter dominant understandings through an analysis of their personal experiences. These two tenets are embraced in order to achieve a more encompassing goal of empowering students and faculty. Instructors approach this goal in different ways, but a common practice is to help students view themselves as active agents of social change. Scanlon (1993) suggests ways to encourage students to become political activists. She recommends several assignments that require students to participate in events outside the classroom as well as group projects that bring feminism alive.

While feminist educators share the vision of liberatory education through cooperative methods and egalitarian relations, the difficulties of applying feminist ideals in educational arenas are highlighted by recent scholars. Feminists educators explore a range of difficulties typically experienced including student resistance (Bohmer and Briggs 1991), classroom dynamics (Cannon 1990), and emotional responses when teaching about oppression and hierarchy (Lee 1993). Others have been critical of the very pedagogical practices typically employed by women's studies teachers. For example, Ellsworth (1989) reveals how many of these practices actually serve to reinforce relations of domination because rationalist assumptions and institutional educational philosophy restrict full escape. She challenges the belief that classrooms are safe spaces for students to speak freely about their experiences because they are essentially microcosms of the larger racist, sexist, and homophobic society in which we live. She also criticizes the ability of teachers to help bring subjugated knowledges to the forefront or center of analysis when they too are not free from their own social locations and internalized oppressions. Ellsworth's criticisms reveal the inherent difficulties of developing a feminist and empowering educational experience within hierarchical institutions. She advocates the use of "affinity groups," groups of students—clustered around particular points of identity—that meet outside of the classroom to provide safer places for students to share their contextual, multiple, and contradictory voices. While her assessment of commonly used pedagogical techniques is helpful, she falls prey to a common problem in women's studies that we discuss in the next section.

Who Should Teach What to Whom

A key debate within multicultural curriculum reform centers on the question of who should teach what and to whom. Specifically, the debate has focused on the appropriate role of white males in teaching about oppression and social inequality (see, for example, Gerschick 1993). The preference for female instructors in women's studies courses is premised on utilizing personal experience as the basis of feminist pedagogy (Culley and Portuges 1985). This preference stems from an implicit assumption that only those who have experienced gender oppression have the knowledge and right to speak about it.

In a classic argument, Jaggar (1977–1978) argues that men should not teach courses on feminism because of men and women's different social locations, privileges, and experiences. While Jaggar concedes that men may learn about sexual discrimination through formal mechanisms, their inability to draw on personal experiences severely limits their effectiveness as teachers. Jaggar also argues that men should not teach courses on feminism because it replicates and reinforces the gendered power differences that typify universities and society at large. This philosophical and political basis has shaped the curriculum and the gendered make-up of women's studies.

Recently, however, feminists have criticized such a politics on several fronts. First, because it rests on a universal notion of women's experiences, a politics of experience ignores the diversity of that experience. The notion of a common oppression based on gender is widely critiqued by hooks (1989), Spellman (1988), and others who highlight the ways in which race, ethnicity, social class, sexuality, and other social locations differentially shape women's lives. The globalization of women's studies only complicates the notion of common oppression. A cross-cultural approach, as we discuss later, helps illustrate the social construction of gender systems and further exposes the extent of diversity of women's experience. However, the number of instructors who can draw from actual cross-cultural experience to enhance their teaching effectiveness is probably minimal.

Secondly, a politics of experience often has the unintended result of reducing one's complex identity into its most visible component. For example, "a male professor . . . is typically reduced to his 'maleness,' an Asian professor to his or her 'Asianness,' a lesbian professor to her 'lesbianness,' and so on" (Fuss 1989, p. 116). A politics of experience essentializes both students and instructors and presumes singular notions of identity. The inadequacy and critique of this presumption, voiced by many feminists of color, is illustrated by the famous title, *All the Women Are White, All the Blacks Are Men, But Some of Us Are Brave: Black Women's Studies* (Hull, Scott, and Smith 1982). The title succinctly captures the historical invisibility of women of color which results from simplified and rigid notions of identity.

Last, in addition to dismissing aspects of experience and facets of one's identity, such a politics masks the relationality, and the accompanying fluidity, that exists between male/female, black/white, and other dichotomously socially constructed identities and social relations. As Lucal (1996) and others note, the traditional approach to teaching about race locates race as something only people of color possess and experience, masking the privileges associated with whiteness. More importantly, the traditional approach to race masks the relationality of racial categories, identities, and privileges. The intelligibility and subjectivity of whiteness, whether consciously articulated as an identity or not, is necessarily based on the constructed boundaries of nonwhiteness.

The same relationality and invisibility of hierarchy exists for gendered and sexual categories, identities, and relations. As members of gender categories constructed in relation to one another, both men and women are gendered beings. Yet, men often lack a gendered consciousness and identity much the same way whites lack a racial consciousness (McIntosh 1992; Kimmel and Messner 1992). This obliviousness is a basic element of the privilege of dominance (Helms and Carter 1990). The lack of male instructors within gender inclusive curriculum implicitly supports the perception of men as genderless, excuses men from taking responsibility for gender privileges, and allows them to evade (or denies them the opportunity to attempt) the often challenging task of teaching emotional and personally relevant topics. In addition, if courses on gender fulfill university curriculum requirements, one must teach these couses to male students. Yet, the logic of a politics of experience would preclude men from understanding oppression, women from teaching it to men, or both.

A key argument for female teachers in women's studies is that the development of rapport based on similarities between students and teachers may increase teaching effectiveness. Rapport between female instructors and female students founded on similarities in the experience of oppression may be one avenue toward teaching effectiveness, but, as we see above, this similarity-based rapport rests on the problematic assumption that the experience is shared. Further, teaching about women or gender is not only about oppressions.[2] Therefore, similarities in the experience of oppression, a politics of experience, does not provide the only, nor perhaps the primary, foundation on which we can build rapport. For instance, one of the most useful foundations we find to build rapport beyond similarity of experience, is through acknowledging the diversity of students' experience. We also develop rapport through an environment of gender equality in the classroom promoted by our interactions with one another as instructors and with students. Later in this chapter we discuss more thoroughly our interactions with one another.

While we are critical of Jaggar's conclusions, we agree that men and women do have different social experiences by virtue of the social construction of gender in our society. Likewise, men teaching about women's experiences can reinforce the gender hierarchy that exists. We agree on these basic fundamentals but believe the insistence on female instructors teaching about women's experiences, feminism, or gender fails to capture adequately the ways in which, men too, are gendered beings or how masculinity is socially (not necessarily) constructed in relation to femininity. It also evades the practical reality that approximately one half of the student population that we are trying to teach about equity is male.

We now turn to our mixed-gendered team teaching approach as an example of one creative, constructive response to the problems outlined by Jaggar and ourselves. We believe a team-teaching model, incorporating the personal knowledge we have as gendered beings, but not relying exclusively on a politics of experience, presents a partial solution to the problems of men teaching about gender. Team teaching allows us to challenge essentialist assumptions about and within gender categorization and to include our lived experiences as a white man and a woman of color in the classroom when appropriate. We also believe that our cross-cultural comparative class content facilitates the problematizing and understanding of gender constructions.

What follows is a discussion of our experiences in a course which focuses on cross-cultural constructions of gender and sexuality. We offer our experiences not as a blueprint for others to follow but as a way to open the dialogue on how to team teach inclusive curriculum in ways that effectively deconstruct the limiting and essentialist notions of gender and sexuality, both in terms of the curriculum and in terms of teaching.

The Course: Culture, Gender, and Sexuality

The Team

One of the advantages of team teaching is the potential to use, when appropriate, the individual areas of expertise, teaching styles, and personal experiences of two or more gendered, racialized human beings. One of our team is a male cultural anthropologist with expertise in American culture and psychological anthropology. The other member of the team is a female sociologist whose expertise is in feminist studies and United States race and ethnic relations. Both of us are well versed in theories of gender subordination and stratification. We use our different areas of expertise to develop a course that examines the social construction of gender and sexuality across cultures.

Course Objectives

In our course we undertake a two-pronged approach to challenge the essentialist assumptions underlying the construction of dominant American gender and sexual ideologies. We first confront static, essentialist and ethnocentric notions of gender and sexuality by exploring the varied historical and cross-cultural gender and sexual constructions. Our inclusive curriculum demonstrates the relationality and fluidity as well as the impact of the sociocultural environment in the process of gender constructions and sexual meanings. We also attempt to move beyond student's essentialist expectations of us, as gendered beings, in terms of our shared abilities and knowledge of the topics at hand. Both of these goals point to the overall higher education project of raising awareness and encouraging students to question and critique their own constructions and meanings, in this case as they pertain to gender and sexuality.

The Social Construction of Gender and Sexuality

In order to reveal the multiple expressions of gender and sexualities, we use an interdisciplinary body of literature including case studies from the field of anthropology (we found the work of feminist anthropologists particularly helpful), history, psychology, queer theory, and sociology. Our exploration of both gender and sexuality within one course stems from the recognition of how these two constructs and relations are linked (Kamano and Khor 1996, 128–31).

We begin the course with a thorough discussion of ethnocentrism and cultural relativism and with an explanation of the essentialist-constructionist problematic (see, for example, Abramson and Pinkerton 1995; Stein 1992). We advance the possibility that much of what students think they "know" to be "true" about gender and sexuality is in fact socially constructed. We also argue that, for various reasons, some of which we think we know and some which we don't know, there is both variation and some consistencies in gender constructions across cultures.

Through the use of historical, anthropological, and sociological evidence, we discuss the construction of gender and sexualities and how they are maintained and changed in various sociocultural contexts. Specifically, we examine the sexual practices, meanings, and identities of men and women in various cultures and times.[3] We continually compare and contrast the student's own culture and the practices of the world's other cultures in an effort to make the strange familiar and the familiar strange (Spiro 1982).[4] An understanding of the variation in constructions of gender and sexuality across cultures challenges students' essentialist views about normalcy and naturalness.

In addition to a cross-cultural survey of gender constructions, we examine in depth the construction of masculinity and femininity along with sexualities within particular cultures. In-depth analysis and description, the hallmarks of ethnography, effectively illustrate the relational nature of masculinity and femininity as well as the range of identities, alternative categories, and practices available in any culture at one time. The variation within a culture and social roles, an element of cultural systems often skirted by ethnography (although less so today), is often as informative as a cross-cultural survey in terms of de-essentializing and destabilizing notions of gender.

While not placing United States constructions of gender and sexuality at the center of analysis, we incorporate the work of postmodern feminists and queer theorists who have been at the forefront of challenging categories of sex, sexuality, and gender. Using their insights, we discuss how dominant beliefs about sexuality result in the invisibility and erasure of those who do not conform to our categories. For example, the categories of homosexual and heterosexual, widely accepted by both the United States general public and social scientists, often force those who are bisexual, or who do not fit into one of the dichotomous categories, to choose their "real" identity (see, for example, George 1993; Lorber 1996). This same assumption is partially responsible for the phenomenon of operative transexuals although certainly the medicalization of sexuality is also a key factor. Examining how our own culture has restricted possible categories and reshaped practices and experiences to fit within conventional dichotomous categories is often a difficult idea for students to accept because these categories have become so naturalized and unquestioned. In addition to discussing transgendered and transsexual experiences in the United States, the cross-cultural component adds to this exploration and questions students' conventional beliefs about the dichotomous and essential nature of our own gender and sexual systems. This examination also encourages students to move beyond a politics of identity as we discuss the variation across cultures. Students' logic that only those who experience certain events should be able to accurately discuss them cannot be applied so easily when we address cross-cultural gender and sexual systems.

The politics of experience is clearly inadequate in the cross-cultural study of gender and sexuality. Both of us, while informed and knowledgeable about cultural practices and meanings, have never experienced many of the practices we discuss. Clitoridectomy, purdah, the experiences of hijras, and transvestitism are topics about which we have read extensively, but not personally experienced. We use ethnographies and case studies that describe and explain the context of such practices and identities.

While these are obvious examples of why a politics of experience is limiting, we believe similar situations exist when female instructors teach about United States gender experiences and inequality. Because women differ in terms of class and racial privilege, sexual orientation, physical abilities, cultural traditions, personal biographies, understanding, self-reflection, and so on, being a woman does not inherently provide female instructors with insight into the diverse and lived experiences of all women within the United States or the ability to teach about it.

Gender and Dominance

A second goal in teaching this class is to challenge the essentialist logic of gendered assumptions as they occur in everyday social interaction. We are particularly concerned with classroom interactions and with students' assumptions about instructors. The course content in which we explicitly and critically consider the gender system of American culture inherently supports this challenge. However, focusing on the interactions in the classroom, we take both explicit and implicit pedagogical steps to contest these gendered assumptions. We actively highlight and challenge assumptions and structure our teaching to minimize the opportunity for gendered assumptions to emerge.

One of the many assumptions typically made about the gendered relations between men and women, one that reflects the history of our culture's construction of gender roles, is that men are more dominant than women. Indeed, women who exhibit masculine-identified characteristics are often negatively evaluated. For this reason, as one of our primary goals in team teaching, we consciously attend to and emphasize equality between instructors.

We take several steps to facilitate equality both in terms of the division of actual work for the class and in terms of the presentation. We divide the labor for developing and preparing for the class equally. Equal labor allows both of us the opportunity to optimize our expertise, to present information, and to lead discussions. This also helps assure that class time is equally spent on our expert areas. We closely monitor the actual time spent in front of students leading the lecture or discussion. We attempt to participate equally in discussion periods with both of us commenting on students' remarks or classroom material.

Students' nonverbal behavior, such as body posture and eye contact, are also possible indicators of assumptions. We find that many female students direct their comments, gaze, and body posture to our female teaching member and that male students attempted to interact more with our male teaching member. This is particularly evident in a course with an even number of both genders. We believe this tendency for students to interact more directly with the same sex instructor is the result of both comfort levels and issues of legitimacy/authority. Course evaluations by students indicate that on some topics students felt more comfortable directing their comments to the same sex instructor.

Another possible interpretation of the tendency on the part of male students to interact more directly with our male team member is that it is less an issue of comfort than it is an issue of authority by virtue of his maleness. The female student's preference to interact more directly with our female team member when talking about female sexuality and femininity in the United States is due in part to students' assumptions that they share similar experiences by virtue of being women. We observe that this occurs less when the class is examining and discussing a sexual and gendered practice outside of the United States. This pattern reveals the difficulty, but not the impossibility, of escaping socialization concerning one's own cultural constructions of gender and sexuality in the limited time frame of one semester or quarter. Students find it less difficult to move beyond their gendered assumptions about which sex is more knowledgeable and appropriate when discussing cross-cultural variations in gender and sexual meanings because these are, in many cases, foreign ideas, thus no one gender "owns" them. In fact, our male team teacher's expertise as an anthropologist serves a useful function in more than simply his ethnographic knowledge. Students perceive his anthropological expertise as a legitimate source of knowledge, even when discussing cross-cultural expressions of female sexuality. We believe that as students "grant" male teachers legitimacy as acceptable "knowers" concerning female experience worldwide, students begin to make similar concessions when critically examining United States cultural practices and meanings.

Through our knowledge base and familiarity with feminist perspectives, we believe we effectively challenge students' assumptions that experiential knowledge is the only effective basis for teaching about sex-specific material. For example, one student shared with us that she was initially hesitant to see a man teaching a women's studies course on gender and sexuality. At the end of the course she was pleased that both instructors were teaching the course. We believe her initial hesitation was based on the politics of experience and assumptions that only women can talk about and be sensitive to issues of female sexuality and femininity.

A key method of monitoring interactions of dominance and passivity is to confer with one another during each class break and after each class. At times, we disagree whether one or the other appears dominant but find it helpful to have a quick discussion during break so that any disparity can be rectified in the remaining class time. The monitoring is not always effective in producing equitable time because, although we also divide class topics relatively equally, some class days are weighted more heavily one way or the other, and the discussions sometimes favor one or the other instructor's expertise. At times, one of us is simply more knowledgeable about a topic or better able to respond to students' questions.

Students' evaluations indicate that there is little perception of dominance of either instructor. Students overwhelmingly show that both instructors equally participate in teaching the course in terms of presenting information, leading discussions, and grading responses. Our careful planning of the course topics is essential in preventing any major disparities to develop—we consciously select topics and case studies with which we are both familiar and we have an equal number of topics about which we are specifically knowledgeable.

In addition to our desire to move beyond dominant/passive assumptions of traditional American gender roles, we want to locate ourselves as gendered beings so we can, when appropriate, bring our personal experiences to bear on the classroom. However, we attempt to escape some of the pitfalls of a politics of experience. We often use our personal experiences to illustrate how we are all socialized with gendered messages concerning appropriate behavior.

Our own experiences effectively demonstrate how engendered we all are. For example, in our first discussions on the "work of gender," we look to our own body postures. We point out our male team member's more open gait and larger surrounding physical space as compared to our female team member's stance, as evidence of how we unconsciously act out gender socialization. We review the literature on styles of communication and verbal patterns of dominance and attend to our patterns and those of others.

While we use personal examples and stories when relevant, we are careful not to represent all men or all women through our own gendered experience, pointing out how other social relations can shape and alter gendered experiences. Since we are trying to move beyond the limits imposed by a politics of experience, we do not divide the class material and presentation along gender lines. Together we provide information and lead discussions about the meaning and construction of masculinity and femininity just as we both talk about same-sex and cross-sex relations. Teaching based on personal experience would limit us to each speaking only about our corresponding assigned gender and sexual orientation within a specific class, race, and regional experience.

Sexuality and Coming Out

In examining sexuality, one of the key topics is the essentialist assumption of the normalcy of heterosexuality. We strive to problematize the often neglected topic of heterosexuality and heterosexual privilege, in a similar way to our discussion of masculinity (see, for example, Richardson 1996).

Historicizing the concept of heterosexuality and heterosexual identities parallels our exercise in historicizing and examining the construction of masculinity and femininity. Including heterosexuality when we discuss the social construction and practices of sexuality effectively displaces the normalcy of heterosexuality and problematizes it in much the same way that other sexual practices and identities are problematized. Escaping essentialism means that we help challenge students' assumptions about homosexual identities and practices (for example, we find that, at the beginning of the course, many students assume same-sex relations are "deviant" and contrary to the essential sexual nature of humans), by investigating the various meanings and practices of same-sex behaviors across cultures and time. Specifically we examine cross-cultural sexual identities, roles, and practices ranging from the berdache and the *hijra* to semen-ingesting practices of the Sambia. Clearly, a politics of experience is not effective or even possible with such a diverse range of practices.

Because we are continually trying to move beyond a politics of experience and because we problematize heterosexuality and homosexuality in the same way, we do not "come out" in terms of our sexual orientations, although we do not attempt to "pass" as heterosexual or homosexual. We do not want to claim or forfeit authority on the topic based solely on our "experience" of it.

We wonder whether concealing our sexual orientation is the most effective method of illustrating the constraining nature of gender roles and sexuality. We do so because we want to problematize heterosexuality and essentialism by displacing assumptions about our own sexuality. The ambiguous state in terms of sexuality forces students to move beyond the politics of experience. However, remaining "sexually ambiguous" limits much of the experiential material that we could bring into the classroom from our personal histories.

Implications for Pedagogical Practice

A major implication of the cross-gender team-teaching model is to broaden the participation, meaning, and practice of gender studies, an area most often explored in women's studies. Given the historical and contemporary neglect of women's experiences, history, and perceptions in the curriculum, we remain deeply committed to the goals of expanding the curriculum to include the experiences of those historically neglected. At the same time, we believe that to further student understanding of the construction of femininity, instructors must examine the fluidity of femininity and how it is related to masculinity, while preventing the construction of masculinity from subsuming examinations of the construction of femininity. This may be a difficult balance, but it is a manageable one. Second, the cross-gender team-teaching model widens the participation of women and men in teaching about gender and feminism. A team-teaching model avoids the problems Jaggar outlines at the same time it makes men responsible for educating students about privilege and oppression.

The cross-gender team-teaching approach is most effective with likeminded, feminist-oriented instructors who share an enthusiasm and interest in deconstructing the oppressive myths of female inferiority and static constructions of sexuality. Exposing essentialism as an explicit topic for classroom discussion helps to reach this goal. This normally occurs when using a social constructionist perspective in teaching about gender and sexuality, but it can also be applied to assumptions students have about who should teach what.

Faculty members who intend to team teach need to be conscious of their interactions with one another, particularly in front of students, so that they do not reinforce gendered stereotypes. In addition to meeting regularly to debrief about classroom interactions and responses, we find it helpful to call attention to gendered actions and behaviors to reveal both the strength of gender socialization and to discuss possible ways to mitigate against oppression. Other techniques we suggest include organizing the class effectively to use a balance of the expertise of both instructors and to distribute class time equally between instructors. Instructors can also defer questions on course topics along the lines of expertise rather than gender and ask one another questions to illuminate issues when appropriate in front of students.

We find, through interaction and observation, two competing models students exhibit for making sense of the comparative empirical examples provided in the class. The interpretive models we observe basically parallel the poles of the dialectic between cultural relativism, on the one hand, and an understanding of basic human rights, or the conception of some universal moral stance from which to judge cultural practices, on the other (see, for example, Peters and Wolper 1995). In our classroom, students, each in her/his own way, play out the drama that has plagued cultural anthropology's idea of cultural relativism at least since World War II. Looking through one of the interpretive models, students tend to understand many of the practices and gender constructions of the world's cultures as subordinating women—even as outrageous oppressive practices, particularly when we discuss purdah and female circumcision. The other view tends to preserve the idea of relativism, a seeming acceptance of diverse cultural practices and constructions of gender and sexuality as part of a cultural context, through a noncritical application and hands-off approach in which students basically say, "to each his/her own." This approach, while relativist on the surface, is primarily employed to justify and preserve the student's native understanding of gender, not to legitimate the practices and views of other cultures. As instructors, we challenge proponents of each of these poles of a very complex issue to embrace the possibilities in an effort to work toward a middle ground.

Our intent is not to dictate students' values. We intend to broaden their understanding of how gender constructions work and how "unnatural" essentialisms can be. Our curriculum raises the issues and provides empirical and theoretical grounds by which to amplify them.

Conclusion

A feminist commitment to liberatory education requires a critique of essentialism spanning not only the essentialist ideas underlying the "nature" of gender and sexuality but also the assumptions about who can best teach what. A critique of both essentialism and a "politics of experience" allows feminists effectively to engender men, to move beyond static notions of femininity and female experience, and to illuminate the dichotomous, relational, and ultimately variant and fluid construction of masculinity and femininity. In addition, this pedagogical approach not only escapes reinforcing the gender hierarchies by equalizing responsibility and legitimacy in the classroom but it is an active part of the solution in working toward nonoppressive gender relations in daily practice and in the lives of our students. We strongly believe that this latter effect, one of contributing solutions to the problems of daily lives in American society and broadening our students' capacity or ability to contribute, should be one of the primary goals of reform in higher education.

Notes

1. This integration reform, however, has not been without debate and critics which have contested both the necessity and the effectiveness of an inclusive curriculum. Conservative scholars such as Allan Bloom and E. D. Hirsch as well as conservative associations (The National Association of Scholars) have argued for a return to an established canon with a firm foundation in Western civilization.

2. The central theme in women's studies is empowerment, not oppression. Even if women's studies were primarily about oppression, which we think it is not, one must learn about the relationality of systems of domination to understand "women's oppression." This does not require that men's experiences or male constructions of sexualities and other forms of identity be given equal attention or should dominate the curriculum, only that they, and their relation to female constructions, be recognized and analytically incorporated in an effort to understanding the cultural foundations of a system of dominance.

3. We draw from a wide range of literature. We have found useful ethnographic information and readings from a variety of anthropological monographs including Abu-Lughod (1986), Bateson (1958), Gorer (1948), Herdt (1987), Levy (1973), Mead (1928), Nanda (1990), Obeyesekere (1990), Sheper-Hughes (1992), Spiro (1982, 1990), and Wikan (1990). A partial but substantive list of further significant theoretical and descriptive readings include the following: Blackwood (1986), Brettell and Sargent (1993), Brown (1991), Callendar and Kochems (1987), Chodorow (1978), Espin (1984), Faderman (1991), Faludi (1991), Freeman (1983), Gay (1986), Gilmore (1990), Gruenbaum (1982), Halperin (1993), Herdt (1994), Lamphere (1993), Laumann et al. (1994), Mayer (1995), Messner (1990), Morgan (1993), Ortner (1978), Ortner and Whitehead (1981), Peiss (1983), Rapp (1993), Rich (1993), Ross and Rapp (1983), Simson (1983), Smith-Rosenberg (1975), Snitow et al. (1983), Spiro (1982), A. Stein (1993), Tavris (1992), Toubia (1995), Walker (1993), Weeks (1986), Weinrich (1987), and Whitehead (1981). There are a number of good books and anthologies on the topic of essentialism and social constructionism including Abramson and Pinkerton (1995), Richardson (1996), Schiebinger (1993), and

E. Stein (1992). Finally we draw from our own research, which covers the construction of identities and the ethnographic history of an American company town.

4. We are aware of the possibility that introducing students to cross-cultural examples has the negative potential of taking the form of "cultural voyeurism." An understanding of cultural relativism, a theme we weave throughout the course, helps to minimize this effect (Engber 1996).

Works Cited

Abramson, Paul, and Pinkerton, Steven (Eds.). (1995). *Sexual Nature/Sexual Culture.* Chicago: University of Chicago Press.

Abu-Lughod, Lila (1986). *Veiled sentiments: Honor and Poetry in a Bedouin Society.* Berkeley, CA: University of California Press.

Bateson, Gregory (1958). *Naven.* Stanford, CA: Stanford University Press.

Blackwood, Evelyn, (Ed.). (1986). *The Many Faces of Homosexuality.* New York: Harrington Park Press.

Bulkin, Elly (1980). Heterosexism and Women's Studies. *Radical Teacher, 17,* 25–31.

Bohmer, Susanne, and Briggs, Joyce (1991). Teaching Privileged Students about Gender, Race, and Class Oppression. *Teaching Sociology, 19,* 154–63.

Brettell, Caroline B., and Sargent, Carolyn F. (Eds.). (1993). *Gender in Cross-Cultural Perspective.* Englewood Cliffs, NJ: Prentice Hall.

Brown, Donald E. (1991). *Human Universals.* Philadelphia: Temple University Press.

Butler, Johnnella E. (1991). Transforming the Curriculum: Teaching about Women of Color. In Johnnella E. Butler and John Walter (Eds.), *Transforming the Curriculum: Ethnic Studies and Women's Studies,* 67–87. Albany, NY: State University of New York Press.

Carby, Hazel (1992). The Multicultural Wars. *Radical History Review, 54,* 7–18.

Callendar, Charles, and Kochems, Lee (1987). The North American Berdache. *Current Anthropology, 24,* 443–56, 467–70.

Cannon, Lynn Weber (1990). Fostering Positive Race, Class, and Gender Dynamics in the Classroom. *Women's Studies Quarterly, 1, 2,* 126–34.

Chodorow, Nancy (1978). *The Reproduction of Mothering.* Berkeley, CA: University of California Press.

Chow, Esther Ngan-Ling (1985). Teaching Sex and Gender in Sociology. *Teaching Sociology, 12,* 299–311.

Culley, Margo, and Portuges, Catherine (Eds.). (1985). *Gendered Subjects: The Dynamics of Feminist Teaching.* New York: Routledge & Kegan Paul.

De Danaan, Lynn (1990). Center to Margin: Dynamics in a Global Classroom. *Women's Studies Quarterly, 1 & 2,* 135–44.

Ellsworth, Elizabeth (1989). Why Doesn't This Feel Empowering? Working Through the Repressive Myths of Critical Pedagogy. *Harvard Educational Review, 59,* 297–324.

Engber, Diane (1996). Evolving a Course on Postcolonial Writings by Women. *NWSA Journal, 9,* 157–70.

Espin, Oliva (1984). Cultural and Historical Influences on Sexuality in Hispanic/ Latin Women. In Carol Vance (Ed.), *Pleasure and Danger,* 149–164. Boston Routledge, 1984.

Faderman, Lillian (1991). *Odd Girls and Twilight Lovers: A History of Lesbian Life in 20th Century America.* New York: Viking Penguin.

Faludi, Susan (1991). *Backlash: The Undeclared War against Women.* New York: Crown Publishers.

Flintoff, Anne (1993). One of the Boys? Gender Identities in Physical Education Initial Teacher Education. In Iram Siraj-Blatchford (Ed.), *Race, Gender, and the Education of Teachers,* 74–93. Buckingham, England: Open University Press.

Freeman, Derek (1983). *Margaret Mead and Samoa: The Making and Unmaking of an Anthropological Myth.* Cambridge, MA: Harvard University Press.

Fuss, Diana (1989). *Essentially speaking: Feminism, Nature, and Difference.* New York: Routledge.

Gardner, Sandra, Cynthia Dean and Mckaig, Leo (1989). Responding to Differences in the Classroom: The Politics of Knowledge, Class and Sexuality. *Sociology of Education, 52,* 64–74.

Gay, Judith (1986). "Mummies and Babies" and Friends and Lovers in Lesotho. In E. Blackwood (Ed.), *Many Faces of Homosexuality,* 97–116. New York: Harrington Park Press.

George, Sue (1993). *Women and Bisexuality.* London: Scarlet Press.

Gerschick, Thomas (1993). Should and Can a White, Heterosexual Middle-Class Man Teach Students about Social Inequality and Oppression? One Person's Experience and Reflections. In David Schoem, Linda Frankel, Ximena Zuniga, & Edith A. Lewis (Eds.), *Multicultural Teaching in the University,* 200–207. Westport, CT: Praeger.

Gilmore, David (1990). *Manhood in the Making.* New Haven: Yale University Press.

Gorer, Geoffrey (1948). *The American People: A Study in National Character.* New York: W. W. Norton and Company.

Gruenbaum, Ellen (1982). The Movement against Clitoredectomy and Infibulation in Sudan: Public Health Policy and the Women's Movement. *Medical Anthropology Newsletter, 13,* 2.

Halperin, David M. (1993). Is There a History of Sexuality? In Henry Abelove, Michele Aina Barale, & David Halperin (Eds.), *The Lesbian and Gay Studies Reader.* 416–31. New York: Routledge.

Helms, J.E. and Carter, R.T. (1990). Development of White Racial Identity Attitude Scale. In J.E. Helms (Ed.), *Black and White Racial Identity Attitudes,* 67–80. Westport, CT: Greenwood.

Herdt, Gilbert H. (1987). *Guardians of the Flutes: Idioms of Masculinity.* New York: Columbia University Press.

———. (Ed.). (1994). *Third Sex, Third Gender: Beyond Sexual Dimorphism in Culture and History.* New York: Zone Books.

hooks, bell (1989). *Talking Back: Thinking Feminist, Thinking Black.* Boston: South End Press.

Hull, Gloria, Scott, Patricia Bell, and Smith, Barbara (Eds.). (1982). *All the Women Are White, All the Blacks Are Men, But Some of Us Are Brave: Black Women's Studies.* Old Westbury, NY: The Feminist Press.

Jaggar, Alison M. (1977–78). Male Instructors, Feminism, and Women's studies. *Teaching Philosophy, 2, 3, 4,* 97–105.

Kamano, Saori, and Khor, Diana (1996). Toward an understanding of Cross-National Differences in the Naming of Same Sex Sexual-Intimate Relationships. *NWSA Journal, 8,* 124–41.

Kimmel, Michael, and Messner, Michael (1992). Introduction. In Kimmel & Messner, *Men's lives* (pp. xiii–xxii). New York: MacMillan Publishing.

Lamphere, Louise (1993). The Domestic Sphere of Women and the Public World of Men: The Strengths and Limitations of an Anthropological Dichotomy. In Caroline B. Brettell, & Carolyn F. Sargent (Eds.), *Gender in Cross-Cultural Perspective,* 67–77. Englewood Cliffs, NJ: Prentice Hall.

Laumann, Edward O., Gagnon, John H., Michael, Robert, and Michaels, Stuart (1994). *The Social Organization of Sexuality: Sexual Practices in the United States.* Chicago: University of Chicago Press.

Lee, Janet (1993). Teaching Feminism: Anger, Despair, and Self-growth. *Feminist Teacher, 7, 2,* 15–9.

Levy, Robert L. (1973). *Tahitians: Mind and Experience in the Society Islands.* Chicago: University of Chicago Press.

Lorber, Judith (1996). Beyond the Binaries: Depolarizing the Categories of Sex, Sexuality, and Gender. *Sociological Inquiry, 66, 2,* 143–59.

Lucal, Betsy (1996). Oppression and Privilege: Toward a Relational Conceptualization of Race. *Teaching Sociology, 24,* 245–55.

Mayer, Ann Elizabeth (1995). Cultural Particularism as a Bar to Women's Rights: Reflections on the Middle East Experience. In Julie Peters and Andrea Wolper (Eds.), *Women's Rights, Human Rights,* 176–188. New York: Routledge.

McIntosh, Peggy (1992). White Privilege and Male Privilege: A Personal Account of Coming to See Correspondence through Work in Women's Studies. In Margaret A. Anderson and Patricia Hill Collins (Eds.), *Race, Class and Gender: An anthology,* 70–81. Belmont, CA: Wadsworth.

Mead, Margaret (1928). *Coming of Age in Samoa.* New York: Morrow.

Messner, Michael (1990). Boyhood, Organized Sports and the Construction of Masculinities. *Journal of Contemporary Ethnography, 18,* 416–66.

Morgan, Tracy (1993) Butch-femme and the Politics of Identity. In Arlene Stein (Ed.), *Sisters, Sexperts, Queers: Beyond the Lesbian Nation,* 35–46. New York: Penguin Books.

Nanda, Serena (1990). *Neither Man nor Woman: The Hijras of India.* Belmont, CA: Wadsworth.

Obeyesekere, Gananath (1990). *The Work of Culture: Symbolic Transformation in Psychoanalysis and Anthropology.* Chicago: University of Chicago Press.

Ortner, Sherry B. (1978). The Virgin and the State. *Feminist Studies, 4,* 19–35.

Ortner, Sherry B., and Whitehead, Harriet (Eds.). (1981). *Sexual Meanings: The Cultural Construction of Gender and Sexuality.* Cambridge, England: Cambridge University Press.

Peiss, Kathy (1983). Charity Girls and City Pleasures: Historical Notes on Working-Class sexuality, 1880–1920. In Ann Snitow, Christine Stansell, &

Sharon Thompson (Eds.), *Powers of Desire: The Politics of Sexuality*, 74–87. New York: Monthly Review Press.

Peters, Julie, & Wolper, Andrea (Eds.). (1995). *Women's Rights, Human Rights.* New York: Routledge.

Rapp, Reyna (1977). Gender and Class: An Archaeology of Knowledge Concerning the Origin of the State. *Dialectical Anthropology, 2,* 309–16.

Rich, Adrienne (1993). Compulsory Heterosexuality and Lesbian Existence. In Henry Abelove, Michele Aina Barale, and David Halperin (Eds.), *The Lesbian and Gay Studies Reader,* 227–554. New York: Routledge.

Richardson, Diane (Ed.). (1996). *Theorising Heterosexuality: Telling It Straight.* Philadelphia: Open University Press.

Ross, Ellen, &. Rapp, Rayna (1983). Sex and Society: A Research Note from Social History and Anthropology. In Ann Snitow, Christine Stansell, and Sharon Thompson (Eds.), *Powers of desire: The Politics of Sexuality,* 51–73. New York: Monthly Review.

Scanlon, Jennifer (1993). Keeping Our Activist Selves Alive in the Classroom: Feminist Pedagogy and Political Activism. *Feminist Teacher, 7,* 8–13.

Schiebinger, Londa. (1993). *Nature's Body: Gender in the Making of Science.* Boston: Beacon Press.

Schniedewind, Nancy (1993). Teaching Feminist Process in the 1990s. *Women's Studies Quarterly, 3, 4,* 19–30.

Schniedewind, Nancy (1985). Cooperatively Structured Learning: Implications for Feminist Pedagogy. *Journal of Thought, 20, 3,* 74–87.

Sheper-Hughes, Nancy (1992). *Death without Weeping: The Violence of Everyday Life in Brazil.* Berkeley, CA: University of California Press.

Simson, Rennie (1983). The Afro American Female: The Historical Context of the Construction of Sexual Identity. In Ann Snitow, Christine Stansell, and Sharon Thompson (Eds.), *Powers of Desire: The Politics of Sexuality,* 229–235. New York: Monthly Review.

Smith-Rosenberg, Carroll. (1975). The Female World of Love and Ritual in Nineteenth-Century America. *Signs, 1,* 1–29.

Snitow, Ann, Stansell, Christine, and Thompson, Sharon (Eds.). (1983). *Powers of Desire: The Politics of Sexuality.* New York: Monthly Review.

Spellman, Elizabeth (1988). *Inessential Woman.* Boston: Beacon Press.

Spiro, Melford (1990). On the Strange and the Familiar in Recent Anthropological Thought. In James W. Stigler, Richard A. Schweder, and Gilbert Herdt (Eds.), *Cultural Psychology: Essays on Comparative Development,* 47–61. New York: Cambridge University Press.

———. (1982). *Oedipus in the Trobriands.* Chicago: University of Chicago Press.

Stein, Arlene (1993). *Sisters, Sexperts, Queers: Beyond the Lesbian Nation.* New York: Penguin Books.

Stein, Edward (1992). *Forms of Desire: Sexual Orientation and the Social Constructionist Controversy.* New York: Routledge.

Tavris, Carol (1992). *The Mismeasure of Woman.* New York: Touchstone, Simon and Schuster.

Toubia, Nahid (1995). Female Genital Mutilation. In Julie Peters and Andrea Wolper (Eds.), *Women's rights, human rights,* 224–237. New York: Routledge.

Walker, Alice (1993). *Warrior Marks: Female Genital Mutilation and the Sexual binding of women.* New York: Harcourt Brace and Company.

Weeks, Jeffrey (1986). *Sexuality.* New York: Tavistock Publications.

Weinrich, James (1987). *Sexual Landscapes: Why We Are What We Are, Why We Love Who We Love.* New York: Charles Scribner's Sons.

Whitehead, Harriet (1981). The Bow and the Burden Strap: A New Look at Institutionalized Homosexuality in Native North America. In Sherry Ortner and Harriet Whitehead (Eds.), *Sexual Meanings: The Cultural Construction of Gender and Sexuality,* 80–115. New York: Cambridge University Press.

Wikan, Unni (1990). *Managing Turbulent Hearts: A Balinese Formula for Living.* Chicago: University of Chicago Press.

CHAPTER FIVE

Not for Queers Only: Pedagogy and Postmodernism

SAL JOHNSTON

I did not explicitly set out to develop a "postmodern" pedagogy. Rather, as I engaged postmodern analyses in my scholarship and taught them in my courses, I became aware of their impact on my teaching practices. I hope this essay demonstrates that these analyses are useful, even crucial, for developing pedagogical practices that resist reinscribing dominant, essentialist constructions of sexuality, race, gender, and class. I focus on sexuality partly because I teach in Oregon where the "religious" right's unholy war is deeply entrenched. Despite assertions that postmodernism is apolitical, I have found postmodern analyses and teaching practices particularly effective for analyzing sexuality and undermining the persuasive rhetoric of the "religious" right.

The postmodern texts that I draw from emphasize breaking down (deconstructing) dualistic models and understandings of sexuality, gender, and race. They suggest that these categories are constructed through relations of power and must be examined with a critical eye. I find these analyses useful because they allow me to go beyond simply defending stigmatized practices, such as homosexuality and problematize sexuality more generally. Deconstructing categories also facilitates articulating the interrelations of race, class, gender, and sexuality.

I begin my discussion with an explanation of the context in which I teach. Next, I briefly review some postmodern analyses: mainly those that show the "natural" to be "cultural." The remainder of the chapter focuses on how I use these tools in constructing two of my courses.

Context: The "Religious" Right and Me

The sociopolitical context in which I teach has a great deal to do with my confidence in the analyses and teaching practices described in this essay. For the past four years I have taught undergraduate sociology courses at the University of Oregon. Oregon has been besieged by battles over proposed antihomosexual legislation sponsored by the Oregon Citizens Alliance (OCA). The OCA is the most prominent Christian right group in Oregon and the most aggressively homophobic. The OCA shares the basic characteristics of the religious right nationally: it seeks to rein-

Originally published in the Spring 1995 issue of the *NWSA Journal*.

force traditional gender roles, patriarchal family structure, and laissez-faire capitalism and to erase the gains of the civil rights movement. The OCA has also targeted women's right to choose, but with little success. In contrast, they've found antihomosexual campaigning politically and financially advantageous.

The OCA's 1992 statewide endeavor, Ballot Measure 9, sought to amend the state constitution to declare homosexuality, collapsed with pedophilia, sadism, and masochism, "unnatural, abnormal, and perverse." The stated goal of the measure was to prevent the state from "promoting" homosexuality by mandating that the "state or its representatives" could not "acknowledge, encourage, or facilitate" homosexuality and other listed behaviors. The legislative intent included preventing Oregon from adding sexual orientation to antidiscrimination legislation, thereby ensuring the "right" of individuals to discriminate in housing, employment and public accommodations on the basis of perceived sexual orientation.

Oregonians rejected Measure 9 in the November 1992 election by a 57 percent to 43 percent margin, but the battle is far from over. The OCA spent 1993 passing local antihomosexual ordinances in communities that voted in support of Measure 9. The OCA placed an antigay referendum on the 1994 statewide ballot, which was narrowly defeated.

The right's preoccupation with the representation of homosexuality and homosexuals in education is evident in the construction of Measure 9, which required educators in all public educational institutions to teach that homosexuality is "abnormal, wrong, unnatural, and perverse." This legislation would have been binding on university classes as well as on grades K–12 and would have criminalized teaching even demographic or scientific "value-free" findings about homosexuality. Further, many people understood Measure 9 as prohibiting queers from teaching.

The passage of Measure 9 would have had grave ramifications for my career. My current research focuses on anti-OCA organizing in Oregon, and I teach courses that examine sexuality, queer theory, and the politics of the secular and religious right. I am also a very identifiable target of the OCA's antihomosexual campaign. When I'm in a room of "normal" looking activists, the camera consistently turns in my direction. I have a flat-top and regularly sport early-1960s men's suits. I present myself in this manner neither to irritate the OCA nor for the thrill of complicating my professional life but because it expresses how I experience my gendered self. Although I understand identity as fluid, changing, socially produced, and performative, I am most comfortable and confident in a butch identity and presentation of self.

My gender identity affects my classroom. The period between when I enter the classroom and when I write my name on the board is both interesting and stressful. As I put the chalk down, the boys in the back of the room have a good laugh and I wonder, "Will this be the class that comes unhinged?" For the rest of the term, I am in the rather strange position of deconstructing the stereotypes and assumed relationships between sex, gender, and sexuality, which I appear to represent. While I do not walk into class on the first day and proclaim my sexual identity, my students see my gender violations and assume it. I don't attempt to leave myself unsituated, but I refrain from coming out through proclamation. I want to thwart "coming out" as an identity claim that privileges myself and other queers to "teach antiheterosexism." As I will argue later, I believe that essentialist identity statements are problematic and I consciously work to undermine them.

Given my physical appearance and the context in which I teach, one would expect me to have a plethora of gruesome tales to report. Yet my classroom experiences are exceedingly positive. The University of Oregon has a "liberal" reputation and a sizable lefty, feminist, counterculture contingent, but there is also a strong Greek system. Both the state and the campus are very racially segregated. Eugene is a "lesbian town," but I've only had one term in which I had more than three or four identifiable queer students in my class (which typically numbers ninety students or more). Youth for Christ is strong enough on campus that we have "Jesus Week" right after "Gay Pride." This suggests to me that my success is not primarily a function of student constituency but instead is due to the theories and pedagogy I employ.

I am unable to "objectively" measure changes in the beliefs or knowledge of students in my courses. What I offer in this essay is a discussion that draws on my perceptions of classroom interactions, on course assignments, and on concrete student feedback from course evaluations.

My course assignments are analytic papers. Students have considerable freedom over what they write about, but they must incorporate course issues, concepts, and readings. I evaluate their work on the basis of logic, depth of analysis, and use of course materials. I consistently remind students that my purpose is to make them better thinkers: they receive no points for polemics. After they get back their first assignment, they believe me. By the end of the term even the struggling students improve in their ability to identify some assumptions underlying a common cultural belief. Because I have only ten weeks with students, I can't personally effect much change. Thus I try to develop critical thinking, with the hope that this skill is carried beyond the classroom.

Course evaluations at my institution include a standardized set of questions and comments written by the students. I ask students to tell me both what they found useful about the class and what was problematic. Students consistently suggest that they found challenging and valuable the class emphasis on learning how to think rather than what to think. Students may cynically be producing what they think I want to hear, but I doubt it. They write their comments anonymously, knowing that I do not have access to them until after final grades are issued.

Pedagogy and Postmodernism

As I have engaged with feminist postmodernist theories[1] and analyses I have had to rethink various aspects of my classroom practices. I discuss three concrete effects of postmodern analyses on my pedagogical practices: (1) I don't grant epistemic privilege to experience; (2) I deconstruct sexuality rather than defending homosexuality; and (3) I work to weave analyses of sexuality (and race, gender, and class) into the substantive issues of the courses I teach.

"Postmodernism" as a referent to a body of theory is largely an American phenomenon and, as Judith Butler argues, it lumps together an assemblage of incongruent theories (1993b, 4). However, Linda Nicholson's characterization of two of the major themes in "postmodern" analyses strongly influences my scholarship and is relevant to my discussion here. Nicholson points to "(1) a rejection of the all-encompassing and frequently teleological theories of human history and social change associated with enlightenment ideas about reason and progress . . . [and] (2) a linking of claims about social life, human nature, and criteria of truth and validity with strategies of power" (1992,–93).

One foundational idea of the Enlightenment is essentialism, defined by Diana Fuss as "the belief in true essence—that which is most irreducible, unchanging, and therefore constitutive of a given person or thing" (1989, 2). Antiessentialists do not simply reject the belief in a core or true essence, they show it to be a historical construction. They show that explanations of sexuality as "natural" (biologically predetermined) are untenable.[2] Instead, sexuality, gender, class, and race are socially produced categories that vary between and within cultures and historical periods. By "denaturalizing" sexuality antiessentialism allows for critiques of the hegemony of heterosexuality. Unless it can be shown that any and every sexual expression is socially produced/mediated rather than natural or innate, procreative heterosexuality remains the normative practice against which all other expressions are measured.

Deconstruction, overly simplified, means breaking down binary oppositions, showing that they are constructed (rather than naturally occurring), hierarchical, and imbricated with relations of power. Meanings are created relationally, as Joan Scott explains, "fixed oppositions conceal the extent to which things presented as oppositional are, in fact, interdependent" (1993, 37). Deconstruction should not be confused with destruction. Unraveling truth narratives, like sociobiology, leaves us with another phenomenon to explain: the production of sociobiology.

Applying deconstruction to sexuality reveals that heterosexuality and homosexuality are socially constructed categories that only have meaning in relation to one another, and that truth claims about sexuality are constructed.[3]

These analyses argue that dualistic categorical schemas function to reinforce existing relations of power. In the case of sexuality, treating the categories as natural or given reinforces the logic that constructs heterosexuality as the only "normal" option. If we wish to resist heterosexism in our classroom practices, then we must analyze the categories along with the effects of categorization. In other words, we can't only direct our classes' attention to the bias and harms against queers to fight heterosexism; we have to show how heterosexuality is historically created and structurally enforced. This critique calls identity categories into question: should we base our identities on categories that function to regulate?

Feminism has posited self-knowledge via experience as central to politics and theory. I am not arguing for the abandonment of the "personal as political" but heed Joan Scott's caution that experience is not self-evident or unmediated. As Scott suggests, there has been a (well-intentioned) tendency in some feminist theorizing to ask the question "What could be truer . . . than a subject's own account of what she or he has lived through?" (25). She argues that the effect of this logic is to naturalize difference; it treats the categories of gender, race, and sexuality as "given characteristics of individuals" (27). The result is that precisely what is to be explained is made essential and that this naturalization reproduces existing ideological systems.

Privileging experience can also lead to constructing experience (and/or identity) as an "ontological foundation" for knowledge or politics (Scott 26–30). Such a perspective assumes that there are sets of experiences that provide the necessary "raw material" for "real" knowledge or political reliability. This homogenizes experience and jettisons difference, thereby rearticulating dominant exclusions. If sexuality is understood as the totalizing experience, for example, then race, class, and gender are marginalized.

Finally, none of us gain knowledge through unmediated experience; there are always different levels of mediation. (While I don't think it is possible to teach straight students what it is *like* to be queer, any more than I could teach male students what it is *like* to be a woman, I do think that students can come to understand relations of power regardless of their position within them.) Not privileging experience is not equivalent to denigrating it, nor does it discount the use of experience as a mode of learning. So while I don't use exercises like "pretend you're gay and write a coming-out letter to your parents," I do examine experiences as a way to reveal and understand relations of power. The distinction is in the proposed relationship between knowledge and experience: my approach does not demand that you personally share an experience to gain knowledge from that experience.

As my self-identification reveals, I am not averse to individual claims for types of identity. However, I am suspicious of essentialist identity claims as a basis for politics or pedagogy. I resist "playing out" identity politics in the classroom. bell hooks suggests abandoning identity politics by advocating feminism rather than declaring oneself a feminist (1984, 29). I advocate, among other things, antiracism, and antisexism, but I do not base my advocacy on my identity. At no point in a class do I ask for antihomophobic comments from students, nor do I seek assurances of my own status as an "oppressed" lesbian. This allows me to abandon essentialist "I am" in favor of "I do."

Deconstructing Experience

"Diversity panels" are supposed to make visible and give voice to those constructed as Other in an effort to challange dominant thinking about race, gender, sexuality, and class. Identity categories are often an important element of these panels. Scott's critique of privileging experience points to the need to be exceedingly careful when forming a panel or bringing in a guest speaker; in particular, we need to think about the implications of the framing of the issue or individual in question. For example, while writing this essay I was invited to be on a student-organized "sexualities panel" for an Introduction to women's studies course. At my institution it appears that "sexualities" panels have pretty much replaced "lesbian panels." While this is an important step, it is insufficient if the construction of the panel is still dependent on an essentialist understanding of identity.

I appeared on the panel with a gay man, a lesbian, and a heterosexual virgin. The make-up of the panel functioned to rearticulate several aspects of dominant discourse. Because all the panelists were Euro-Americans our race was not discussed, a fact that may have made identity appear to be singular. By not including self-identified bisexuals, the panel replicated an understanding of sexuality as a hetero-homo binary. Having three of the four panelists represent homosexuality reinforced the notion that only homosexuality, not all sexualities, needs explanation. This impression was further reinforced by the fact that the panel's one heterosexual was a virgin, implying as it did that active heterosexuality is simply self-evident. The primary problem was that we were each selected to "represent" our "identity."

Although labeled a "sexualities" panel, we were not there to discuss sex but rather to discuss our respective sexual *identities.* I naively agreed to appear on the panel with hopes of disrupting the usual proclamations of "truth" through sexuality. The first question that the students had us answer, however, basically amounted to "What is your sexual identity?" So much for deconstruction. I answered that I identify most with the terms "butch" and "queer." I then briefly stated that the former references a gender construct (one among many) and the latter a very loose sexual identification.

When questioned about these terms I explained that I use "queer" because it is self-evidently ambiguous. Although "lesbian" is assumed to imply specific meanings, it doesn't even say anything specific about people's sexual practices, much less about the rest of their lives. I suggested that desire is more complicated than sexual categories allow; for example, I'm not attracted to "all women" or "all lesbians" but to femmes (and not exclusively, though predominantly, to women). So, I asked, what then is the appropriate basis on which to assign someone to a sexual category? Desire? Fantasy? Behavior?

I went on to explain that it is my violation of certain gender norms that produces the tendency to code me as lesbian. However, the cultural stereotypes about "what a lesbian looks like" are based on deviations from stereotypical femininity and do not determine sexuality; being a "tomboy" doesn't make you a dyke and playing with dolls doesn't make you straight. Gender doesn't predict sexuality.

I was rather pleased with myself, thinking that I had nicely resisted homogenizing labels until the questions from the class made it clear that they understood me to be "a Lesbian" and understood my attempts at ambiguity and deconstruction as internalized homophobia. After all, I look like a dyke, I walk like one, why wouldn't I quack? Was I ashamed? I thought of Scott's caution about naturalizing difference, about the implications of constructing categories as "given characteristics of individuals," and knew I was trapped.

I responded by reiterating that my categorization was not prompted by "lesbian shame" but by the very real differences between gender and sexuality. Further, the harassment that I endure is based on gender. The most dangerous situations I have been in are those in which people think I am biologically male and then discover that I am not. I am not suggesting that my "gender trouble" is not consistently linked to sexuality (once discovered) but rather that in my case it is gender that gets me in the most trouble.

Those skeptical of postmodern analyses could read this as proof of the unintelligibility and impracticality of these analyses. However, I understand my difficulty on the panel as a function of the uncritical use of identity categories. Stereotypes based on totalizing identities are not dismantled by presenting individuals as representative of an identity group, even if the participants are chosen to confirm the humanity of their group. I have been much more successful (and comfortable) discussing my research and activism than I have appearing as "petri dish Q." Presenting individuals under totalizing signs/labels closes the door in effect to a critical examination of the meanings and production of the latter. As Scott suggests, the result of such a presentation is that what needs explanation is understood as an inherent aspect of the individual and is thus inaccessible to scrutiny.

Theory in Practice

I'd like to undermine heteropatriarchy, but this commitment does not manifest itself in my "teaching antihomophobia." I do not teach about homosexuality per se; I don't attempt to provide a rationale or a justification for sexual practices, nor do I pose value-laden questions about sexuality. Instead, I work to disrupt popular understandings of sex, gender, and sexuality. I direct student attention to particular issues and questions in order to reframe them in ways that challenge dominant understandings of sexuality.

Sex and Identity is an upper-division course, small for my institution (with thirty to sixty students, mostly majors), and it tends to more women than men. The course, as I structure it, is an examination of theories of sexuality with readings, assignments, and discussions that deconstruct the latter. Race, gender, and class are always part of our analysis, even though the course situates sexuality as a central concern. The logic of the course moves from antiessentialist scholarship to various social-constructionist positions and concludes with deconstructive analyses.

A key concern is the critical examination of the production of knowledge concerning sex, categories, and assumed meanings and relationships. We engage in a basic examination of how different theories explain/construct sexuality and attempt to analyze how they produce what they purport to explain. Central questions posed by the course include: Who produces knowledge concerning sexuality? How and why do they do so? What relationship between sex, sexuality, gender, and identity is posited by the theories under investigation? What relationship can we see between sexuality and race, class, and gender? How are sexual practices, meanings, and identities produced and reproduced? What is the relationship between sexuality and power?

To introduce students to the idea that sex, gender, race, and sexuality are social constructs rather than fixed biological "realities," and that science does not produce "objective truth," I have students read Ruth Hubbard's *The Politics of Women's Biology* (1990) and Jeffrey Weeks's *Sexuality* (1986) by the end of the second week. Students find these texts conceptually challenging but readable. In conjunction with the readings

I use two small-group exercises that seem to help students understand the analyses presented. For the first exercise I ask students to try to determine what all women have in common. Students quickly conclude that there isn't a singular defining characteristic. They realize that even biological criteria have exceptions. For the second exercise, drawing on Weeks's overview of the sexuality literature and Hubbard's analysis, I have students examine a newspaper article on Anne Moir and David Jessel's *Brain Sex* (1991), which argues that there are male and female brains and that "homosexuals" have the "wrong" brain. Students analyze the text on a number of levels, including the author's underlying assumptions; the assumed relationship between sex, gender, and sexuality; the construction of gender; the gendering of hormones and organs; and the usefulness of studying rats. This exercise makes evident some of the social consequences of theoretical and scientific assumptions.

We then move into an analysis of psychoanalytic theory, an examination of the "repressive hypothesis," and a summary of social-constructionist analyses. The readings grouped under "social construction" are primarily historical and function to reveal the multiple constructions of sexuality very concretely. Many of the readings are in Ann Snitow, Christine Stansell, and Sharon Thompson's *Powers of Desire* (1983); they reveal that including race, class, and gender in analyses of sexuality render singular, totalizing explanations untenable. For example, Kathy Peiss discusses the class differences in sexual norms and regulation during the late nineteenth century. Jacqueline Dowd-Hall disrupts the ahistorical and unidirectional understanding of rape (seen as a timeless form of control over women) by revealing the effects of race, class, and gender on the construction and practice of rape and lynching.

In the final section of the course we examine Michel Foucault (1980), deconstructive analyses, and identity politics. In conjunction with readings from Judith Butler (1990, 1993a, 1993b) I show *Paris Is Burning* (Livingston, 1991) and k.d. lang videos.[4] *Paris Is Burning* is an excellent film showing the imbrication of race, class, gender, and sexuality and illustrating Butler's concept of "performativity." Politically, I think this film is important as well; it blends performance with the tangible effects of oppression. Students often comment that it is a "sad movie." I counter by saying that the film certainly reveals some of the tragedies heaped on transsexuals but that it is also about resistance, survival, pride, and power. I challenge them to recognize the dangers and oppression without falling into "pity." The k.d. lang video also shows that gender does not link up to biology in a predetermined way. It has been useful, and fun, to play with the question of when k.d. is in "drag" and when she is not. Is it drag when she is in campy "country" skirts? A serious dress? Or a man's western suit?

I taught Sex and Identity twice during fervid antihomosexual campaigning by the OCA. It was tempting, given the right's pathologizing typifications of queers, to fall into "defending" homosexuality; but to argue that homosexuality "isn't bad" reinscribes the same heterosexual-homosexual binary that fuels heterosexism and the current attacks by the right. My occasional anxiety attacks over the political utility of the analyses provided in my course were assuaged by the very cogent analyses of my students.

The Sex and Identity course is atypical. I have an entire term to specifically deconstruct sex, gender, race, and sexuality. While many courses would not as readily accommodate the critiques I describe above, it is still possible to weave analyses of sexuality into the substantive issues of courses seemingly about other topics.[5] A statistics course could dissect the inane statistics the religious right propagates or examine Fritz Klein and colleagues' (1985) study of bisexuality. A course on the family can historicize families and show how the employment of different definitions of "family" constructs and maintains specific race, class, gender, and sexual scripts and relations of power. I cannot offer a formula for integrating antiessentialist analyses of sexuality into the entire curriculum, but I will provide a discussion of how I wove analyses of sexuality into a course in which students were not expecting to engage with these issues.

My experiences teaching Social Change confirmed for me the efficacy of deeply contextualizing issues of sexuality. I taught the course the term after the 1992 election using Measure 9 as a focus for examining the dynamics of social change. A typical topic for this course is an examination of the changes in Eastern Europe. I chose Measure 9 as a frame both to allow us to examine multiple levels and types of social change and, because I planned the course before the election, as resistance to the academic censorship proposed by Measure 9.

About half of the 120 students in the course were nonmajors, ranging from sophomores to seniors, and the gender distribution was about equal. On the first day of class I explained that we would examine multiple levels and types of social change (from national to regional to local as well as economic, political, and social) and that the course would focus on various changes related to the emergence of Measure 9. Students challenged the appropriateness of this focus as "too narrow" or "irrelevant to their lives." I countered by stating that the three major issues we would examine were (1) national economic trends and Oregon's timber economy, (2) the social changes due to the progressive movements of the 1960s and 1970s, and (3) the emergence and agenda of the religious right. I suggested that if anything, this was a ridiculously large amount of material to attempt to cover in ten weeks. I explained that Measure 9 provided a concrete point of convergence.

I framed my discussions of sexuality in reference to the agenda of the religious right, the social changes produced by the social movements of the 1960s and 1970s, and ongoing changes in the meanings and expectations of gender, race, and sexuality over the course of this century. A significant shift in student attitudes occurred when we began reading Sara Diamond's book *Spiritual Warfare* (1989). The book alarmed my students. They clearly had little prior information about the political significance of the rise of the right or about the breadth of the right's agenda. Students began to see some logic in understanding sexuality and power, and their links to race, gender, and class.

So, for example, in examining the right's family agenda we looked at how, why, and to what extent the family structure in this country has changed. This involved, first, articulating the multiple factors contributing to changes in family structure, from the economy to changes in gender norms to increased mobility. Then we examined the race, class, and gender relations inherent in the "traditional" family. Contextualizing the issue provided students with tools to analyze the situation in Oregon for themselves. Students began offering analyses of how and why the right uses scapegoating and why their rhetoric is persuasive. I am, without question, leading students along an analytical path, but students are free to focus on the issues of their choice and to contest the analyses presented in the readings.

I use similar analyses in Social Change that are similar to but less sophisticated than those used in Sex and Identity. For example, we explore the relationship between knowledge and power through the simplified proposition that power is inherent in categorical schema. We then discuss contemporary social movements as contesting the meanings and content of categories. I try to use methods and materials that resist evaluating individual identities and instead consistently focus on the broader social relations: how identities and experiences are produced.

This framework helped produce an important shift later in the course when we were examining changes in Oregon's timber communities. I assigned Iris Young's (1990) article "The Ideal of Community and the Politics of Difference," which argues that community forms through exclusions. In addition, students read a portion of a doctoral dissertation that examined community, identity, and change in Oregon timber communities. Students could then analyze the use of social and economic change and crisis by political movements. We examined the structural factors producing support for Measure 9, instead of constructing rural Oregonians as "rednecks." Student responses to our examination of "timber communities" solidified for me the importance of presenting issues in complex ways and not adhering to political bifurcations. This was not a liberal "show both sides of the issue" response but a commitment to examining the production of social, political, and economic relations.

Student comments on evaluations of Social Change consistently noted that "students were expected to come to their own conclusions" and that this facilitated their engagement with the course. Students reported that focusing on critical thinking, rather than taking an emotional inventory, allowed them to grapple with challenging issues. Additionally, I am in the position of evaluating not students' feelings or compassion but rather the logic of their arguments.

Weaving issues of sexuality deeply into the structure and logic of the course, deconstructing categories and rhetoric, being honest about what I advocate politically but having the course focus on critical analyses and demanding clear thinking, all allowed students to become less defensive and actually engage the material. One student wrote in the anonymous course evaluation:

> I was skeptical of the intent of the course as you outlined it in the first class. I was leery that you were taking advantage of the forum of the class to push your own agenda. . . . However, the readings and lectures were fascinating and I realized that these issues were the best topics for social change.

Conclusion

I do not mean to portray postmodernism as a panacea, but I find its analyses pedagogically and politically useful. Antiessentialist and deconstructive critiques allow us to move beyond a dualistic construction of sexuality and to examine the relations of power constructing categorical schema. If we want our pedagogical practices to resist heterosexism, then we must avoid rearticulating the logic that underlies it. Moving out of a bifurcated analytical structure also facilitates examining the multiplicity of experience rather than reified categories.

Deconstruction does not leave us with nothing to teach but rather allows us to focus on how categories and truth claims are constructed. As Cindy Patton (1993) suggests, it is postmodernity, not postmodern theory, that has made it "problematic to posit ourselves as subjects" (175). Further, the most important reasons to question, analyze, and theorize essentialist constructs are political and pragmatic: the political and social agenda of the right is dependent on essentialist constructions of gender, sexuality, and race. Effective resistance is dependent on a complex understanding of how these meanings and relations of power are constituted and deployed. Postmodernism is not at odds with a pedagogy focused on critical analyses; I think it demands it.

Acknowledgments

An earlier version of this chapter was presented at the Pacific Sociological Association Meetings, San Diego, CA, April 14–17, 1994. This essay has benefited greatly from the insights and critical comments of friends and colleagues and five anonymous reviewers. I am particularly grateful to Julia Wallace for suggesting that I write this piece and for cogent comments on multiple drafts of this essay. My thanks also go to Diane Dunn, Linda Fuller, Kristin Pula, Lycette Nelson, Roderick Williams, and Sue Wright. Finally, I must thank my students for the hard work, patience, and thoughtful comments that made this discussion possible.

Notes

1. See, for example, Butler and Scott, *Feminists Theorize the Political;* Nicholson, *Feminism and Postmodernism;* and Alcoff and Potter, *Feminist Epistemologies.*

2. For an excellent overview of antiessentialist arguments see Jeffrey Weeks, *Sexuality.*

3. Within this dichotomous schema, heterosexuality and homosexuality consistently envelop bisexuality.

4. Since I taught this class last, Butler's *Bodies That Matter* has been published; and chapter 4 discusses *Paris Is Burning.* Other films and videos that can be used in classes include *Changing Our Minds: The Story of Dr. Evelyn Hooker, Love Makes a Family, On Hate Street* (48 Hours special that includes information on the OCA), *One Nation Under God* (on conversion therapy), *Sacred Lies, Civil Truth, Straight from the Heart, Silent Pioneers, The Times of Harvey Milk,* and *Torch Song Trilogy.*

5. The resources available for teaching about sexuality are expanding. One book I highly recommend is *The Lesbian and Gay Studies Reader,* edited by Abelove, Barale, and Halperin. This anthology contains a very thoughtful compilation of important articles and an extensive bibliography. Another important resource is the Center for Lesbian and Gay Studies (CLAGS), which has an archive of course syllabi that can provide examples of how to incorporate analyses of sexuality into various substantive areas. To add your name to the *CLAGS Newsletter* mailing list write to CLAGS, The Graduate School and University Center, City University of New York, 365 Fifth Ave. New York, NY 10016.

Works Cited

Abelove, Henry, Michele Barale, and David Halperin, eds. *The Lesbian and Gay Studies Reader.* New York: Routledge, 1993.

Alcoff, Linda, and Elizabeth Potter, eds. *Feminist Epistemologies.* New York: Routledge, 1993.

Butler, Judith. *Bodies That Matter.* New York: Routledge, 1993a.

———. "Contingent Foundations: Feminism and the Question of 'Postmodernism.'" In *Feminists Theorize the Political*, ed. Judith Butler and Joan Scott, 3-21. New York: Routledge, 1993b

———. *Gender Trouble: Feminism and the Subversion of Identity*. New York. Routledge, 1990.

Butler, Judith, and Joan Scott, eds. *Feminists Theorize the Political*. New York: Routledge, 1993.

Diamond, Sara. *Spiritual Warfare: The Politics of the Christian Right*. Boston: South End P, 1989.

Foucault, Michel. *The History of Sexuality, Volume 1: An Introduction*. New York: Vintage, 1980.

Fuss, Diana. *Essentially Speaking*. New York: Routledge, 1989.

hooks, bell. *Feminism from Margin to Center*. Boston: South End P, 1984.

———. *Yearnings: Race. Gender, and Cultural Practices*. Boston: South End P, 1990.

Hubbard, Ruth. *The Politics of Women's Biology*. New Brunswick, NJ: Rutgers University Press, 1990.

Klein, Fritz, B. Sepekoff, and T. J. Wolf. "Sexual Orientation: A Multivariable Dynamic Process." In *Bisexualities: Theory and Research*, ed. Fritz Klein and T. J. Wolf, New York: Hayworth, 1985.

Livingston, Jennie. *Paris Is Burning* [motion picture]. Los Angeles: Off White Productions, 1991.

Moir, Anne, and David Jessel. *Brain Sex: The Real Difference between Men and Women*. Brooklyn, New York: Delta, 1992.

Nicholson, Linda. *Feminism and Postmodernism* New York: Routledge, 1990.

———. "On the Postmodern Barricades: Feminism, Politics, and Theory." In *Postmodernism and Social Theory*, ed. Steven Seidman and David Wagner. Cambridge, MA: Blackwell, 1992.

Patton, Cindy. "Tremble Hetero Swine!" *Fear of a Queer Planet*. Ed. Michael Warner. Minneapolis: University of Minneapolis Press 1993. 143–77

Scott, Joan W. "Experience." In *Feminists Theorize the Political*, ed. Judith Butler and Joan Scott, 22-40. New York: Routledge, 1993.

Snitow, Ann, Christine Stansell, and Sharon Thompson, eds. *Powers of Desire: The Politics of Sexuality*. New York: Monthly Review, 1983.

Weeks, Jeffrey. *Sexuality*. New York: Routledge, 1986.

———. *Sexuality and Its Discontents*. New York: Routledge, 1985.

Young, Iris. "The Ideal of Community and the Politics of Difference." In *Feminism and Postmodernism*, ed. Linda Nicholson, 300-23. New York: Routledge, 1990.

CHAPTER SIX

Feminist Pedagogy, Interdisciplinary Praxis, and Science Education

MARALEE MAYBERRY AND MARGARET N. REES

As a theoretical and methodological practice, feminist pedagogy embraces a commitment to incorporating the voices and experiences of marginalized students into the academic discourse as well as educating all students for social justice and social change (Kenway and Modra 1993; Maher 1987; Rosser 1990; Shrewsbury 1993). At its core, feminist pedagogy is a commitment not only to the development of cooperative, multicultural, and interdisciplinary knowledge that makes learning inviting and meaningful to a diverse population but also to the development of a critical consciousness empowered to apply learning to social action and social transformation.

Although the theory and practice of feminist pedagogy is an increasingly familiar concept to women's studies educators around the country, few science educators have yet to acknowledge its potential to transform the traditional conceptualizations of scientific thought that fail to investigate the role of culture in the production, dissemination, and utilization of scientific knowledge (Bleir 1991; Harding 1993; Shulman 1994).

This article focuses on our vision of how social, scientific, and feminist inquiry and teaching can be drawn together to create a new vision of science education. What follows reflects our experience as two feminist educators teaching a unique interdisciplinary course, Earth Systems: A Feminist Approach. Earth Systems infused geological education with the insights of sociological inquiry and feminist pedagogy and was offered in Spring 1995 for credit through the departments of geology, sociology, and women's studies at the University of Nevada, Las Vegas. Seventeen white undergraduate students (fourteen women and three men), ranging from sophomore to senior level, enrolled for and completed the course. Twelve students were social science or humanities majors; three students were women's studies majors; two students were natural science majors. In addition, we granted permission to one female graduate student from the environmental studies program to enroll in the course. She received graduate credit for developing and implementing a session on "ecofeminism." It is also important to note that Earth Systems was developed and team taught by a geologist and a sociologist, while most science education programs at the high school and college level remain under the direction of scientific experts and science education research teams who

Originally published in the Spring 1997 issue of the *NWSA Journal*.

rarely, if ever, include academicians from either the social sciences or humanities.

Our methodological approach is experiential. We weave our experiences as well as the experiences of our students—male and female, natural and social science majors—into all aspects of our account. Personal experiences, therefore, provide the lens through which our discussion is refracted. We analyzed the written narratives of eight students collected from journal accounts compiled throughout the semester. We also conducted oral interviews with six students who volunteered to discuss the impact of the course on their knowledge of the relationship between earth processes and society as well as their commitment to social and environmental change. Finally, to provide an account of our experiences we draw on journals that we, the instructors, kept throughout the course and subsequent works that we produced about the course.

Rationale for Teaching Earth Systems: A Feminist Approach

Earth Systems: A Feminist Approach emerged from our awareness of recent feminist scholarship that presents a challenge to traditional Western scientific scholarship and science education (see the works of Harding; Rosser; Fausto-Sterling; Rosser and Kelly). Our approach to the development of the course was informed by the two interrelated issues that are central to this scholarship: (1) the "masculinity" of science and science education, which has contributed to the attrition of women, men of color, and people from working-class backgrounds from science courses and careers, and (2) the failure of scientific inquiry and education to situate scientific knowledge in a social, political, and historical context.

Numerous pedagogical implications for the transformation of the teaching and curricula in science education are embedded in these issues. As an increasing number of studies clearly suggest, elements of science education that need reform include the culture of competition that characterizes many science classrooms (Henderson 1993, Hollenshead et al 1994; Manis 1994; Seymour and Hewitt 1991; Tobias 1990); the lack of curriculum images that reflect diverse cultural and gender experiences and are relevant to the daily lives of students (Otto 1991; Trankina 1993; Kelly 1985); and low teacher expectations about the ability of women and men of color to successfully participate in scientific inquiry (Hollenshead et al 1994; Spear 1984). Furthermore, programs across the nation, such as Miami University's Project Discovery, the University of Michigan's Women in Science Program, and Sue Rosser's University of South Carolina System Model Project for the Transformation of Science and Math Teaching to Reach Women in Varied Campus Settings, illustrate, to varying degrees, some ways in which science classrooms and science curricula can be redesigned to empower marginalized students, acknowledge different ways of knowing, and provide a safer environment within which students' experiences and concerns will become central to the learning process. While changing particular curricular content and pedagogical techniques may increase the diversity within the pool of scientists, it will not necessarily alter the theoretical, philosophical, and political perspectives upon which science is based—a concern central in recent scholarship on feminism and science.

The work of feminists on science challenges Western scientific epistemology's inability to situate scientific knowledge in its historical, social, and political context. According to this view, what is wrong with Western science is that the social causes of scientific belief and behavior are neither exposed nor discussed in science domains. Sandra Harding and others (1991, 1993) have drawn attention to how the purportedly objective and value-free nature of science not only obscures the historical and social context of science but in fact may hide an androcentric bias (Bleier 1991 Fausto-Sterling 1981, Keller 1985, Rosser 1990, Shulman 1994). The politically regressive consequences that follow from this position are clear: the scientific establishment's insistence on the "purity" of science supports the claim that scientific findings improve human welfare, and it protects the establishment from claims that scientific research could be used to work against the welfare of certain social groups (Harding 1993, 53–54).

In addition, an awareness of how scientific knowledge is socially constructed is considered an important beginning for the development of the competencies that enable disempowered groups to become critically resistant readers and writers of their social, cultural, and educational environments. The pedagogical challenge for feminists is to create a feminist science that acknowledges and critically addresses the social study of science and the associated power relations embedded in the scientific community as well as the manner in which science is traditionally taught. To this end, the creation of a contextualized science in science education not only will begin to speak to the interests of women and men of color but will challenge us all to examine the role science plays in shaping definitions of knowledge, power relations, and social inequalities and to recognize our capacity to act within the world. As Sandra Harding stresses, "It seems to me that for nonscientists, the failure of the sciences to show that they are *for* us and have always been committed to and reasonably successful at increasing human welfare—to show science in historical context in that sense—goes a long way toward explaining why not only many women but also the majority of men in the U.S. are scientifically illiterate" (1993, 49).

In order to address these concerns, the primary goals of Earth Systems: A Feminist Approach were twofold. First, we wanted to create a cooperative, noncompetitive learning environment where all student voices could be heard and where the collaborative production of geological knowledge was linked to daily lives through the lens of sociology and feminist theory. Second, we wanted to develop a curriculum that would strengthen the ability of students (including those marginalized from previous science education) to play an active role in transformative learning and environmental, social, and political action.

"Doing" Geology, Sociology, and Feminist Pedagogy: Reflections from the Field

Our course was based on the principles of feminist pedagogy. Feminist pedagogy is not, as implied in the conventional view of pedagogy, merely a teaching method that transmits the content of knowledge but a pedagogy that signifies what Frances Maher and Mary Kay Thompson Tetreault call "the entire process of creating knowledge, involving the innumerable ways in which students, teachers, and academic disciplines interact and redefine each other in the classroom, the educational institution, and the larger society" (1994, 57). Thus the foundation of the course was built on the collaborative production of knowledge about the interrelatedness of earth and social systems in an environment that would demystify "doing sociology" and "doing geology."

We found that a combination of institutional requirements, such as course outlines and grades, and a lack of models and materials designed to develop cooperative, multicultural, and interdisciplinary knowledge often impeded our attempts to implement these goals. Many moments throughout the course, however, convince us that the blending of our pedagogical and intellectual commitments was successful. Although we cannot provide definitive ways to overcome institutional barriers to the implementation of feminist pedagogy or to bridge the gap between the social and natural sciences, our experiences offer some starting points.

(Un)enclosed Knowledge

A central organizing tool in traditional educational settings is the course syllabus, but it becomes a problematic tool when feminist pedagogy is implemented as the primary principle around which the classroom is structured. For example, professors at many universities are required to submit their course syllabi to their department chairperson before the beginning of each semester, and, at most universities, the course syllabus becomes the contract between student and professor, detailing the professor's expectations and requirements. Learning and knowledge, therefore, are organized, prearranged, and transmitted from the professor to the student. Paulo Freire refers to this approach as the "banking" method of education, in which "knowledge is a gift bestowed by those who consider themselves knowledgeable upon those whom they consider to know nothing." In this model, students are anonymous, interchangeable "containers" or "receptacles," to be "filled" by the teacher (1983, 58). In opposition to the "banking" method, women's studies practitioners have developed the practice of feminist pedagogy (Weiler 1991). Sitting in a circle underscores, visually and kinesthetically, the decentralization of authority in the women's studies classroom. So does the fact that everyone in the room has a name and a voice. Each member of the classroom is a learner and a potential teacher. Each member brings something to contribute to the collaborative construction of knowledge, and the knowledge they collectively produce should, ideally, exceed what any member thought they knew when they arrived. Obviously, a preplanned course syllabus, specifying each week's class content, and a traditionally organized classroom limits the implementation of this process.

Committed to feminist pedagogy, we started our course with a vaguely structured syllabus that would allow for collectively developing course content and direction throughout the semester with the students. The syllabus did, however, specify the course goals, provide a set of guidelines for how classroom discussions and negotiations would be implemented, and stipulate a set of criteria for grading. In addition, it listed the dates of each class period but did not provide topics or readings.

As instructors, we immediately recognized our discomfort with beginning the course without a detailed outline. What would we do each class period? How could we guarantee that the course would cover the "necessary" information? Most unnerving, how could we assure our preparedness each class, given our other academic responsibilities, if we had to think through each class period on a week-to-week basis? We commonly felt that this was the "scariest classroom endeavor" that we had ever undertaken.

As we began to feel comfortable about our decisions regarding the syllabus and the unstructured nature of the course, class began. We discussed the syllabus with the students and emphasized that they would collectively help build the curriculum and could participate in reconstructing the grading criteria. The students quickly made us aware of their discomfort, which was not unlike our own. In the first week's journal entries, we discovered their fear about not being provided with a "banking" model of education:

What outline? This makes me very nervous. We haven't even closed the date for the field trip. I would prefer things to be more set. I haven't been unsyllabied [*sic*] since high school. It makes prioritizing assignment times difficult. I'm used to structuring my week relative to my work load. This makes me think of *Zen and the Art of Motorcycle Maintenance*: A thing is either good or not good and we don't need an enforced system of letters to tell us what is what. On the other hand, life without letters could be difficult. I'm used to comparing myself to the class averages and I'm truly frightened of flying blind.

There is one thing I find disturbing—grading. Most institutions require grading and therefore teachers of feminist pedagogy must grade. Why should one participant in a class receive a higher grade then [*sic*] another for a journal entry?

At the outset, some students were also unsure about the "transformed" classroom setting. In particular, the natural science majors expressed great discomfort about sitting in a circle and opening all inquiry to discussion. After class the first evening, a geology major confided to Peg (Margaret) that sitting in a circle and verbally participate in class discussions felt uncomfortable and foreign because she had been so well schooled in traditional science classrooms. Because of her discomfort, she was unsure whether or not she could continue in the class. In contrast, the social science and humanities majors in the course were quite familiar with this arrangement. Upon hearing about the discomfort that some students felt about the classroom organization, a women's studies major commented, "I wouldn't know what to do if I walked into a classroom and the chairs were not in a circle or if there wasn't a lot of discussion!" In time, however, we all became more comfortable with the classroom environment and the emphasis on "process" learning. Students soon started to provide us with a wealth of ideas about topics that they desired to explore. In response, we designed class periods to incorporate their interests and concerns. The strong classroom emphasis on experiential, collaborative, and self-directed learning, however, presented us with a web of other challenges.

(Un)connected Knowledge

Providing to students, and ourselves, the experience of a process-oriented learning environment was only one of the hurdles that we faced in our attempt to infuse the classroom with a feminist pedagogy and collaboratively constructed knowledge. Early in the course, we recognized that achieving the goal of constructing a truly interdisciplinary course was hindered by our own academic backgrounds. The following example illustrates this problem: Peg, trained as a geologist, *knew* the importance of understanding plate tectonics, the hydrologic cycle, the rock cycle, the composition of the earth, and geological hazards and processes. For students to become scientifically and environmentally literate, she maintained that these concepts should be discussed. Maralee, trained as a sociologist and women's studies scholar, *knew* that any solid interdisciplinary knowledge would need to include discussions about epistemology, feminist critiques of science, policy formation processes, and the relationship of race, class, gender, and power to scientific and environmental inquiry. She adamantly stated, "the students *must* understand the concepts of epistemology, ideology, hegemony, and standpoint before the end of the semester." During the first few weeks of the course, each of us was determined to center class discussions on many of the concepts that make up our introductory classes. As we struggled with allotting time for each of the various discussions that *must* occur, our joke became, "two-two-two introductory classes in one."

Students, however, did not find this humorous. They found jumping between discussions of feminist critiques of science and sessions devoted to earth processes quite unnerving. For example, after several weeks of discussing feminist critiques of science, we wanted to illustrate how a variety of perspectives could be employed to examine a scientific concept. We decided to discuss the concept of "plate tectonics" by exploring the numerous ways in which this theory is presented at the introductory level and then trying to understand the relationship between the history and development of plate tectonics and our everyday lives and culture. We had expected students to be fascinated by the idea that scientific knowledge can have a subjective, cultural, and historical component. What we discovered, however, was their hunger for more "scientific" inquiry. A female social science major commented in a journal entry:

> If the continents never sink and they keep pushing against each other and erosion keeps happening, do the continents get smaller? Or is there enough volcanism to prevent this? Do new continents ever form? Have their shapes changed much? This subject fascinates me. Are there any classes on this that I could take as a non-science major?

Another student, a male biology major, obviously tiring of our attempts to always look at science within a social context, wrote this about the plate tectonics session:

> This was the best class session yet. Hopefully, this will continue. It is very relieving to finally get into earth systems, which I thought was to be the mainstay of the class rather than feminism. I thought it is from a feminist approach we are to learn the earth systems, not to learn the feminist approach itself. If I solely wanted to learn the feminism, I would have enrolled in women's studies 101, not this class.

As feminist educators, we were thrilled by the fascination with science expressed by our female student who, we later learned, had shied away from science courses since her early high school years. We were less pleased by the reaction of our male science major. Why had the approach failed to be of interest to him? What could spur his desire to learn how feminist critiques of science could be a new approach to evaluating, understanding, and conducting science? It wasn't until the last two weeks of the course that we would begin to be able to answer these and other questions. In the meantime, we were slowly becoming aware of how difficult it is to develop integrated knowledge.

Our inability to create interdisciplinary knowledge continued to haunt us. At one point, the students agreed to spend two weeks researching the relationship between concentrations of nonrenewable natural resources and political economies. They were to find literature that addressed why a particular resource (e.g., diamonds or copper ore) was concentrated in one part of the world (e.g., South Africa or South America) *and* the relationship between the presence of that resource and the country's political organization (e.g., apartheid or revolutions). After the two-week period, one student reflected the sentiment of many others by commenting:

> I found more than 300 entries in the library [relating to the mineral I wanted to study], some even in English, but none made any sense. I knew that science was not an easy subject, but I get the feeling I'm reading a foreign language. In another section of the library, I found that the De Beers people [an international family cartel] are known as the syndicate and insulated themselves into the financial fabric of a recalcitrant Australian government. They then threatened to disrupt the Australian economy if they [the syndicate] were not allowed to control newly discovered diamond mines. I understand some of what is being said, but I can't put it into words I understand or integrate what I am reading. This is an impossible task.

Furthermore, the resource librarian called us on the telephone during this stage of the course to convey her dismay at the graying of her hair as she worked with many of the students individually trying to help them locate the resources necessary for the successful completion of the project.

Solving the problem of "integrating knowledge" became a class goal. Students listened for and worked intently toward the moment that knowledge about earth and social processes would feel integrated.

Connected Knowledge

It was not until the last several weeks of the course that we began collectively to feel the integration of knowledge. On one occasion, we were engaged in an oil-exploration game intended to demonstrate the geological concepts of oil reservoirs and traps. The game was designed to get students interested in learning about sedimentary strata, faults, folds, and the difference between petroleum resources and reserves by having them play the role of an independent petroleum company with geologists and economists who needed to make business decisions about where to purchase land and drill for petroleum exploration. What our students gained, however, was a new understanding of capitalist consciousness. The game resulted not only in an increased knowledge about where petroleum may be trapped but also in a clearer understanding of the social and economic forces that shape our utilization of the earth's natural resources. The students identified the relationship between natural resources and economic imperatives, as evidenced by these journal entries:

> When we first started the game, I had a few unvoiced objections. [I wanted to ask,] what about the environment, ecology, and social consequences of drilling for petroleum? However, these were quickly forgotten as the excitement mounted. Our team wanted to be the first to "strike gold." So we bought information about the land, searched for the best places to drill, bought land, and drilled. We made a profit so we did it again. Soon we were up to $950,000, we were rolling in money and profits were soaring. Could we stop? No! Did *I* have any reservation about continuing? No. We went absolutely crazy with greed and power. We bought and drilled and bought and drilled. . . . I felt horrified at the greedy little capitalist I had become (and so easily)!

> My desire to finish first and make a profit clouded my thinking. Never once did I think about the flora or fauna on top of the earth, only what was underneath. I looked at risk factors in terms of dollars only, and never once thought of human penalties.

Perhaps one of our most successful efforts at integrating fields of knowledge occurred during a weekend excursion into Death Valley to see and experience many of the geological processes and features discussed in class. Sedimentary deposits, limestone, sandstone, and basalt, in the words of one student, "are easier to understand when they're tangible." We also encouraged the students (and ourselves) to pay attention to the group's social dynamics, hoping to develop a sense of camaraderie between individuals. The weekend experience, although trying because of seventy-two hours of strong winds, rain, and snow, effectively connected knowledge and process. The connectedness was experienced by many students as an "active" learning process. This journal entry reflects the comments made by many of the students:

> The field trip to Death Valley was a great application of feminist pedagogy. It incorporated much of what we have learned in class into an understanding of geological processes with a societal and personal perspective. To be able to reach out and touch rocks that are 1.6 billion years old means so much more

than hearing that rocks of such a great age exist. Physical involvement [with the earth] alone, however, doesn't guarantee a more holistic approach. The questions and comments and the camaraderie of the group was certainly a crucial part of the learning process. That process would not have had such impact if it had been presented in the same dry, sterile method so common to the usual scientific field trip.

During the second day of the field trip, we entered Mosaic Canyon and observed faulted, brecciated, and polished limestone that is beautifully displayed in the steep-sided, narrow, curving passage into and through the mountains. We stopped to consider how the history of a fault (and its nature) cannot be captured by observing a limited rock section. Suddenly, and spontaneously, the students began to discuss the unforeseen environmental problems that could result from the spatially limited geological study being conducted at the proposed Yucca Mountain Nuclear Repository site, which is located a hundred miles north of Las Vegas: a site marked by numerous active and inactive faults. To the onlooking tourists, students discussing the geological research at Yucca Mountain may have seemed disassociated from the geological story told by the rocks in Mosaic Canyon. To our group, however, the limited history of deposition, faulting, fracturing, and fluid flow that was recorded in the Mosaic Canyon outcrop constituted a warning. The important questions became apparent to us all: What geological questions were scientists at Yucca Mountain addressing? What geological evidence was being overlooked on account of the limited area within which geological observations were taking place? Should other questions be asked? Can geological questions truly be evaluated through "site assessment" or should more regional investigations be required? Who was being allowed (funded) to study the geology of Yucca Mountain? Do the questions asked, investigations conducted, and conclusions formed vary with funding agents? What are the potential human consequences? Have scientists not already destroyed the sacred land of the Western Shoshone by building roads, drilling wells, and digging tunnels for scientific inquiry to justify the disposal of human waste? Geological processes, the construction of scientific knowledge, power, influence, and human consequences all emerged as important topics of discussion while we observed the faults and fractured limestone of Mosaic Canyon.

After observing how our discussion had moved from the effects of local faulting to a critique of the geological studies being conducted at Yucca Mountain, one student commented:

The field trip from heaven and hell. We are integrating a world view with a world we are only beginning to know. The discussion in Mosaic Canyon had the quality of synthesis that we search for when we reach out to read a book, touch a leaf, quench a thirst, or to hold the hand of another.

This is just one of many stories to emerge from our attempt to develop a truly interdisciplinary course and to teach it from a feminist perspective.

(De)constructing Knowledge

Developing interdisciplinary knowledge requires a collaborative effort and a commitment to process learning. Moreover, this process forces both students and teachers to engage in a continuous effort to invent new knowledge.

The significance of process-based learning became clear to us after a frustrating small-group exercise aimed at demonstrating the various types of information scientists need for determining the epicenter and focus of an earthquake. During this exercise many of the social science and humanities majors, who were mostly women, had difficulty working through a series of arithmetic and algebra problems, using ruler and compass, and plotting to scale on a map. The angst built to such a level that the exercise manuals were literally being pushed to the corner of their desks and shoved into backpacks—pushed away and out of sight, where they could not intimidate. One student lost all interest in scientific inquiry during this agonizing session:

> The inner workings of how an earthquake occurs and how its epicenter is calculated seem understandable. However, once I tried to do it, with the compass and equation in hand, I was dumbstruck. For the life of me I couldn't grasp what was seemingly an easy task. Is it really so important to know where the epicenter of an earthquake is?

We felt that the level of math anxiety and student disengagement with the project, which surfaced during the session, needed to be addressed. The following week we decided to place our central focus on this issue and "do math anxiety." Maralee, recognizing her own difficulty with the project, walked the students through the various mental images and thinking processes that she herself had had to use in an attempt to solve the mathematical equations. The presentation forced her to discuss her fear of confronting a problem that could not be contextualized or historicized and made her carefully prepare a step-by-step description of how a "mathematically challenged" mind might go about thinking through the problem. This strategy, we hoped, would allow students to see that fears and anxieties brought on by confronting math are neither unusual nor limited to the "uneducated." Furthermore, we hoped that the strategy would expose students to a multitude of ways to perform mathematical procedures.

The results were striking: the students fearful of math were now fully engaged in the problem-solving process; other students began to offer their classmates a variety of approaches to solving the equation, thereby helping us all develop a better appreciation for the multitude of ways that "scientific" procedures can be conducted; and Maralee learned that even she could "teach math." In addition, the experience underscored the importance of a classroom environment in which all members of the class care about each other's learning as well as their own.

In relation to this exercise, we also wanted to develop a sense of the social and political aspects of earthquakes in order to address the question "Is it really so important to know where the epicenter of an earthquake is?" We assembled a set of readings to demonstrate the human and social dimensions of earthquakes and illustrate the importance of distinguishing between natural occurrences and natural "disasters." The discussion that ensued allowed each of us to begin to understand the relationship between scientific knowledge, social policy, and social inequality. Throughout these sessions the language of sociology was spoken. For instance, the concept of "disaster" was revealed to be a socially constructed concept, one that varies historically, culturally, and regionally. We called into question the "naturalness" of disasters by discussing which segments of the population are most vulnerable to natural disasters and observed that such events overwhelmingly kill poor people in poor countries. The discussion illuminated how scientific language often obscures the social, political, and human consequences of scientific knowledge and provided us a new way to think about the social context of science. When students (and ourselves) posed questions about how scientific findings play out in everyday life, the distance between the natural and social sciences shrank.

By the end of the unit, we had discussed the science of earthquakes and how scientists locate and evaluate earthquakes, as well as how social policies regarding earthquake occurrences are formed. We discovered that an earthquake's impact on human life is interrelated with a variety of social policies and social conditions. Scientific procedures and findings were now joined with the question of who benefits from "science" and who doesn't. Reflecting on her newly acquired knowledge about where earthquakes are likely to occur, how scientists study them, and the social and political implications of earthquakes, one student wrote:

> Almost like a puzzle where the scene is at first confusing and obscure, then suddenly becomes clear and obvious when completed. The discussion and reading led me to put together bits and pieces of information that I already had into a complete picture. I said "of course" when I finally recognized that, although we can do little about natural "occurrences," we can do a lot about how humans are impacted by them, and the social inequities of how different groups are affected by natural phenomena.

Implications for Social Transformation: Fostering Praxis

At its core, feminist pedagogy is a commitment not only to interdisciplinary knowledge and process learning but also to the development of a critical consciousness empowered to apply knowledge to social action and social transformation. Nancy Schniedewind suggests that a fundamental component of feminist pedagogy is "learning a process for applying theory to practice, attempting to change a concrete situation based on that learning, and recreating theory based on that activity" (1993, 25). Without this component, commonly known as praxis, feminist pedagogy merely becomes, in the words of Jane Kenway and Helen Modra, "wishful thinking" (1992, 156).

Five months after the course had ended, we wanted to better understand the impact Earth Systems: A Feminist Approach had had on the students', and our own, social and political awareness. Had the class affected day-to-day understandings of either the earth or society? Did the class have an impact on a student's intellectual and personal life? Had the content and pedagogy of the class inspired new attitudes about environmental and social change?

Kristin Kampschroeder, a sociology graduate student working as a research assistant in the Department of Geoscience, interviewed six students from our class, asking them to discuss these questions. When students discussed their understanding of the interrelatedness of earth systems and social systems, some expressed concern over the role natural resources play in the development of foreign policy:

> Anytime I hear about national policy or military policy (like in Rwanda), I am always wondering what is it that our country wants to export from the other country. What do they have that we want? I'm not as naive.

> I think the most important thing that I gained was a new insight into how geology and sociology are interrelated and how social policies don't naturally evolve from things that we are taught to think of as beyond human control, such as mineral deposits.

A number of students also expressed a new awareness of the social context within which scientific "knowledge" is produced:

> I have a greater interest in the structure of scientific knowledge and how it has shaped our culture and political policies.

> Most important to me was the idea that science is not objective. That was a new concept for me at the time.

> The course greatly changed my perception of society. I was always earth-centered and it certainly helped me refine my feelings of frustration with en-

vironmental issues; particularly in regard to how capitalism and science shape our environmental policy.

For other students the course reinforced previously held beliefs and, for some, helped them better articulate their environmental and social attitudes:

Because I have a major that is interdisciplinary, women's studies, before the class I was always looking for things that were interrelated. The class was solid proof that everything is interrelated, even geology and sociology. Since being a women's studies major, I have become more active in my community. The Earth Systems class is definitely a part of my continued involvement, since it was a class in my major field.

I had a lot of knowledge about the earth and U.S. society before taking this class. What the class did was to clarify what I knew and also to give me the facts and figures to back up my general knowledge and intuition.

Everything in your life, any bit of learning has some effect. The course reinforced my feminist feelings and gave me more confidence in them. I now have fewer doubts about what I want to do, where I want to go, and what I want to accomplish.

For many students the awareness of earth processes and social systems had an impact on their daily activities. By engaging in individual activism, most students felt they could be effective agents of social change in everyday life:

I have stopped dying my hair! I wear cotton clothes now. It's not a good thing but I still get my nails done, you cannot make me stop. You don't know how much guilt [the class] made me feel. I cannot do anything in my house. I cannot throw away styrofoam containers, I cannot open my refrigerator without realizing the effect it is having on the ozone layer. When I take my one bag of garbage out a week, for both me and my husband, which I don't think is all that much, I feel guilty because it is in a Hefty bag that probably *will* way outlive me. I live differently. I don't leave the water running when I brush my teeth. I don't take bubble baths as often. OK, once in awhile I do. I deserve them, it's a right. I put in desert landscaping in my backyard. I mean this class had a profound effect on me, preppy USA.

I quit shaving my legs while the water was running in the shower. That was my big thing.

When I found out that the water table is diminished to the point it is, now every time I turn on the faucets I look over my shoulder.

Statements such as these suggest just how quickly students respond to new ideas about the interrelatedness of earth and social processes.

Nonetheless, as we mentioned above, the emancipatory potential of feminist pedagogy is often subsumed in feminist classrooms by what Kenway and Modra refer to as the "over-valorization of consciousness-raising" (156). While consciousness-raising—or awareness that the personal is political—is certainly a mission of feminist educators, consciousness itself is not readily transformed into a plan for social action or social change. The potential of feminist classroom dynamics to succeed in raising consciousness and fail in engaging people to act collectively upon the world was clearly demonstrated by a number of the students enrolled in Earth Systems: A Feminist Approach. Several students did articulate a plan of action, however, and expressed a commitment to becoming politically involved in groups and organizations dedicated to environmental and social transformation. It is not surprising that these students had previously been community activists for whom confronting the particular environmental and social issues examined during the course became one more challenge. One student, a former local chapter president of NOW, expressed a new interest in becoming involved in environmental issues:

> I think I would like to become more involved in environmental change than I have been in the past. I have always stayed away from environmental issues, not really understanding them. My political involvement in the past revolved around women's rights and I think that this class showed me a lot of things interrelated to women's rights and clarified to me that relationship.

Another student, a self-defined environmental activist, commented upon her new interest in women's issues:

> I branched out my memberships in groups. I have always been an environmentalist and belonged to a lot of environmental groups. However, I recently joined NOW. Although I don't have time to really do a lot of things, my interests are a little broader now and I now make donations to environmental *and* women's organizations and help out on a local level in whatever ways I can.

One woman saw new challenges ahead:

> So now I have another cause to which to commit my efforts. Not only will I be a crusader for environmental awareness, but I will also try to show people how the same misguided value system, and the controlling interests that helped create that value system, has led to not only environmental degradation, but are destructive to the cultures and the lives of people around the world.

We noted earlier that feminist pedagogy premises the student as student-teacher and the teacher as teacher-student. We have thus asked ourselves the same questions we asked our students: Did the class affect our understanding of the earth and social systems? Did the class have an impact on our intellectual and personal lives? Did the class inspire us to act upon the world? As with many of our students, the movement we are making toward transformative knowledge and transformative social change is largely built upon our particular life situations. Peg currently teaches a moderately large section of Introductory Physical Geology, and she now weaves feminist pedagogy into this much more traditional classroom. As part of this change, she is committed to making the curriculum more environmentally oriented and more oriented toward the students' lives on a local and global level. In addition, Peg is a guest lecturer in Maralee's sociology classes, where she presents a deeply moving portrayal of her own experiences as a woman trained as a scientist, a scientist who is now questioning many of the assumptions upon which her academic and personal development are based. Peg describes her transition as, "scary, but once you start to question who you are and what you know, you can never go back." Maralee is now fascinated by exploring new ways of implementing feminist pedagogy in all her courses. More important, perhaps, is her new understanding of how sociology and the natural sciences can inform one another. She is developing sections on science in both her introductory sociology and women's studies courses. She is also giving seminars to geoscientists on the ways one can build bridges between feminism and science. Furthermore, her sabbatical leave is dedicated to further exploring the intersections of knowledge. Most recently, Maralee and Peg have received funding from the National Science Foundation to launch a three-year educational project, the Social Study of Geology.

Clearly, fostering praxis is a complicated and difficult task. However, we believe that any attempts to integrate social and scientific knowledge promote a better understanding of the ways in which knowledge can begin to be transformative.

Conclusion

We, as feminists, as well as many others, believe that the creation of a contextualized science education together with feminist pedagogy will speak to the interests of many people and will challenge us all to examine the role science plays in shaping definitions of knowledge, power relations, and social inequalities. Our experiences developing and participating in the teaching of Earth Systems: A Feminist Approach demonstrated that the gap between the social and natural sciences can be narrowed. Furthermore, our effort to implement feminist pedagogy in an interdisciplinary "science" classroom strengthened the ability of all students (and ourselves) in the class to play an active role in transformative learning and environmental, social, and political action. As we have pointed out throughout this chapter, science education may be the pivotal arena in which theory and practice can become powerful agents of social change.

From our perspective, the course Earth Systems: A Feminist Approach and others like it are important additions to the academy providing new educational opportunities for faculty and students, illustrating the need for institutional change, and stimulating debate. We think that institutional changes must include supporting team teaching for faculty education, funding interdisciplinary resource development, and rewarding curriculum reform. From the perspective of women's studies, our course provided to students an educational experience that reflected the fundamental tenets of feminist education: it was interdisciplinary, it emphasized social transformation, and it allowed students to play a central part in the construction of their education. Furthermore, it illustrated why it may be important to integrate natural science concepts into the traditional women's studies curriculum. From the perspective of conventional science, however, there may be some question regarding whether it was a "science course," regarding the degree to which students were prepared to enter the next level geology course and the need for the course in the curriculum. We are convinced that Earth Systems is a science course that prepares students to bring new perspectives to other science courses and provides an important educational component for all of us who live in a technologically advanced society.

Judging from the students' written work and journal entries, it is clear that their understanding of geological concepts and social processes had increased to widely varying degrees by the end of the semester. The social science and humanities majors demonstrated only a modestly increased understanding of geological concepts, but they had developed a much more complex understanding about how capitalist and hegemonic processes shape scientific inquiry and the uses to which science is put. The natural science students, by contrast, had developed at least an elementary understanding of how social systems shape scientific enterprises and had begun to recognize the importance of discussing scientific concepts in a historical and social context. We believe these changes are important. It remains unclear, however, to what degree this class inspired students to pursue other geology, sociology, or women's studies courses.

These considerations and questions bring us to suggest several broad areas for improvement within the academy and within our course. We believe that the significance of "doing science" and "doing social life" becomes clearest when course content and discussion continually illuminate the connections between everyday happenings and science and provide students the opportunity to construct connections between science and day-to-day experiences. Thus the primary point to consider is how educational activities, readings, and exercises can be developed and implemented to demonstrate, across disciplines, why the learning of scientific, sociological, and feminist concepts is important.

We have identified a number of specific areas for improvement for our course that may be applicable to other courses on the social study of science as well as to many other courses across the curriculum. First, a variety of well-planned field trips to sites within the local Las Vegas community must be designed to expose students to the connections between their everyday life and natural science processes. Outings of this kind may be more useful than one culminating field trip. Second, a broad range of interdisciplinary projects and experiential, hands-on labs need to be developed that require the active engagement of students and instructors at every step. The projects and labs would aim to help participants construct scientific and sociological understandings from their own observations and experiences. Third, numerous collaborative group projects that bring science and nonscience majors together, allowing them to be both teachers and learners, must be developed to create the space for a dialogue to begin between diverse types of knowledge. Finally, new interdisciplinary literature (especially from the environmental sciences, women's studies, and the humanities) combined with the knowledge base of earth scientists could be used to highlight the relationship between technology and geological or natural science processes and our everyday lives (especially those of indigenous peoples and women).

Our discovery of new ways to develop a relational and interdisciplinary science pedagogy and curriculum is an important first step in motivating students to broaden their social and scientific knowledge. We hope, also, that curricular changes like the ones we implemented may begin to alleviate the fears and misconceptions many conventional scientists have about interdisciplinary projects of this nature. These changes, combined with a growing awareness that science education needs to reach a more diverse audience in order to improve science literacy and to diversify the pool of scientists, may foster the building of "two-way streets" (Fausto-Sterling 1981) between social, feminist, and scientific inquiry.

Acknowledgments

The authors would like to thank the *NWSA Journal* reviewers and Ellen Cronan Rose for their helpful comments on an earlier version of this chapter. The final preparation of this chapter was, at least in part, supported by the National Science Foundation under Grant HRD-9555721.

Works Cited

Bleier, Ruth, ed. *Feminist Approaches to Science.* New York: Teachers College Press, 1991.

Fausto-Sterling, Anne. "Building Two-Way Streets." *National Women's Studies Association Journal* 4.3 (1992): 5–15.

———. *Myths of Gender: Biological Theories about Women and Men.* New York: Basic Books, 1985.

———. "Women and Science." *Women's Studies International Quarterly* 13 (1981): 30–32.

Freire, Paulo. *Pedagogy of the Oppressed.* New York: Continuum, 1983.

Harding, Sandra. "Forum: Feminism and Science." *National Women's Studies Association Journal* 5.1 (1993): 56–64.

———. *Whose Science? Whose Knowledge? Thinking from Women's Lives.* Ithaca: Cornell University Press, 1991.

Henderson, Rebecca. *Female Participation in Undergraduate Math, Science, and Engineering Majors: Organizational Features.* Paper presented at the annual meeting of the Pacific Sociological Association, San Diego, CA, 1993.

Hollenshead, Carol, et al. "Women Graduate Students in Mathematics and Physics: Reflections on Success." *Journal of Women and Minorities in Science and Engineering* 1.1 (1994): 63–88.

Keller, Evelyn Fox. *Reflections on Science and Gender.* New Haven, CT: Yale University Press, 1985.

Kelly, A. "The Construction of Masculine Science." *British Journal of Sociology of Education* 6 (1985): 133–54.

Kenway, Jane, and Helen Modra. "Feminist Pedagogy and Emancipatory Possibilities." In *Feminisms and Critical Pedagogy,* C. Luke and J. Gore 138–66. New York: Routledge, 1992.

Maher, F. A., and M. K. T. Tetreault. *The Feminist Classroom.* New York: Basic Books, 1994.

Maher, Frinde. "Toward a Richer Theory of Feminist Pedagogy: A Comparison of 'Liberation' and 'Gender' Models for Teaching and Learning." *Journal of Education* 169.3 (1987): 91–100.

Manis, J. M., et al. *An Analysis of Factors Affecting Choices in Majors in Science Mathematics, and Engineering at the University of Michigan.* Ann Arbor: University of Michigan Center for Continuing Education of Women, 1989.

Otto, P. "One Science, One Sex?" *School Science and Mathematics* 91.8 (1991): 367–73.

Rosser, Sue. *Female-Friendly Science.* New York: Pergamon, 1990.

Rosser, Sue, and B. Kelly. "From Hostile Exclusion to Friendly Inclusion: University of South Carolina System Model Project for the Transformation of Science and Math Teaching to Reach Women in Varied Campus Settings." *Journal of Women and Minorities in Science and Engineering* 1.1 (1994): 29–44.

Schniedewind, Nancy. "Teaching Feminist Process in the 1990s." *Women's Studies Quarterly* 21.3–4 (1993): 17–30.

Seymour, N. M., and E. Hewitt. *Factors Contributing to High Attrition Rates among Science, Mathematics, and Engineering Undergraduate Majors.* Report to the Alfred P. Sloan Foundation, 1991.

Shrewsbury, Carolyn. "What Is Feminist Pedagogy?" *Women's Studies Quarterly* 21.3–4 (1993): 8–16.

Shulman, Bonnie. "Implications of Feminist Critiques of Science for the Teaching of Mathematics and Science." *Journal of Women and Minorities in Science and Engineering* 1.1 (1994): 1–15.

Spear, M. G. "Teachers' Views about the Importance of Science to Boys and Girls." *Science for Girls.* Ed. A. Kelly. Philadelphia: Open University Press, 1984.

Tobias, Sheila. *They're Not Dumb; They're Different.* Tucson: Tucson Arizona Research Corp., 1990.

Trankina, M. L. "Gender Differences in Attitudes toward Science." *Psychological Reports* 73 (1993): 123–30.

Weiler, Kathleen. "Freire and a Feminist Pedagogy of Difference." *Harvard Educational Review* 61.4 (1991): 449–74.

PART II   **Pedagogical Practices in the Feminist Classroom**

CHAPTER SEVEN

Small Group Pedagogy: Consciousness-Raising in Conservative Times

ESTELLE B. FREEDMAN

In the fall of 1988 I began teaching the introductory course in the Feminist Studies Program at Stanford University. "Introduction to Feminist Studies: Issues and Methods" (FS101) had grown from a small discussion class to a medium-sized lecture course with separate section meetings for sixty-six students. The subject matter ranges from the origins of sexual inequality and the history of feminism to contemporary paid and unpaid labor, race and feminism, reproductive rights and sexuality, and violence against women. Because many of these topics raise both emotional and political sensitivities, I felt that FS101 required a forum in which students could discuss their personal reactions to classroom learning. Even more than the U.S. women's history classes I had taught previously, "Introduction to Feminist Studies" permitted, and indeed necessitated, the integration of the personal and the academic.

In preparing the course, I wondered how I might use consciousness-raising in the classroom to achieve this end, and whether my 1970s experience of consciousness-raising would work with the more conservative students of the late 1980s. By consciousness-raising I mean the sharing of personal-experience with others in order to understand the larger social context for the experience and to transform one's intellectual or political understandings of it. Once before, in a women's history class, I had experimented with the explicit use of consciousness-raising in the classroom. On the day we discussed documents from the feminist movements of the 1960s and 1970s, I spontaneously turned the class into a consciousness-raising session. We formed a circle and spoke in turn about how one article or idea in the readings had affected each of us personally. The experiment took over an entire week of the course, as students shared feelings of both anger and inspiration, revealed personal experiences with sexism on campus, and reacted to the differences that emerged in their views. The evaluations of the exercise were enthusiastic, so the next year I built a consciousness-raising session into the syllabus. Again, the students reported that they not only understood the historical experience of feminism more clearly, but that they also made important connections between the past and the world around them.

In addition to this and other positive models, I had more defensive reasons for incorporating consciousness-raising into the introductory

Originally published in the Autumn 1990 issue of the *NWSA Journal* course.[1] The preceding year, a hostile male student had tried unsuccessfully to disrupt FS101, and at the University of Washington, one male student had the class placed the entire women's studies program under attack by claiming that classes discriminated against men. I wanted to forestall such disruptions as much as possible by creating a place outside of the classroom where emotional responses might be shared with peers and not simply directed at faculty. Aside from hostile students, I worried about the feelings of alienation that students of minority race, class, ethnicity, sexual identity, or physical ability would experience in a predominantly white, middle-class, heterosexual, and able-bodied classroom.[2] Consciousness-raising groups might allow these students to acknowledge their feelings and make personal and intellectual connections between gender and other forms of social hierarchy.

To faculty who are veterans of 1970s women's studies classes or who work in public universities or small liberal arts colleges committed to teaching, my rationale for incorporating consciousness-raising into the classroom may seem unnecessary. But I work within an extremely elitist university in which pedagogy is rarely discussed, and academic advancement depends almost exclusively on scholarship. At this university, opponents of the term "feminist studies" shudder at such a self-conscious reference to the political nature of knowledge and associate feminist scholarship with a political radicalism they consider anti-intellectual. Indeed, even a colleague at a feminist studies meeting reacted to my plans for setting up consciousness-raising groups by warning that it was inappropriate and unprofessional for me to attempt to do "therapy" in my classes.[3] Students who signed up for FS101 arrived in a state of extreme fear of feminism. Most associated the term with an unpleasant militancy and refused to accept the label "feminist" even if they believed in the liberal goals of the movement.

In this setting, I feel that the use of consciousness-raising has to be handled carefully, not only for its pedagogical value but for the political well-being of the course and the program. Even on more liberal campuses, these conservative times might make faculty wary of the explicit use of consciousness-raising groups. I believe that now more than ever, however, we need to confront students' fears of feminism and of social change. As women's studies courses become part of general education and distribution requirements on many campuses, we can expect more conservative or nonfeminist students in our classes. From my experience teaching FS101, I believe that consciousness-raising can be an extremely effective way to address the fear of feminism held by many of these students. This chapter then, is an effort to share my own and the students' experience with consciousness-raising in the late 1980s in order to encourage the careful incorporation of personal experience into academic classes wherever this might be appropriate.

* * *

With advice from feminist colleagues, I devised a structure for making consciousness-raising central to FS101. Required biweekly group meetings supplemented an already demanding course—three lectures, heavy reading, a discussion section weekly, and three papers during the quarter.[4] Thus, to make clear from the outset that the groups were not extracurricular but integral to the process of learning, I spelled out on the syllabus the rules for attendance and the format of sessions; and I stressed the importance of a final paper evaluating the groups. On the recommendation of several colleagues, this paper would not be graded, lest students feel judged for either their emotions or their politics. Knowing Stanford students' sensitivities about language and politics, I called the process "small groups." Although I referred to consciousness raising in my lectures, students continued to speak of their "small groups" rather than "consciousness-raising groups."

The major dilemma I faced, however, was not about naming, but whether to create random groups that would mix students from various backgrounds or to create minority support groups—for women or students of color, lesbians and/or lesbians and gay men, disabled, male, ethnic, or working-class students. As much as I wanted to diminish minority alienation, I felt that it was more important for each group to confront the issues of difference with as much firsthand information as possible. In addition, many students had multiple or overlapping identities; constructing separate groups would force them to choose only one basis of support. For these reasons, the groups were formed by a random sorting of names into thirteen sets of four or five students each. (I hoped that the small size, compared with discussion sections of up to twenty-one students, would make scheduling easier, allow students to meet in a dorm room, and help to build friendships.) Each group had to meet five times during the ten-week quarter, for a session lasting about two hours, at a time to be arranged by group members.

I assigned readings for the first session only: Pam Allen's "Free Space" and Irene Peslikis's "Resistances to Consciousness."[5] I also recommended a rotating timekeeper, leaderless groups, and an uninterrupted five to ten minutes for each member to speak at the outset of sessions. Suggested topics paralleled the syllabus and attempted to link course readings and lectures with everyday life. "How does your personal experience of race, class and ethnicity affect your response to what you are learning?" followed the lecture on race and feminism and coincided with a required "unlearning racism" workshop.[6] When we studied women and work, the suggested question asked students to relate readings and lectures to jobs, families, and campus life. I left one week open for student topics and closed with a question to parallel our reading of Marge Piercy's utopian novel, *Woman on the Edge of Time*: "What one thing would you most want to change about our current world?" Students were asked to keep private journals after groups but not to submit them. The final paper evaluating the groups was to draw heavily upon the journal.[7]

During the quarter, several incidents on campus, in the community, and in the classroom intensified the importance of consciousness-raising and expanded it beyond the groups and into the lecture sessions. On campus, two white students posted racist slurs in the Afro-American theme house, igniting a yearlong debate over the action and the administration's response, and heightening awareness of racism. Then, against the backdrop of the Bush-Dukakis campaign, a few antiabortion activists mobilized conservative women to join Operation Rescue's blockade of local abortion clinics, while campus feminists formed a prochoice alliance. Within the classroom, students responded to the readings on lesbian feminism with such a profound silence that I felt compelled to challenge their homophobia. Borrowing a technique from a colleague at an even more conservative university, I asked students to write hypothetical "coming out letters" to their parents, drawing on their readings about lesbianism and homophobia.[8] At the same time, the students' presumption of their instructor's heterosexuality made me extremely uncomfortable about "passing" as straight and raised my own consciousness to the point that for the first time I came out in a classroom as a lesbian.

Thus for me, as well as for the students, FS101 took unexpected turns. On two occasions, for example, students raised my consciousness about issues that personally affected them. First, shortly before my lecture on sexual violence, I received a call from an incest survivor in the course who had been distressed by the lack of readings on incest. I asked her permission to discuss the call, anonymously, in class, and used the episode to talk about my own preconceptions about violence.[9] Secondly, in anticipation of the lecture on women and food, a student volunteered to speak in class about her own struggles with anorexia and bulimia. Her moving, expert presentation provided both personal testimony and information about support groups on campus. Inspired by her offer, I invited other students in the class to speak about their personal involvement in issues we studied. Members of the Rape Education Project did so, and since no students came out in the lecture class, I invited representatives from the Gay and Lesbian Alliance to speak on available student support services.

Meanwhile, students managed the small groups independently. Every other week I asked for feedback on the groups during lecture. Although students made few concrete comments at the time, they suggested that the groups were going well and were important to them. Only at the end of the course, after I read the set of sixty-six papers describing and evaluating the groups, did I realize how critical they had been to the educational process. Several students felt that the groups were as important as the class itself; for some, they were "the best part," and for at least one, "the most personally enriching part of the class."[10] Not every group, however, succeeded in establishing a sense of purpose and facilitating growth. Several groups had difficulty finding meeting times or sharing personal experiences; their members felt disappointed when they compared their experiences with those of the majority of students. Generally though, papers from eleven of the thirteen groups testified to the power of the small groups for enhancing student understanding of issues raised in class and for contributing to both self-understanding and greater understanding of others.

As they did for second-wave feminists of the 1960s and 1970s, consciousness-raising groups in FS101 functioned to move students from silence to speech, from isolation to community, and sometimes from political ambivalence to political commitment. Once empowered to explore ideas and feelings, a number of students were able to confront personal dilemmas, especially those concerning sexuality and race. As a result, their definitions of feminism expanded. By the end of the course, the majority of students reported that they had shifted from discomfort with feminism to enthusiastic embrace of the term and its complexity. A few made commitments to political activism. One small group continued meeting throughout the year to support the feminist activism of its members.

Although the degree of change varied greatly, the majority of students reported that initially they had been "skeptical," "wary," "a little leery," "worried," "nervous," or "doubtful" about going to these "weird" and "extra" groups. "Initially, I honestly dreaded the meetings," one student who was "skeptical about [their] value" confessed; and another thought she would "dread going every other week." A freshwoman felt "intimidated at the thought of having to talk to such knowledgeable people" and went to the first session "with a slight feeling of apprehension." For several groups, the first meeting was "awkward," but rather quickly, most students recounted, they were "pleasantly surprised," particularly by "the high level of engagement and interest." Students "truly began to look forward to the sessions." Repeatedly, the papers used the term "comfortable" to describe the atmosphere in which students found themselves "eager to talk" and to listen to others. As one woman explained after the first meeting, she "was actually excited to discuss new ideas openly and honestly with the members of my group."

Throughout the small group papers, students expressed wonder at their ability, even need, to talk about course issues. "We all began by saying that we could not possibly talk as long as we were supposed to," one woman recalled. "We then proceeded to talk longer than that, amazed that we each had so much to say." Similarly, a member of another group initially felt "Are we really supposed to just sit around and talk for an hour and a half? That's such a long time and I've got real work to do for other classes." Here, too, the group ran over time and "had no problem of thinking of things to say." The student "came away from that meeting with a sense of urgency that I had to tell others about this revolutionary concept of small groups."

Students quickly adapted to this unusual assignment, in part because the groups provided a safer place to try out ideas than did the traditional lectures or sections. A woman of color in her first year of college found the groups "extremely helpful" in discussing course topics "perhaps because I am not a very outspoken person, yet these groups were very comfortable, so I could express my feelings openly." Many other students reported on the importance of meeting informally outside of the classroom. The first group session "made me feel slightly more comfortable expressing myself in [the lecture] class because I had some idea of how others might react," one woman wrote. "Basically, I didn't feel as alone with my viewpoints after the first meeting." An Asian immigrant compared the "sense of well being" in the group meeting to "times I used to share my thoughts and dreams with my mom, my sister, my woman friends." The experience was "empowering" for her because "I, a minority woman, was taking part in naming myself, in taking control of my life." The personal gatherings, she explained, represented "a political statement."

The creation of safe space for talk rested upon the ability to listen. "A very important part of making the discussion groups work so well was that we really listened to each other, and let each other speak," one woman wrote. For her, having uninterrupted time "was good practice listening to people." A senior felt "comfortable speaking to an audience that was listening, not judging," while a highly articulate sophomore felt that "Small groups gave quieter people a chance to talk (unlike 'loudmouths' like myself)." Reciprocity of speaking and listening seemed to characterize all groups, easing my fears that certain students would dominate. As a senior wrote of her group: "All of a sudden I had four therapists to listen to me. I in turn, could speak to their problems, or simply listen to them." Like therapy, groups relied on speech to achieve consciousness; but unlike therapy, they included neither experts nor leaders. Because students preferred a natural flow of speech and felt their groups achieved balance among members, evaluations overwhelmingly rejected the opening five to ten minute format. Students also criticized the assignment of topics, preferring to choose their subjects spontaneously.

Student papers provide many clues about why the groups offered safety so quickly. For one, a supportive environment was especially necessary for members of this class, given the hostility to feminism in the culture at large and the university itself. Even enrolling in a feminist studies course could be stressful. Because many students "met with nervous responses from family and friends over taking the course," they "found it was helpful to discuss these problems with others" in the small group. Most members of one group thought that "our fathers felt threatened by our studying feminism," and the students shared their responses from family members.

Male students, who made up just under one-fifth of the class, may have been particularly vulnerable to stigma. A freshman explained at his first group meeting "how difficult it was being a guy feminist," for "not only did he get badgered by guys, but also he got heat from women who saw his feminist comments sometimes as pickup lines." Another man discovered from the different reactions of male and female friends "the extent to which" his enrollment "was viewed as a political decision." The experience of one male student illustrated the extent of male resistance on campus. While distributing pamphlets from the Rape Education Project in his dorm, men typically asked "Oh, are you going to teach us how to rape?" In another group, every member wrote about an incident that showed them firsthand the kind of chiding directed at male students who took feminist classes. While they met at an outdoor eating area, a student described by one woman as "a domineering white male" approached his buddy in the group. Learning what the small group was doing, the outsider "started to tease" his friend, "hollering disbelief." After one woman accused the intruder of sexism, the group had a forty-five minute debate on the meaning of the attack, the usefulness of her counterattack, and the way the incident clarified points about oppression made during the unlearning racism workshop.[11]

As might be expected, for men the experience of groups tended to be more intellectual than personal. One man wrote that he "felt somewhat alienated" in group because he didn't share the experience of gender with others. Another felt at the first meeting that the issues "did not always seem to affect me directly"; but at a later session, discussions of the readings on the politics of housework engaged him quite personally.[12] By the third meeting he "spoke at length" of the struggle to create an "equalitarian" relationship in living with a woman. At least one man, already aware of being a member of a "targeted" racial group, now saw how gender affected women daily. "I've come to realize what kind of stuff women have to go through," he wrote, "and more importantly, how gender affects me."

In addition to feeling conflicted about enrolling in the class, reading about issues such as rape, racism, sexual identity, body types, and standards of beauty proved disturbing to many students. Other instructors had warned me that heightening student consciousness of discrimination and sexual vulnerability often creates emotional stress in women's studies classrooms. The students echoed this theme in their papers. "We all agreed that [by the] third meeting the class had changed our lives in a profound way; we now felt surrounded by sexism." Or, as another student explained, "the material in this class was overwhelming, which made it particularly important to have a place to express reactions to it as we went along."

Anger was a primary reaction to the readings but one that evoked deep conflict, especially for women. At the beginning of the course, many students stereotyped feminists as "angry" and feared being so-labelled. The small groups functioned to legitimize anger and make it less overwhelming. "Our first group meeting can be summed up in one word: ANGER," a student recalled. "Unfortunately," she continued:

> most of us felt defensive when speaking about feminism, as if we needed to prove something to men, but could not channel the anger into well articulated arguments. . . . We hoped that this class and our upcoming small group meetings would help articulate our thoughts, explain why we were angry, and how we could feel "offensive" by presenting a clear definition of feminism and its goals.

Even a student who was more reluctant to identify as a feminist shared similar feelings: "Being able to air my feelings and hear the impressions of the other women in the group helped me to resolve some of the anger that I formed while reading the materials on violence against women." Another student recalled thinking that "At last, here were some people who I could talk to about those things that make me angry that no one seems to understand. I felt somewhat empowered." Speaking about the experiences of the past week "was good for me," a minority woman wrote, because "I found that I had a lot of unvented anger that I could let loose at these meetings." One group applied the reading of Virginia Woolf's *Three Guineas* to the problem of anger. Because Woolf "encouraged people to understand the background people are coming from," a student wrote, she talked of her father's traditional upbringing. "The group discussion," she concluded, "helped bring out that I should be angry at the socialization structure that my father grew up in, not merely at my father himself."[13]

Finding the support for taking the course and for processing both the knowledge of sexism and the anger it evoked made meetings valuable and a source of growth. As one student explained, "As a result of the support I received during the meetings, I quickly began to look forward to them. If I were religious I might say that the meetings were a bit like going to church, in that I felt stronger, more self-loving, and more confident after leaving." The sole man in another group wrote that he had "the courage to persevere in my studies because I had a support group. I had the drive to share so that I could see reflections of myself in others, even if the reflections had the faces of a different gender." Drawing on Bernice

Johnson Reagon's ideas in "Coalition Politics," one student described the small groups as "the 'room' that we all went back to in order to discuss strategies on how to change the world."[14] The ability to feel safe, relaxed, and candid, was due "no doubt," one student suggested, "to the absence of a TA or other authority figure."

For some students, feeling empowered to speak, learning to listen, and growing more confident were not ends in themselves. Members of several groups reported a new comfort with carrying their feminism outside of the classroom. All of the students in one group discovered that they had become known as the "dorm feminist" in their residences. One woman "decided to confront some people on my floor who were constantly making sexist remarks . . . and I probably would never have done it had we not had the discussion in our small group." Three members of another group decided to take a women's self-defense course together. A resident assistant distributed questionnaires from the women's center to the frosh in her dorm and asked her group for affirmation that she was helping the cause. At least one woman planned to be "challenging my parents on a lot of things I never thought about before." In contrast, one student felt relieved simply to meet: "I used to wonder why I was not planning or participating in demonstrations, but have realized that I am comfortable listening to other people and sharing with other people on a personal level. Both aspects are necessary and I don't believe one to be more valuable than another."

Activism brought its own lessons about feminism. Well into the quarter, one group of five white women devoted a meeting to writing a collective letter to the student newspaper to criticize "examples of sexist humor and negative depictions of women" in a recent campus production. The effort brought out group differences that surprised them. As they struggled "to transform our anger into a well-articulated argument," the group learned firsthand the difficulties of feminist process and politics. They debated language and strategies, and they discovered their limits when some members were reluctant to sign the letter. "Many of us," one member explained, "although willing to speak up in a small group, still feared taking a 'feminist' stance and being labelled a 'feminist.'" The group never produced a letter "that satisfied us all" and at least one member left discouraged. Another woman felt, however, that the "exercise was still an important one" because the group had collectively articulated its feelings, which, she believed, was more important than publishing a letter. "From the standpoint of political consciousness-raising," a member began her evaluation paper, "we may not have been very effective, but the group was invaluable as a place to laugh and sound off without having to justify our feminist point of view." Although the letter was never sent, she wrote, "it was a wonderful, and sometimes tense, exercise in coalition-building."

* * *

Reflecting the feminist politics of the 1980s, when women of color moved feminism from its white, middle-class focus to a more inclusive political worldview, FS101 attempted to emphasize the intersections of race and gender inequality. Along with the readings on race and feminism, the unlearning racism workshop and campus incidents made race and racism highly charged topics within the class. Small groups offered a potential space for understanding racial difference and patterns of domination. The demographic composition of the groups, however, strongly influenced the tone and depth of their discussions of race. Because three-quarters of the students were white, minorities were either absent or rare in small groups. Predictably, all-white groups had the least insightful discussions; highly unbalanced groups placed the burden of education on the single minority student; and highly mixed groups had the most valuable sessions on race.

The all-white groups tended to focus on the shared experiences of women and on nonracial differences between members. A man in one of these groups regretted its racial composition. Although he enjoyed the comfort and intimacy of his group, he realized that it "felt more like a womb than a coalition," in the terms of Reagon's article. Had the group been more diverse, he felt, members would have been forced to deal with differences in other ways. Often, these groups sought ways to resolve their discomfort over white privilege, with some interesting results. For instance, one white student used the concept of "simultaneous oppression" in her own way. Rather than referring to the multiple and simultaneous oppression of women of color (by gender, class, and race), she took the term to mean that white women were both oppressed and oppressors. With this interpretation, she identified through her gender with subordinate groups, while she accepted responsibility for her position of racial dominance.

For both mixed and all-white groups, the themes of white guilt and feelings of helplessness recurred in the papers.[15] White students in a mixed group felt immobilized by the realization, as one wrote, that "at one time in our lives we are all the oppressor." "Our group teeters on the brink of an intellectual abyss," she wrote of the unsatisfactory conclusion. "We say nice things to each other and depart." Or as the one black member of the group put it, the white women "all admitted to feeling guilty for being white." As another white member acknowledged, recognizing difference within feminism "was really very eye-opening and made some of us feel as though we had been pretty spoiled and blind." Similarly, a white woman in another group commented after listening to a Chicana describe the dual effects of racism and sexism: "It was hard for the white people in our group to accept that we would never be able to truly identify with the minority women's experience."

The racial imbalance in mixed groups placed a special burden of explanation on black, Asian-American, and Chicana members. "It seemed that [X] and I, who were the two people of color in our group," wrote one man, "did most of the talking on the subject of racism." The woman to whom he referred illustrated the educator role when the group discussed Betty's Friedan's attitude toward housework. Other students, she explained, "felt sorry for housewives," but since her own mother had been on welfare and then struggled in a service job, she longed for "my mom to be a housewife and to live in a house like the 'Brady Bunch.'" The man in the group shared with her "the alienation minority children feel when they are taught by the media to value a white, middle-class lifestyle over their own."

Other women of color reported the frustrations they felt when placed in the role of racial educators. When the four white women in one group "all looked to" the one black member to discuss race, "she turned the question around" by asking her classmates if "we would all have the same response given our similar whiteness." In another group a woman of color learned that her white classmates were surprised when she spoke of the internalized racism that leads to straightened hair and plastic surgery among minorities. "Although it hurts to have these things go unnoticed," she reflected, "I was encouraged by their acknowledging that when you have a prevalence of white, blond, blue-eyed skinny models, dolls, and characters in story books, these facts should not be shocking." Similarly, a Chicana resented "the duty of minorities to teach others, and particularly their oppressors"; however, at the same time she "valued this opportunity to enlighten people who were truly interested and regretful of their own ignorance." Some racial educators changed their views. At first, for example, a campus activist found that the burden of educating others made her resistant to meetings and "impatient" because she had "already dealt with" many of the issues that white women were "struggling to understand." By the last two sessions, however, she felt that her attitude had shifted from feeling "condescension" to valuing the discussions "not just for other women in the group, but for myself as well." An initial confidence in her superior knowledge about race gave way to a realization that she, too, needed a place "to process the things that we were reading" in ways that discussion section did not allow.

The most successful discussions of race—that is, the ones that elicited deep responses, as well as conflicts—occurred in the most diverse groups. A group with two minority women, two white women, and one white man achieved a degree of safety in discussing difference and racism. As the Chicana member wrote, the group "seemed to me to be a microcosm of the feminist movement—where people work for many of the same goals for differing reasons." Having made her "'foreign' experiences and ideas accessible to people through small group," she now felt ready to "move to this next stage of a potentially more hostile environment" in the world at large.

Another diverse group illustrated the different perceptions of white and minority students. After discussing readings about the cycle of poverty in which many black mothers are caught, a white upper-class woman expressed both dismay and a potential role for herself:

> To say that racism and poverty is disturbing will never explain the empty feeling in my stomach as the discussion progressed. However, I realized at least my stomach was full. This discussion reminded me that since I was blessed with educational opportunities and economic resources it is my duty to ensure others have the same.

Despite this student's attempt to identify with the poor, her attitude left one of the minority women in her group feeling "peeved" and fearful that another woman of color "was about to cry, and so was I, a little." The problem, she explained, was that the privileged students "sound like such do-gooders, as if racism and prejudice don't really affect them—as if racism were some immoral practice which must be abolished." The assumption that whites could "take themselves out of the arena of racism" struck her as "superior and condescending," and as a betrayal of the common bond of feminism. Racism, she implied, is everyone's problem; the good intentions for uplift expressed by some white students alienated minority students in her group.

These episodes reflected the dilemmas of mixed groups. On the one hand, these groups did most to educate white students and sometimes helped alleviate their guilt. In the process, they risked relying on students of color as racial educators who explained differences among women, rather than addressing the deep personal and structural barriers to race equality. On the other hand, the few minority students in these groups learned a great deal about white attitudes toward race and how these attitudes affect them personally. Given the race and class stratification of our society, students of color will no doubt confront these views throughout their lives; small groups can serve as testing grounds for clarifying their responses. Overall, the racially mixed groups worked at identifying the dilemmas of difference better than the all-white groups; but they would have been even more effective if they had a greater proportion of students of color. That way the minority students would feel less isolated and less targeted as racial educators. At a more racially mixed campus, or in a course with greater minority enrollment, groups could go even further in raising consciousness about racism. In this setting, mixed groups can go only so far toward exploring the relationship between gender and racial inequality.

* * *

Whatever progress the lesbian and gay movement has made since the 1970s, for most Stanford students, lesbianism remains a frightening topic. In signing up for FS101, a woman student risked being labelled, in the words of one, as "the feminist dyke." Or, as another woman told her group, she "felt funny because people who knew she was taking the class would think of her as a lesbian." The association of feminism with lesbianism ran deep among students who brought to the class strong prejudices about homosexuality. Several expressed their religious opposition to gay sex, or, in response to viewing the film "Choosing Children," to lesbians or gay men raising children. Even liberal students wanted to distance themselves from homosexuality by defending feminists against the label of lesbianism.

Not surprisingly, the coming out letter challenged the class enormously and proved to be "harder than we had thought." Everyone expressed discomfort about doing the assignment. Students who had thought they were tolerant of lesbians and gay men found themselves hiding the assignment from roommates; some wrote " 'Fem-Stud Assignment' across the top in big letters," in case friends passed by as they wrote. In the words of one student, we "were continually worried that somebody was going to look over our shoulder and misinterpret what we had written."

The small group following the letter writing assignment was, for many, "by far the most tense of the quarter." One of the most highly political groups seemed to spend little time discussing the letters. One member was reportedly "speechless" and "couldn't imagine how others managed to do it." Another woman became "very depressed" writing hers, and for telling reasons: "I knew my parents would go off on another fit, and that once again I had to face the fact that their love and financial support is conditional." Fear of parental disapproval loomed large in the discussions and helps explain the tone of so many of the letters, well summarized by a freshman who wrote critically that several members of his group had made "a total emotional plea to their parents telling them of their misfortune and asking for acceptance." The members of another group "all agreed that it took a while to finally get around to actually saying 'I am lesbian' "—a term that many letters avoided altogether.

However difficult, the exercise, and especially the group discussion of it, brought home the depth and the costs of homophobia. "If we feared so much that someone might find our letter, did that indicate that we were homophobic?" The discussion of the letters led another group to realize that "by denying our feelings of homophobia, we were only perpetuating them." It also helped to undermine homophobic responses. During the discussion of hiding the assignment, for example, one woman "gradually realized that my fear of being stereotyped wrongly had greatly diminished since the beginning of the course."

For other students, the assignment brought homosexual feelings to the surface. The group discussion forced one man to "think about my own homophobic fears—did I harbor those feelings because being homosexual is not being a man?" Another group asked the question "Have you ever thought about being homosexual?" which produced "some defensive reactions." At least one woman admitted to the thought but found that she could not "envision a sexual relationship" with another woman. In response to the question, another woman contemplated her unsatisfactory relationships with men and wondered if she might be lesbian. At that point, she recalled:

> Two of the other members looked like they thought I was going to come out right then and there and didn't know what to do, and the other member looked grateful that I had responded to her question honestly, and did seem to sincerely understand my confusion at the time.

The speaker found it a "rewarding moment" because she was not ostracized for her honesty or her suspicions about her sexuality.

If the coming out assignment created the most tension, it also seemed to have had the most consciousness-raising effect. In one group, a woman who had recently "stopped identifying . . . as heterosexual" rated this session as the "best meeting" because it "produced the most consciousness raising." Other members (a straight man and two straight women) agreed that it was the "most rewarding," in part because the letter gave a "concrete experience" about which to relate feelings and "a bonding experience" for students who struggled with the assignment. In several groups, attitudes towards coming out seemed to have changed for many students. One group member "concluded that many more people would come out if there weren't such a stigma in society. We admired those who are strong enough to."

Only two students came out in their groups. In one case, a gay man was relieved to find that he was "among pretty gay-sensitive people." The group later turned to him to tell them what was and what was not "offensive" in their behaviors and whether their fear of having their coming out letters seen constituted homophobia. Accepting the educator role, he both criticized and reassured his peers. "We all sort of agreed," he wrote, "that this was another form of homophobia but acknowledged too, that individuals are forced to make choices under duress in a deeply homophobic society." In another group, a woman catalogued the responses when she "told the group that I am a lesbian":

> Unfortunately, the person who I expected to have a negative reaction had to go to a funeral . . . One seemed unimpressed . . . one asked me what lesbians looked like, was obviously uncomfortable, but made a very noble attempt to pretend that she wasn't, and the other felt very comfortable and proceeded to ask me lots of questions.

The discussion shifted when this same student also revealed that she was an incest survivor and explained that she was not alone among Stanford students. Group members, she reported, "were more shocked by this than the lesbianism, and had a hard time dealing with it. . . . As for myself, I didn't think I could deal with talking about either subject without being honest about it. I also felt I owed to other lesbians and to other incest survivors to speak out." In the small group setting, she was able to do so.

Just as all-white groups had more superficial discussions of race, the overwhelmingly heterosexual groups often began with the question of homosexuality but soon moved to the general topic of sexuality and relationships. In two of the women-only groups, the coming out discussion turned to comparable fears of rejection or exposure among straight people. "Just as gay people are expected to be ashamed of their sexuality, fat women are supposed to view their weight as a transitory state," explained one student. Another group moved from discussing lesbians' fear of rejection by their families to memories of their own childhood rejections by other girls and the lasting fear of being different. The parallels gave them insight into homophobia in the absence of firsthand accounts from lesbian or gay male students.

I was surprised by how few lesbian and gay male students either took this class or came out in it; fear of disclosure by association with feminism may have kept them away or in the closet. Nonetheless, the predominantly straight groups learned more about homophobia than they had expected, in large part due to the letter writing assignment. Despite their resistance, once students tried on a homosexual identity, they had at least a glimpse of the firsthand experience that was missing in most groups. Forced to identify with the sexual minority, students seemed to confront their homophobia more personally, and with less guilt, than they confronted their racism. Thus, although the presence of minority students within groups did not necessarily raise consciousness dramatically, an assignment that encouraged personal identification with minority vulnerability had strong potential to do so.

During the first lecture of the quarter, before I distributed the syllabus, I had asked each student to write a paragraph or two about how they defined and reacted to the term "feminist." The overwhelming majority of the class described the goals of liberal feminism positively, but they found the label "feminist" too frightening to adopt for themselves. At the beginning of the small groups, students addressed these feelings. "All of us stereotype a feminist negatively," one black woman explained, "that is, as a militant person." Or, as one student summarized the reaction to feminists voiced by each member of her small group: they "hated men," "did not want to appear attractive," and "were radical and rebellious."

In analyzing their prejudices in class discussion, many students credited the media with shaping their image of angry, militant feminists. I would add that Stanford's student culture not only emphasizes the importance of being attractive to the opposite sex but also encourages conformity to a model of self-satisfaction (the "no one has problems at Stanford" syndrome, as a counselling center flier labels it). In this atmosphere, political rebelliousness—especially when it addresses personal issues rather than, say, U.S. foreign policy—can be dismissed as a sign of personal failure.

FS101 challenged stereotypes by exposing students to a variety of feminist ideas and strategies and by stressing the political nature of the personal. Lectures on the history of feminism and readings in *Feminist Frameworks* explored the diversity of liberal, radical, and socialist feminist politics and the issues raised by women of color and men in the movement. Reading Virginia Woolf's *Three Guineas* early in the course provided a context for relating discrimination against women to traditional political concerns, such as war and peace. Johnetta Cole's *All American Women* further emphasized the ways that feminism spoke to the concerns of a variety of women. These readings and the lectures no doubt contributed to student reevaluations of feminism. It is also possible that exposure to the diversity of their instructors helped some students identify as feminists, for we (myself and two graduate teaching assistants) represented female and male, black and white, and gay and straight.

Despite these classroom influences, I sensed from the student papers that the small groups were perhaps the most critical element in the process of unlearning earlier stereotypes. "I used to think that all feminists were either lesbians or militant man-hating women," wrote an Asian-American woman. "After taking this class, I am proud to say that I am a feminist and I also do not hesitate to inform others of my feminist views and beliefs." Similarly, another woman confessed that "I'm quite sure that I wrote one of the least flattering definitions of and reactions to feminism at the beginning of the quarter," and that she "would certainly never have said that I was a feminist." During the course she had adopted a definition of feminism that made her able to identify with the term: "a feminist recognizes differences between men and women, but does not always value either male or female attributes and qualities more than the other." She concluded her paper by embracing a new identity: "Now all I have to do to know how I respond to the word feminist is to look in the mirror and see someone whom I respect and like very much." One male student shifted from "a negative gut reaction" to a positive one; "I now consider myself a feminist, which I hadn't even considered before the class." Or, as another man reported, "for the first time, I openly consider myself a feminist—with pride."

The disappearance of defensive reactions to feminism recurred as a final theme in the small group papers. "Now I really consider myself a feminist, it has become a part of who I am. I am not defensive about it. The word has lost its negative connotations," wrote one woman. In another group a feminist studies major explained that "Now more than ever, when I hear or see the word 'feminist' I feel proud. Most of my defensive reactions are entirely gone and I feel positive and connected with the title and its meaning to me." Yet another student felt that she "no longer need[ed] to back away from this name or label. I no longer need to put it in quotes." More rare was the commitment to advocating feminism in public, such as the student who declared feminist studies as her major and felt "very relieved that I have exorcised most of my fears about defending [feminism] publicly."

The final paragraph of a paper typically spoke of pride and even joy in the student's transformation into a feminist:

> When I see the word "feminist," I feel like celebrating and crying at the same time. I feel a sadness because I know that many people will react to it negatively . . . I also respond with a feeling of happiness because I know that through education, the incredible ideas of feminism have and will break through the negative stereotype
>
> Now, when I see or hear the word feminist I invariably respond positively. I feel a bond with the person it is directed toward, and proudly feel a renewed women-centered identity.
>
> When I hear the word feminist, I think: this is a person I want to get to know.
>
> To be sure, when I see or hear the word feminist, I respond with a proud, warm, connective feeling. I myself am a feminist and it's nice to know that I have sisters and brothers who are the same.

Students from several groups echoed this last student's historical insight: "I now understand why feminist consciousness-raising groups in the 1970s were so effective in generating women's energies."

While most students claimed a greater willingness, to identify as feminists, to themselves or to others, and a more complex definition of feminist constituencies and goals, others addressed the limits of their politics. Unlike the generation that initially adopted consciousness-raising in an era when radicalism was fashionable, today's students shy away from any taint of political rebelliousness. "Even after having taken this class," a woman wrote, "I have yet to conquer my enduring uneasiness with the word 'feminist.' . . . I do still feel a deep and vague discomfort with the word . . . and continue to have difficulty saying 'I am a feminist' " because of the connotation of "radicalism, rebelling, and a touch of 'man-hating' that I am not yet able to accept or overcome."

In a different way, other students expressed how, by the end of the course, they had become acutely aware of their political limitations. As one woman of color reported of her group: "Each of us were entrenched in our inner conflict about our own capitalistic desires and urges." The most frequent conflict women addressed concerned standards of beauty. "We agreed that since taking this class we have often felt like complete hypocrites as we put on our makeup," one white woman revealed of her group. "I grapple with my difficulty of redefining beauty," wrote another woman, "perhaps I need to accept my silly definitions of beauty as dictated by the society I live in." The challenge of differentiating between the messages of the culture and their own beliefs confounded this woman's group, as it did other feminists of the 1980s. The free classroom copies of *Ms.* magazine drove home the point—today's political feminism came packaged with contradictory messages extolling traditional femininity and consumer capitalism.

Whatever the limitations of student political consciousness, this experiment in the use of small group, personally based learning proved even more rewarding than I had anticipated. I agreed with the student who wrote that while she "expected these consciousness-raising sessions to change each of us, the rate and degree to which it occurred surprised and inspired me." Small groups had clearly played an important role in allowing internal, emotional shifts to occur gradually in students who had been resistant to feminism. Although the purpose of the groups was to enhance classroom learning and not necessarily to achieve political conversion, the two seemed to happen simultaneously. The intellectual challenge of readings, discussions, and papers certainly contributed to the process, but consciousness-raising provided something that traditional academic work could not: a safe space for discussing personal difference and connecting these differences to gender inequality. Given the complexity of feminist identity that emerged in the 1980s, as well as the negative stereotypes of feminists that persist among students, consciousness-raising offers a unique method for learning the very things feminism espouses.

Finally, in addition to emphasizing the importance of consciousness-raising as a form of pedagogy and urging its adoption in other classes, I want to credit the students in this course with making consciousness-raising work. Those who were willing simply to enroll in FS101 at a campus that was generally hostile to feminism had to be exceptional students. Revealing their own fears of feminism, their anger and guilt about racism, and their discomfort with homosexuality took courage and entailed risks. The requirement of attending consciousness-raising groups may have motivated change, but the students themselves made possible the personal and political growth that their papers document. For a feminist teacher, their learning has been an inspiration and a source of faith that feminism will survive, even in these conservative times.

Acknowledgments

In planning this course, I benefited especially from the experience of my colleague Jane Collier (Anthropology), who had previously taught FS101, and from my two graduate teaching assistants, Lisa Hogeland (Modern Thought and Literature) and Kevin Mumford (History). I thank them, along with the following other members of the feminist community at Stanford, for their responses to this paper: Laura Carstensen, John Dupre, Mary Felstiner, Regenia Gagnier, Patricia Gumport, Margo Horn, Susan Krieger, Diane Middlebrook, Adrienne Rich, Alice Supton, and Sylvia Yanagisako.

Notes

1. Two experiences outside my own classroom influenced my use of consciousness-raising in FS101. I learned a great deal from sociologist Susan Krieger's example when she successfully incorporated small groups in a class of conservative prebusiness students. Her students wrote self-reflective papers about small group dynamics, rooted in personal experience. If such groups could work with these students, the groups seemed to have great potential for feminist studies. Another model was an unlearning racism workshop I had attended at the Stanford women's center some years earlier, facilitated by the late Ricky Sherover-Marcuse. In order to require such a workshop of all FS101 students, the feminist studies program hired an experienced facilitator to conduct workshops for members of this class.

2. Of the sixty-six students who took this course for credit (not counting auditors), 74 percent were white and 26 percent black, Asian, or Chicana. Men constituted 17 percent of the entire class, 12 percent of minorities and 18 percent of whites. Students tended to identify themselves in terms of race and gender. Similarly, in this paper I refer to students by gender and race, unless a student has indicated another identity.

3. On earlier resistance to the use of consciousness-raising by women's studies faculty, and for a review of the theoretical basis for consciousness-raising in the classroom, see Renate D. Klein, "The Dynamics of the Women's Studies Classroom: A Review Essay of the Teaching Practice of Women's Studies in Higher Education," *Women's Studies International Forum* 10, no. 2 (1987): esp. 189–93.

4. I assigned the following readings: Johnetta Cole, ed., *All American Women: Lines that Divide, Ties that Bind* (New York: Free Press, 1986); Emily Honig and Gail Hershatter, eds., *Personal Voices: Chinese Women in the 1980s* (Stanford, CA: Stanford University Press, 1988); Buchi Emecheta, *The Joys of Motherhood* (New York: George Braziller, 1979); Virginia Woolf, *Three Guineas* (1938; reprint, New York: Harcourt, Brace, 1963); Marge Piercy,

Woman on the Edge of Time (New York: Fawcett Crest, 1976); Alison Jaggar and Paula Rothenberg, eds., *Feminist Frameworks: Alternative Theoretical Accounts of the Relations between Women and Men* (New York: McGraw-Hill, 1984); and a thick course reader.

5. Pamela Allen, "Free Space," in *Radical Feminism*, ed. Anne Koedt, Ellen Levine and Anita Rapone (New York: Quadrangle, 1973), 271–79; Irene Peslikis, "Resistances to Consciousness." In *Sisterhood is Powerful*, ed. Robin Morgan (New York: Vintage Books, 1970), 379–81.

6. In this three-hour workshop, an experienced facilitator helped students to explore their personal class, race, and ethnic backgrounds and to dispel unconscious stereotypes about various groups. The workshop attempted to affirm the value of difference, address the costs of discrimination, and create a nonjudgmental space for students to acknowledge the racial fears and misinformation they had acquired in the past. Ideally the students should attend a series of workshops, but because of time and budget limitations, the small group meeting served as a follow up to reinforce the workshop.

7. Despite my effort to make the group meetings required, several papers complained of members who appeared irregularly, because it seemed "almost like a luxury—and when it comes to a clash between 'real' classwork . . . and therapeutic classwork, it's hard to break the Stanford mold and take the ungraded activity seriously." Evaluation papers suggested that attendance would improve if I scheduled group meeting times rather than leaving it to students. They also complained about the rigid format I outlined and convinced me that in the future the groups could determine their own process and discussion topics. After the second year of teaching this course with consciousness-raising groups, I have decided that it is essential to structure the meeting times into the course schedule in advance. Doing so would be especially important for nonresidential schools, where it is even more difficult for students to find informal meeting times and places.

8. John D'Emilio constructed this exercise at the University of North Carolina–Greensboro, and it has been used by several other faculty members around the country. Several students discussed their letters with parents. One of my favorite responses was from the mother of a straight son; the son called to say he was writing a coming out letter to her, "hypothetically real" and wondered what she would say if he sent it. Her reply: "The same thing I said when you went to college: always use a condom." I am grateful to such mothers for sending their daughters and sons to my classes.

9. After the lecture, which did discuss the problem of incest, two other incest survivors identified themselves to me privately, and one suggested readings for the next year. From this experience I learned about the importance of making sensitive topics visible on the syllabus in advance and not only in the lecture class.

10. In quoting from the student papers, I have corrected typographical errors but have left grammar and punctuation intact. Students did sign the papers, so they may have had an interest in presenting a positive evaluation of the groups in order to please the instructor. The papers, however, did not affect grades, and many students offered criticisms about the structure or timing of groups, alongside their reflections on how groups influenced them.

11. To my surprise, coming from the separatism of the 1970s, mixed-gender groups evoked no protest and in fact satisfied almost all students. One all women's group did report a special openness, and members tended to discuss childhood memories and sexuality more freely. But members of other all-female groups said they missed a "male perspective." In mixed gender groups, no women complained of male dominance and many expressed gratitude for the "male insight." Their comments may have been due to the respectful attitude of the men in the class, as well as to women's often expressed fears of being labelled man-haters.

12. These readings included: Pat Mainardi, "The Politics of Housework." In *Feminist Frameworks*; excerpts from Lenore Weitzman, *The Marriage Contract* (New York: Free Press, 1983); and interviews with domestic workers in Cole, *All American Women.*

13. Another student wrote that when she described her father to the group, she understood why she couldn't get angry: "I realized that as a child, it seemed to me that my father was constantly yelling. He scared me most of the time with his anger, and for this reason, I think that I express my anger quietly and in a somewhat controlled fashion." She did not elaborate on whether she wished to change this behavior, but she felt that the insight was "an important step toward an understanding of myself."

14. Bernice Johnson Reagon, "Coalition Politics: Turning the Century." In *Home Girls: A Black Feminist Anthology*, ed. Barbara Smith (New York: Kitchen Table Press, 1983), 356–68.

15. For example, a white woman who missed the meeting on race in her mixed group wrote: "I suppose I could have talked about the white guilt everyone tells me is not healthy to have but that I have anyway. I just don't understand why I can go to Stanford while other people are starving."

CHAPTER EIGHT

Bringing Different Voices into the Classroom

JULIA T. WOOD

In illuminating the patterns of women's moral thinking, Carol Gilligan's *In a Different Voice* (1982) redressed conventional moral theory's long-standing disregard of women's experiences and ethical stances. Arguing that traditional moral theory ignored women, Gilligan demonstrated that women's moral reasoning is distorted systematically when it is interpreted within a framework that embodies a predominantly male perspective. *In a Different Voice* advances a model of women's morality centered on sustaining relationships and responding caringly to others.[1]

In addition to generating substantial research, Gilligan's ideas fundamentally altered our understanding of women and their ways of thinking, valuing, and experiencing. By now a significant body of work informed by multiple disciplines and methodologies documents two discrete paths by which identity and conceptions of morality evolve. Growing out of these are distinctive, gender-associated senses of self, interpersonal stances, and orientations toward others and moral choices. In addition to the two moral voices Gilligan recognizes, others may exist.[2]

As feminist scholars reflected on Gilligan's work, its pertinence to a number of teaching interests became clear. Incorporating her material into courses, however, has sometimes been difficult. It is one thing to describe distinct moralities in ways students understand and quite another to enhance affective appreciation of different voices. Yet, as Audre Lorde (1984) reminds us, only when teaching involves hearts as well as minds, emotions as well as thinking, can it inspire engaged living. Other voices in behalf of this perspective such as Estelle Disch and Becky Thompson and bell hooks insist teaching should involve students' needs and feelings as well as their intellects.

Last year in my women's studies course Gender and Communication, I serendipitously discovered a way to involve students vitally and personally in understanding and valuing distinctive moral voices. In this chapter I describe this discovery and explain how it led me to develop a unit that aims to encourage all students, male and female, to understand and appreciate different moral perspectives. Because the classroom incident that occurred reveals key issues of content and pedagogical process, I recount it in some detail. From this example, I derive intellectual and personal values that inhere in teaching designed to enhance awareness of distinctly valid moral voices.

Originally published in the Spring 1993 issue of the *NWSA Journal*.

My course focuses on myriad ways and contexts in which communication recurrently creates and re-creates gender ideals. Unlike most courses in women's studies, this class typically enrolls about 10 to 20 percent men and roughly the same proportion of minority students; and, as one might expect, the views and voices of the male minority threaten to dominate classroom discussion. As Amy Shapiro has pointed out, "Because of his positioning in our culture, the man often sets the tone and conveys the agenda" (1991, 70), an issue earlier recognized by Treichler and Kramarae. When this occurs in a classroom, the learning environment itself can become another arena of oppression for women instead of achieving its goal of liberating and enabling all individuals.

This chapter has been prompted by an occasion when male students attempted to define the agenda in a class, but responses from women students thwarted their attempt and transformed the classroom into a laboratory for personal discovery and expansion. At the midpoint of the course in the fall semester of 1990, we were discussing gender and personal relationships as part of a unit that typically includes attention to gender-differentiated roles, expectations, and bases of satisfaction. "Myra," who was completing her senior requirements, volunteered her experience. She told the class that her widowed father had recently suffered a heart attack and could no longer live alone. He had asked her to forgo graduate school in order to move home and care for him. Relating this to class topics, Myra explained that since he clearly needed her, she had decided she should do what he asked. At the same time, she disclosed that she resented being pulled away from her own goals and felt guilty and selfish for feeling resentful.

Almost before she had concluded her comments, a male student, "Joe," asserted, "He has no right to expect that of you." And another, "Bill," reinforced this judgment by adding "You have your own life to lead, and it's not fair for his problems to interfere with that." Myra looked mystified, but offered no further comment: She had been silenced and seemed now to be doubting the integrity of her own views. This was not surprising since the whole weight of our culture—as well as accepted theories of moral reasoning—lay behind the male students' comments.[3]

At the time, my initial inclination was to intervene in support of her choice and gently to rebuke Bill and Joe for presuming superior knowledge and the prerogative to offer advice. Before I could arrange my response, however, an adage in my field came to mind: "I know you think you understand what I said, but what you thought you heard is not what I meant." This led me to a different response, one that relied less on my role as an authority who directs classroom content and more on my role as a facilitator who enables students to discover their own "truths."

Explaining that there are often misunderstandings in communication, I proposed an experiment to find out what each communicator thought the other meant by her or his comments. Then I asked every student, not just those who had spoken, to write out answers to three questions:

1. What did you hear Myra say? Explain what you understood her to be thinking and feeling about her situation.
2. What did you hear Joe and Bill say? Explain what you understood them to be thinking and feeling about this issue.
3. What do you think Myra wanted as a response to telling us about the situation with her father?

The students' responses fairly consistently reflected patterns distinguishing male and female moral orientations along the lines indicated by researchers in this area (see Belenky et al. 1986 and Gilligan et al. 1988). Four of the five men and four of the women in the class thought that Myra described a situation of conflicting rights: "She thinks [her father's] rights supersede her own and she's willing to let his problems infringe on her life." Twenty-one of the twenty-five women in the class along with one man phrased Myra's predicament in terms of personal needs and relational responsibilities: Myra felt her father's needs and wanted to respond to them compassionately.

Students' interpretations of Joe and Bill's comments fell similarly in line with gender generalizations about patterns in moral thinking. Four of the men and four of the women "heard" Joe and Bill as being concerned about Myra's rights in the situation and as thinking her father was out of line in his request that she take care of him. Twenty-one of the women and one man "heard" Bill and Joe as disregarding the father's needs and ignoring the responsibilities of being involved in a family where members are supposed to look out for each other.

In responding to the third question I had posed, a similar pattern emerged. The majority of men and a minority of women thought Myra wanted advice; they defined a constructive response as giving her counsel on what she should do. Yet the majority of women and one man thought that Myra wanted someone to listen to and understand the conflict she was experiencing between her personal goals and her desire to take care of her father.

The next step in this experiment was my asking Myra to tell us what *she* had written in response to the first question. This was her answer: "I am feeling really torn about wanting to pursue my education now and needing to take care of my father. He is ill and scared and needs me now, so I can't turn my back on him, but I'd really counted on starting my graduate studies." I then asked her whether what she felt about the situation was addressed by the responses from the four men and four women who heard her talking about rights. "No," she replied. "I don't see what rights have to do with the situation. It's not a matter of rights. I don't even think that applies to us."

Again, Bill and Joe assumed center stage by launching into justifications of their responses as both appropriate and correct. At this point, however, I did intervene, asking them to withhold defense of their responses. I then introduced the class to the concept of different voices and explained the distinctive natures of the voice of caring and the voice of fairness. The voice of caring emphasizes the responsibilities people have by virtue of their relationship with each other. From this perspective the titular moral goal is to respond to others in caring ways. Conversely, I pointed out, the voice of fairness assumes that what we "owe" to others and are entitled to expect from others depends on our rights and the highest moral goal is to be fair in how we treat others by honoring their rights while not violating our own.

Following my theoretical summary we entered into a discussion that was to last three class periods. During this time I outlined differences between the voices of caring and fairness (see table 1). Early responses from students made it clear that many thought there was a better or right voice that I simply wasn't revealing to them. This led me to emphasize repeatedly throughout our discussion that the voices are best understood as distinct and that both represent valid ways of understanding oneself as well as relationships with others. Using phrases like "different and equal," "not comparative," and "equivalently valid," I stressed the inappropriateness of judging the two voices hierarchically.

An incident that occurred during the second day of our discussion clarified the thesis of our evolving unit on different voices. One student, after another unsuccessful effort to persuade me to reveal which voice was "right," burst out in frustration with the challenge, "Well, if you're not trying to teach us what is right and what we ought to do, then what are we supposed to learn from all of this?" After several students offered their perspectives (some of which echoed the speaker's frustration), I suggested there were two purposes: understanding and respect.

Understanding I defined as being able to comprehend another person's perspective even if it is different from your own—just to understand without judging it. This purpose seemed most comprehensible to students when I likened it to learning another language and being able to translate from one language to the other. Respect I defined as recognizing that a perspective other than your own can be legitimate, equal in validity to the way you view the world. Respect does not require personal acceptance of another's position, yet it goes beyond mere toleration. This seemed to click best for students when I suggested that the kind of respect we were talking about was analogous to admiring someone who does a job well that you yourself couldn't or wouldn't do. Whether or not we want to do what the other does, we can still respect his or her abilities.

As students realized I really didn't have a "hidden right answer" and that I was not judging any of the responses to Myra's comments as right

Table 1
Gender Differences in Developmental Patterns

Developmental Issue	Voice of Caring (usually women)	Voice of Fairness (usually men)
Basis of identity	Identity develops within relationships with others creating permeable ego boundaries that allow others into self.	Identity develops by differentiating from others, creating rigid ego boundaries that keep others out.
Basic interpersonal stance	Connections with others are desired and enhance personal security; separation feels unsafe while interdependence feels familiar and safe.	Connections with others are not so desired and may threaten personal security; independence feels safe.
Orientation toward others	We have responsibilities that grow out of our relationships with others and that we meet to sustain the connection and ourself.	Others have some rights, which we should meet as long as they don't conflict with our own.
Moral principles that guide	One should show *care* by responding compassionately to others' *needs*.	One should be *fair* by impartially respecting others' *rights*.
Criteria for deciding how to respond	We have to understand each person, relationship, and situation on its own terms; what is caring in one case may be inappropriate in another context. Caring is personal and individual.	We should judge a situation, person, or relationship by generally accepted rules; to base acts on each individual case is ad hoc and too relativistic to ensure fairness.

or wrong, defensiveness was replaced by interest and genuine excitement about learning. Students shifted from protecting their own positions to being curious about other ways of perceiving situations. They engaged in remarkably open dialogue with each other as they explored different ways of understanding and responding to people and situations. There were also moments in which the "Aha! experience" occurred, as when one man exclaimed, "Finally, my girlfriend makes sense to me!" or when a woman student told us "This is the first time anyone has described how I think and relate to people and said what I do is okay. Now I can finally explain the way I think to my father!"

By the third day of our discussion, we moved on to consider the last question I had posed: what kind of response was Myra looking for when she made her comment? After I'd introduced this focus for discussion, Joe volunteered that he now understood what had been "wrong" about his response. He proceeded to explain quite eloquently that rights and needs are different vocabularies that refer to different ways of thinking about relationships so that his response about Myra's rights was oblique to her concern about her father's needs. Others in the class joined in to elaborate Joe's insight, making the points that showing care and being fair reflect different understandings of what relationships are and that helpful responses are contingent on the perspective of the person talking.

I then asked Myra whether she agreed with Joe's critique of his response. Now more enabled to claim her voice than she had been three days before, Myra confirmed Joe's recognition of the difference between needs and rights views and added that his response was unhelpful in another way. She noted she also hadn't appreciated his giving advice since she hadn't asked for any. Once again, the class split with the majority of women nodding in understanding while most of the men expressed mystification and anger, insisting that if Myra hadn't wanted advice she shouldn't have brought up the issue and that Joe was only trying to help her.

This allowed me to introduce material that describes differences in how women and men use communication and, relatedly, differences in what they generally desire from others. We talked about what Deborah Tannen (1990) has called "troubles talk," the kind of conversation in which one person describes something that is frustrating him or her. Drawing upon a wealth of research in communication and linguistics, Tannen demonstrates that women most often engage in troubles talk to connect to others and the response they desire is evidence that their conversational partner understands their feelings and cares that they are troubled. Men, however, engage in troubles talk less frequently; when they do, they tend to want advice on how to resolve a problem. (This is, of course, but another variant on the well-established distinction between expressive and instrumental goals in communication that tend to diverge along gender lines.) Further, Tannen points out that men feel compelled to solve problems others present and especially feel so when women express dilemmas since the male role of protector is "at stake" in their capacity to take care of whatever is bothering a woman.

After I had summarized research on communication styles, I sketched conceptual distinctions for students, showing how these differences in desired responses corresponded to the different voices we had been discussing. Women in the class became highly vocal in confirming the distinction and in almost uniformly declaring men's penchant for doling out advice and not attending to their feelings to be one of the most frustrating things about talking with guys. The men in the class, perhaps feeling some defensiveness at what felt like an attack, countered that they found it frustrating when women insisted on "processing every-thing to death" and focusing on feelings when all they wanted was to resolve whatever problem they had.

This led us back to our earlier discussion of "translation" as critical in communication. Both men and women are generally trying to be helpful, we concluded, but without understanding the other's "language," their efforts often are ineffective. From this the class derived the principle that in communication the goal is not to do for others what you want them to do for you, but rather to do for others what they want you to do for them. When I pushed students to consider other communication principles that might grow out of our discussion, they came up with two additional ad-visories. First, they agreed it's a good idea to decode language for others so that they know what you want from them; second, they realized it's useful to ask others what would help them if they don't say what they want. Both of these principles, like the first one, are well supported by research and theory on interpersonal communication, so my instruc-tional role was simply to affirm what the students discovered on their own.

At the class's instigation we devoted the remainder of the period to informal role plays in which students took turns being "speaker" and "listener" and practiced the three principles we had distilled: telling partners what kind of response would be helpful, asking partners what kind of response would be helpful, and responding in different ways—using rights and needs language and understanding and advising re-sponses. This proved an effective culminating experience for the unit on different voices.

The philosophy underlying teaching about different voices as well as much of the content of such teaching is implicit in the foregoing descrip-tion of how that "communication" module came into being in my own course. Now I want to present a more formal rationale that might be both persuasive to administrators and clearly communicable to students.

There are four arguments for teaching undergraduate students about gender differences in developmental paths and moral voices. The first is especially pertinent in research institutions: this material must be in-cluded in instruction in order to offer students the most intellectually complete and current understanding of how humans develop and how they conceive and respond to ethical issues. Teaching either Kohlberg's model of male development or Gilligan's model of female development alone provides only a partial and, thus, an inaccurate understanding of human behavior.

A second argument invokes the importance of teaching students to honor differences on their own terms rather than to rank them hierarchi-cally (see Brummet 1986). Particularly relevant in environments committed to humanistic education, the argument here is that teaching about diverse ethical perspectives promotes awareness of and respect for human diversity. In its nonjudgmental presentation of distinctive developmental patterns and outcomes, instruction fosters in students sensitivity to pluralistic ways of defining the self and acting in relation to others.

Third, teaching about different voices enhances the coherence of many courses in women's studies by supporting and extending other instructional topics. For instance, many women's studies courses cover gender socialization as a process that is enacted in part by differential treatment of male and female children. Well-established differences in the socialization of male and female children can be integrated into the explanations of how different moral voices evolve: The voice of caring's emphasis on responding to others and preserving relationships would certainly be promoted by a socialization in which female infants are touched more and kept physically closer than are male. Conversely, the voice of fairness reflects a view of humans as essentially individual and separated, a stance that is firmly cultivated by typical patterns of male socialization, which stress independence and individual action. Similar connections may be made with topics such as self-esteem, assertiveness, salience of relationships, managerial styles, and so forth. In many instances instructors will find that discussing different moral voices supplements material already covered and introduces significant independent understandings.

Finally, instruction about different moral voices enlarges students' insights into themselves and others with whom they interact. When students do not understand that there are distinct, equally valid ways of conceiving and expressing selfhood and connections with others, they naturally perceive their way as "right." Consequently, they tend to perceive ways other than their own as deficient, uninformed, or otherwise inferior. Knowledge of multiple, equally valid voices that reflect different conceptions of the self, relationships, and behavior enables students to broaden their understanding of the range of human thought and action and to learn diverse ways of interpreting and responding to others in order to be more personally and socially effective and constructive.

The serendipitous experience described in this essay was effective in a particular class. It was one of those rare and magical moments in teaching when people, ideas, and a particular situation seem to jell spontaneously. Yet, unplanned and unexpected moments in education, however inspiring, cannot be counted on to inform teaching routinely. What I want to do now is explain quite briefly how the unit I now regularly include in my courses both makes use of and varies from the one that spontaneously occurred in the fall of 1990.

In the three times I've taught this unit since its spontaneous occurrence in the fall of 1990 I have experimented with variations in content, length, and teaching process. These experiences have led me to two variations from the original format. First, it is important to initiate the unit with a concrete example within students' experiences, but a richly detailed illustration cannot be expected to emerge spontaneously as it did in my 1990 class. For this reason I developed a case study that I now use to launch the unit.

A second change I have made is in the application section of the unit, where my goal is to involve students in actually trying out the different viewpoints of rights and needs and the distinct response styles of advising and understanding. Again, I have found that not all classes are as amenable to experimenting with new skills as was the fall 1990 class. Consequently, I now rely on role plays to provide structure and the safety of assigned roles.

The final change I have made is to position the unit toward the beginning of my course rather than at the midpoint where it originally emerged. Understanding different ways of conceiving the self and relationships is fundamental to appreciating many other dimensions of gender and communication, which is the focus of my class. Alternative ways of contextualizing the unit might well be more appropriate in other courses that grow out of other disciplinary bases.

Despite these variations, what emerged the first time I taught this material remains the basic blueprint for the unit as I have developed it over the past two years. The fundamental structure and themes that unfolded in the impromptu situation survived largely intact for the unit I now routinely present. Currently I allot three days for the unit, and this has continued to provide adequate time for discussing and processing ideas. To inaugurate it, I present a case study based on the original incident involving Myra, Bill, and Joe. Rather than situating their conversation in a classroom as it actually occurred, however, the case represents them as three friends involved in a conversation over lunch. After students have read the conversation, I pose to them the same questions that I used in the original class. This inevitably provokes a discussion entailing clashes between moral viewpoints based on needs and rights and response styles based on advising and understanding. I conclude this opening session by offering a conceptual overview of the basic models developed by Kohlberg (for male development) and Gilligan (for female development). To provide students with a summary of information in this unit I hand out a chart that has been adapted from my work with Lisa Lenze (see table 1).

Following this, we spend the second day talking about response styles as well as reasons why men and women may have both different tendencies and preferences for responding. The principles I've previously identified are explicated at this point, and the class and I engage in discussion that focuses on the distinctiveness of styles and the equal validity of each.

The final day of the unit is devoted to application. Since I premiered the unit, Lenze and I have developed role-play exercises to illustrate effective and ineffective ways of articulating what is wanted from a conversational partner and responding appropriately to another's "troubles talk." Students participate in critiquing the role players, which allows us to exercise critical judgment without creating defensiveness in role players. During the remainder of the period I repeat the "practice session" that culminated the original teaching of this material. Students talk with each other and practice stating what they want in a response, asking what kind of response another would find helpful, and reacting to their partners with either understanding or advising communication.

The extent to which students value this unit is clearly demonstrated in their final evaluations of the course. This unit, in whole or in part, is routinely the most frequent response to the question, "What parts of the course were most valuable to you?"

If a central purpose of liberal education is to expand students' appreciation of differences among people, then this unit advances this goal. It does so in at least two ways. First, it discourages the misperception that gender and gender-associated behaviors are rigidly fixed by biology. Invariably students' comments reveal that most women and some men adopt the voice of care, most men and some women endorse the voice of fairness, and some members of each sex employ voices that blend attention to caring and fairness. Using students' own comments as illustrations, instructors can emphasize the point that moral voice is gender-influenced, not sex-determined.

Second, a unit on moral voices provides an opportunity to think beyond the two voices that Gilligan recognized and the variations on them noted by Belenky and her colleagues. Gilligan has been legitimately criticized for implying that only two modes or voices exist when, in fact, there may be multiple ones beyond what encrusted androcentric perspectives have allowed us to envision. Extended class discussion of moral issues discloses perspectives that do not fit neatly into the dichotomous model Gilligan proposed. Thus, students are encouraged to continue the process of discovering moral voices beyond the classroom.

The residual message of the unit I have described here is not that there are two moral voices but that there is more than a single one: how many we have yet to know. When students emerge from a class with increased insight into themselves and others and with greater respect for distinctive modes of thinking and acting, then perhaps we come closer to bell hooks's vision of education as an experience that liberates us by reaching both our minds and our hearts.

Notes

1. Although Gilligan claims that "The different voice I describe is characterized not by gender but theme" (2), the narrative weight of the book argues
   otherwise. Both Gilligan's own descriptions throughout her work and interpretations of her findings by others represent the different voice she identifies as at least strongly associated with, if not the product of, gender.

2. For extensions of Gilligan's theory see: Apter; Belenky et al.; Eichenbaum
   and Orbach; Gilligan, "Moral Orientation and Moral Development"; Rubin;
   and Wood.

3. Not only has male authority been privileged, but also most men in my class
   responded in a manner consistent with conventional moral theory's emphasis on individual autonomy and rights. Uninformed by women's experiences
   but nonetheless universalized to them, accepted views of morality grow out
   of classic works by three men widely regarded as the "great" moral theorists
   of this century: Eric Erickson, *Childhood and Society*; Lawrence Kohlberg,
   "The Development of Modes of Thinking and Choices in Years 10 to 16";
   and Jean Piaget, *The Moral Judgment of the Child*.

Works Cited

Apter, Terri. *Altered Loves: Mothers and Daughters during Adolescence.* New
  York: St. Martins, 1990.
Belenky, Mary, Blythe Clinchy, Nancy Goldberger, and Jill Tarule. *Women's
  Ways of Knowing: The Development of Self, Voice, and Mind.* New York:
  Basic, 1986.
Brummett, Barry. "Absolutist and Relativist Stances toward the Problem of Dif-
  ference: A Model for Student Growth in Public Speaking Education." *Com-
  munication Education* 25 (1986): 269–74.
Disch, Estelle, and Becky Thompson. "Teaching and Learning from the Heart."
  NWSA Journal 2 (1990): 68–78.
Eichenbaum, Luise, and Susie Orbach. *Between Women: Love, Envy and Com-
  petition in Women's Friendships.* New York: Viking, 1988.
Erickson, Eric. *Childhood and Society.* New York: Norton, 1950.
Gilligan, Carol. *In a Different Voice: Psychological Theory and Women's Devel-
  opment.* Cambridge, MA: Harvard University Press, 1982.
———. "Moral Orientation and Moral Development." In *Women and Moral
  Theory*, ed. E. Kittay and D. Meyers. Savage, MD: Rowman and Littlefield,
  1987. 19–33.
Gilligan, Carol, Janie V. Ward, and Jill M. Taylor, with Betty Baldridge, eds. *Map-
  ping the Moral Domain.* Cambridge, MA: Harvard University Press, 1988.
hooks, bell. *Talking Back: Thinking Feminist, Thinking Black.* Boston: South
  End Press, 1989.

Kohlberg, Lawrence. "The Development of Modes of Thinking and Choices in Years 10 to 16." PhD diss., University of Chicago, 1958.

Lorde, Audre. *Sister Outsider: Essays and Speeches.* Trumansburg, NY: The Crossing Press, 1984.

Piaget, Jean. *The Moral Judgment of the Child.* 1932. Rpt. New York: The Free Press, 1965.

Rubin, Lillian. *Just Friends: The Role of Friendship in Our Lives.* New York: Harper and Row, 1985.

Shapiro, Amy. "Creating a Conversation: Teaching All Women in the Feminist Classroom." *NWSA Journal* 3 (1991): 70–80.

Tannen, Deborah. *You Just Don't Understand: Women and Men in Conversation.* New York: William Morrow, 1990.

Treichler, Paula, and Cheris Kramarae. "Women's Talk in the Ivory Tower." *Communication Quarterly* 31 (1983): 18–32.

Wood, Julia T. "Different Voices in Relationship Crises: An Extension of Gilligan's Theory." *American Behavioral Scientist* 29 (1986): 273–301.

Wood, Julia T., and Lisa Lenze. "Gender and the Development of Self: Inclusive Pedagogy in Interpersonal Communication." *Women's Studies in Communication* 14 (1991): 1–23.

CHAPTER NINE

Teaching about Domestic Violence: Strategies for Empowerment

SAUNDRA GARDNER

The burgeoning literature on feminist pedagogy has led many of us to examine critically not only what we teach in our courses but also how we teach.[1] Struggling to create a learning environment that empowers all students, feminist faculty have been particularly concerned with the structure and dynamics of the classroom, the personal and emotional impact of course materials, and the development of teaching methods that facilitate personal and social change.[2] While such concerns are certainly germane to any feminist classroom, I believe they are particularly salient in courses that center on sensitive topics such as domestic violence.[3] The emotional intensity of the subject, the strong sense of powerlessness many students feel, and the high proportion of survivors who enroll in such courses, all produce a unique set of challenges to those teaching in this field.[4] For example, how do we talk about domestic violence without revictimizing members of the class who have experienced it? How can we counteract feelings of hopelessness and despair, which intensify as we explore one form of domestic violence after another?

Given the nature of traditional academic training, many of us are not prepared to answer such questions or even to anticipate them. To help bridge this gap, I would like to share my experiences teaching domestic-violence courses over the past six years. While there is obviously no single "right way" to organize or teach any course, we can learn from each other's mistakes and successes and it is in this spirit that I offer the following overview of my course. In addition to highlighting the types of problems and issues that frequently emerged in my classes, I discuss specific teaching strategies developed to mitigate them. I also present a detailed description of my current syllabus as well as discuss how course requirements have changed over time, and why.

I first taught the course described here, Domestic Violence and Social Structure, in 1985. It is an upper-level sociology course as well as an approved elective in the Peace Studies and Women's Studies programs on campus. The course presents a feminist analysis of various forms of domestic violence (e.g., wife beating, physical violence against children, incest, lesbian battering, etc.) and critically examines how the patriarchal structure and ideology of society function to create and perpetuate

---

Originally published in the Spring 1993 issue of the *NWSA Journal*.

violent behavior. The course is offered every three semesters and enrollment is limited to forty.

While the class attracts students from a wide variety of majors, the fields of education and social work are often overrepresented. The majority of students are middle-class, and nearly all students are white. Students' ages typically range from eighteen to fifty-five, but the majority are under twenty-three years old. My classes also tend to be disproportionately female. Since I have taught the course, only thirty out of a total of 144 students have been male.

Of all my courses, domestic violence is among the hardest to teach and it certainly is the most emotionally draining. This is due, in part, to the subject matter of the course, but another key factor is the high proportion of students in the class who have experienced physical and/or sexual violence during childhood or as adults. Typically, about one-third of those who enroll in the course "know" they are survivors and another third come to this realization about midway through the semester. Although these figures are relatively high, they are not unusual. Others who have taught domestic violence or related courses, such as Janet Lee (1989, 543–44) and Brenda D. Phillips (1988, 289), report similar patterns. Thus, for many students, the course either opens up old wounds or triggers an awareness of past experiences with violence that have been buried for years.[5] For those who have not directly experienced violence, the course is also a struggle since it directly challenges their taken-for-granted and, oftentimes, idealized conception of the family. Most initially respond to this challenge by either doubting the prevalence of domestic violence or by blaming the victim for such behavior. Although these patterns of resistance begin to disappear by the third or fourth week of the semester, frustration and depression often take their place.

For those teaching courses on domestic violence, especially for the first time, these responses to the course can create a great deal of personal anguish. I remember, for example, seriously questioning whether it was even appropriate to teach a course that focused on such an emotionally volatile and sensitive topic. Were the costs to myself, and to the students, just too high? I also remember feeling confused about my ethical responsibilities, particularly in relation to survivors in the class. As I struggled with these issues, I sought the advice of others, including colleagues, members of the class, representatives of a local battered women's project, and personal friends who were survivors. All offered valuable suggestions for how I could reduce the personal trauma experienced by survivors in the class as well as minimize the resistance and fatalism so common among the other students. These early discussions allayed my anxieties about the course and, perhaps more important, they provided the impetus for many of the curricular changes and teaching strategies outlined in this article.

The issues and concerns that emerged during my first semester of teaching about domestic violence dramatically increased my awareness of what I call the "politics of syllabus construction." I am referring here to the notion that every syallabus we create is more than just a map of the course; it is a highly political document. Each of its components, ranging from the texts we choose to the particular topics we cover, conveys very specific messages to the student about our values and priorities. And, given the painful histories of many students enrolled in domestic-violence courses, these messages take on a heightened significance. As a result, those of us who teach such courses need to construct our syllabi with great care.

In terms of texts and readings, I believe it is important to choose materials that provide a strong conceptual framework for analyzing domestic violence yet, at the same time, do not objectify those who have experienced it. In this regard, I have found that qualitative studies work best. Two that I use and highly recommend are: *Violence against Wives* by Emerson Dobash and Russell Dobash (1979) and *Father-Daughter Incest* by Judith Herman (1981). I have also taught the course using more quantitative texts but stopped doing so for several reasons. First, I found that such texts did little to increase students' understanding of the dynamics or social context of violent behavior, and this was especially true for those who had not directly experienced violence. As a result, it was much easier for such students to maintain their "us versus them" mentality, often expressed in comments such as "I'd never stay in an abusive situation" or "There must be something wrong with these people." As Phillips notes, such remarks are quite common among nonsurvivors and, for those who have experienced violence, they are quite painful (291). In my classes, this situation frequently produced hostile interactions between survivors and nonsurvivors, with neither group being "heard" by the other. Secondly, quantitative texts elicited consistent negative feedback from survivors in the class. Most viewed such texts as yet another form of victimization; many reported feeling objectified, "unreal," and lifeless. Or, in the words of one survivor, "Rather than illuminating my experiences or those of other survivors, page after page of charts and tables just seemed to erase it." Both of these problems were alleviated when I switched to qualitative texts that offered a more subjective and contextual analysis of violence.

Given the numerous myths and stereotypes associated with domestic violence, I believe it is also important to include materials that highlight the theme of cultural diversity. In my course, I address this concern in several ways. First, in my presentations to the class, I pay particular attention to how differences in race, sexual identity, socioeconomic status, and age affect the various types of domestic violence covered in the course.[6] Secondly, I assign several reserve readings that address how the dynamics of battering are affected by sexual identity and by race (i.e., Uzzell and Peebles-Wilkins [1991], 131–38, and Hart [1986], 173–89).

The course also includes several optional books, such as *Voices in the Night,* edited by Toni McNaron and Yarrow Morgan (1982), and *I Never Told Anyone,* edited by Ellen Bass and Louise Thornton (1983). These texts are mainly first-person accounts of violence written by survivors. As such, they serve to validate and affirm the experiences of students with similar histories and, in particular, those just beginning to explore their past. These experiential readings also help others in the class gain a deeper understanding of what it means to be victimized by people you love and trust. Despite these advantages, I believe such texts work best as optional rather than required reading. Given the graphic descriptions of violence discussed by the authors and what this might, in turn, trigger for the reader, I feel each student should have complete freedom of choice regarding if and when to read this material.

I also think it is important for the syllabus to include the names and phone numbers of local resources and services (e.g., crisis centers, battered women's shelters, counseling centers, etc.). In my course, I discuss this list on the first day of class as well as my rationale for including it. As part of this discussion, I talk about the types of students who typically take the course and how important it is for those who experience difficulty with the class to seek assistance. Like Phillips, I find that this type of discussion increases peer sensitivity to survivors' experiences and, as a result, helps to create a more positive learning environment (291). I also remind students of the resource list throughout the semester and make a special effort to do so whenever we begin to discuss a new topic, such as incest and battering.

Since most students are quite anxious about taking the course, and this is particularly true for survivors, it is helpful if the syllabus is very explicit about what issues will be discussed within each topic area of the course and when. In my experience, such information reduces student anxiety stemming from "fear of the unknown" and, in addition, it helps students with violent histories to make an informed choice about whether to attend class on a specific day. Although I view class attendance as important, I also know that some topics may trigger intense emotional pain as well as flashbacks for some students. Thus, I do not require attendance as I do in all other courses I teach. At the beginning of the semester, I inform students that they may miss class, and do so without penalty, whenever they feel this choice is emotionally necessary. I also suggest that they get notes from a classmate or meet with me privately to discuss the material covered in class during their absence.

In terms of deciding what to discuss and when, I typically use the first few weeks of the semester to highlight conceptual and theoretical issues central to the course. Aside from introducing students to the analytical framework we will be using throughout the semester, this type of discussion creates a relatively nonthreatening environment within which the class can begin to develop a sense of community and trust. It has been my experience that the feeling of safety engendered by such a classroom atmosphere clearly facilitates later discussions of more experiential course materials. Also, when discussing each form of domestic violence, I have found that creating a balance between analytical and experiential approaches to the topic works best. Shifting back and forth between these frameworks helps to ensure that students do not get too lost in abstractions nor become too emotionally drained. Over the years, students have frequently commented that the more theoretical discussions provided an important "emotional time out" for them, and I should add, for myself as well.

Another way to offset the gloom that can paralyze a class is to add what I call a "social response" section after each form of violence discussed. Here the emphasis is on social action and, in particular, current programs and services aimed at reducing the various types of domestic violence. To highlight this theme, I schedule a variety of guest speakers throughout the semester. Among those I typically include are police officers, a victim-witness advocate from the DA's office, representatives from Parents Anonymous, local therapists who specialize in the area of domestic violence, caseworkers from the Department of Human Services, and staff from a local battered women's shelter. In addition to these professionals, several incest survivors and formerly battered women speak with the class. Based on student feedback, these presentations are clearly viewed as the most significant of the semester. Some students note, for example, how the speakers' personal stories made many of the concepts and issues of the course "come to life"; others describe how the presentations enabled them to stop "blaming the victim"; and comments from survivors in the class typically highlight the importance of such speakers as role models.

With regard to specific assignments, I have had the most success with those that encourage cooperative and collaborative learning. Two I highly recommend are in-class discussion groups and student-initiated social-change projects. Both activities help to create a sense of community within the classroom, and they also provide time for students to talk with each other about their thoughts, feelings, reactions to the course, and so forth. The in-class discussion groups are formed at the beginning of the semester and meet about every two weeks. Students are randomly assigned to these groups and, each time they meet, one member serves as discussion leader. This person is responsible for preparing a presentation on a topic or issue relevant to the course and for leading the group discussion. Fulfillment of this assignment is worth 15 percent of the student's final grade.

The other assignment, student-initiated social-change projects, is one I introduced several years ago as an option to the more traditional term paper. A key benefit of these projects is that they offer students a way to effectively translate their anger and frustration regarding the prevalence of domestic violence into concrete social action designed to reduce it. In doing so, these projects enable students to create their *own* answers to a question that frequently dominates class discussions of domestic violence: "What can *we* do to help stop this behavior?"

Early in the semester, students who elect to work on a social-change project in lieu of a term paper are asked to submit a brief description of their ideas for possible social-change projects.[7] Students with similar interests are placed together in groups typically consisting of four to six people. Each group is given about two weeks to prepare a preliminary proposal outlining the specific goals of their project and how they plan to achieve them. To ensure that the projects are both appropriate and ethically sound, I review the proposals and request revisions if necessary. I also serve as a resource person by linking groups to relevant campus and/ or community organizations.

My evaluation of this assignment is based on two sources of information, each accounting for 15 percent of the student's final grade. The first is a group report, written collaboratively, that describes the rationale and goals of the project, any problems the group encountered regarding the project's design and/or implementation, the outcome of the project, and what the group views as the short- and long-term impact of their project. The second required paper is an individual project report submitted by each group member. Here students are asked to describe what they learned from working on the project, what they might have done differently and why, and their own thoughts and reactions regarding the process of creating social change.

The majority of student projects developed over the past several years have focused on creating social change within the university community. Of these, most have either attempted to increase student awareness of domestic violence or to create additional services for members of the campus community who have experienced such violence. One group, for example, organized a university-wide Incest Awareness Day, which became an annual event for several years. Others presented workshops in residence halls on such topics as emotional and physical abuse, courtship violence, and incest. And, some students worked to establish campus-wide therapy and support groups for survivors of violence.

There have also been a variety of off-campus projects aimed at creating social change within the larger local community. Most of these projects were developed in consultation with the local battered women's shelter, and all have focused on obtaining information designed to stimulate social change. One group, for example, organized a court watch to ascertain the circumstances under which judges were most likely to grant a protection-from-abuse order. This information was then shared with staff of the local shelter and others who provide legal services for battered women. In a related project, another group interviewed formerly battered women to assess how well current shelter and community services met their needs and to ascertain how such services could be improved. Other students interviewed local police officers regarding the strengths and weaknesses of current domestic-violence laws, problems associated with their enforcement, and ways to improve the existing statutes.

Student evaluations of the social-change assignment have been extremely positive. In fact, many have described this aspect of the course as one of the most empowering and transformative experiences of their college careers. For instance, one student wrote: "This is the first time in four years that the work I've done for a course has actually been relevant to the *real* world." Others commented more directly on the link between theory and praxis and, in particular, how it affected their emotional response to the course: "I don't feel stuck or paralyzed anymore since we were able to use our knowledge to do something positive and concrete about domestic violence. We didn't just talk; we put our education to work." Such comments clearly suggest, that in courses on sensitive topics like domestic violence, it is particularly useful for students to become actively involved in their education and this includes the process of social change. By working with others who share their concerns and by having the opportunity to design and implement projects such as those described here, students soon realize they *can* effect change; they *can* "make a difference." Thus, by incorporating assignments designed to promote social activism, faculty can help reduce the feelings of despair and powerlessness so common among students in their domestic-violence classes.

In conclusion, one of the most difficult tasks facing those of us who teach domestic violence or related courses is to create a learning environment in which students feel both safe and empowered. There are obviously countless ways to achieve this goal, and the most successful are likely to be those that take into account students' emotional as well as intellectual needs. In this regard, I hope the teaching strategies and course curriculum outlined here prove to be useful resources.

Notes

An earlier version of this paper was presented at the annual meeting of the National Women's Studies Association, June 1989, in Towson, MD.

1. For an excellent overview of this literature, see Weiler; Ryan; Culley and Portuges; and Bunch and Pollack.

2. For further discussion of the dynamics of feminist teaching, see Rakow; Disch and Thompson; Lewis; Gardner et al.; and Rothenberg.

3. As defined here, domestic violence includes all forms of emotional/psychological, physical, or sexual violence that occur within intimate, familial, or familylike relationships. Thus, unlike the more frequently used term "family violence," this conceptualization includes violent behavior between individuals unrelated through blood or marriage (e.g., dating violence, lesbian battering, etc.).

4. It is important to note that these issues can emerge in any course that includes one or more class sessions on the topic of domestic violence. See, for example, the works by Lee and Phillips.

5. This knowledge is based on information shared with me by students via private conversations, written assignments, and course evaluations.

6. My lectures draw on a wide variety of materials, but I have found the work of the following authors to be especially useful: Gelles and Cornell; hooks; Gordon; Lobel; and Russell.

7. Typically, about seventy-five percent of the class choose this option.

Works Cited

Bass, Ellen, and Louise Thornton, eds. *I Never Told Anyone: Writings by Women Survivors of Child Sexual Abuse.* New York: Harper and Row, 1983.

Bunch, Charlotte, and Sandra Pollack, eds. *Learning Our Way: Essays in Feminist Education.* Trumansburg, NY: Crossing Press, 1983.

Gulley, Margo, and Catherine Portuges, eds. *Gendered Subjects: The Dynamics of Feminist Teaching.* Boston: Routledge and Kegan Paul, 1985.

Disch, Estelle, and Becky Thompson. "Teaching and Learning from the Heart." *NWSA Journal* 2 (1990): 68–78.

Dobash, Emerson, and Russell Dobash. *Violence against Wives.* New York: Free Press, 1979.

Gardner, Saundra, Cynthia Dean, and Deo McKaig. "Responding to Differences in the Classroom: The Politics of Knowledge, Class, and Sexuality." *Sociology of Education* 62.1 (1989): 64–74.

Gelles, Richard J., and Claire Pedrick Cornell. *Intimate Violence in Families.* Newbury Park, CA: Sage, 1990.

Gordon, Linda. *Heroes of Their Own Lives.* New York: Viking Penguin, 1988.

Hart, Barbara. "Lesbian Battering: An Examination." In *Naming the Violence: Speaking out about Lesbian Battering,* ed. Magda Lobel, 173–89. Seattle: Seal Press.

Herman, Judith Lewis. *Father-Daughter Incest.* Cambridge, MA: Harvard University Press, 1981.

hooks, bell. "Violence in Intimate Relationships." *Talking Back*. Boston: South End Press, 1989. 84–91.

Lee, Janet. "Our Hearts Are Collectively Breaking: Teaching Survivors of Violence." *Gender and Society* 3 (1989): 541–48.

Lewis, Magda. "Interrupting Patriarchy: Politics, Resistance, and Transformation in the Feminist Classroom." *Harvard Educational Review* 60 (1990): 467–88.

Lobel, Kerry, ed. *Naming the Violence: Speaking Out about Lesbian Battering*. Seattle: Seal Press, 1986.

McNaron, Toni A. H., and Yarrow Morgan, eds. *Voices in the Night: Women Speaking about Incest*. Pittsburgh: Cleis Press, 1982.

Phillips, Brenda D. "Teaching about Domestic Violence to an At-Risk Population: Insights from Sociological and Feminist Perspectives." *Teaching Sociology* 16 (1988): 289–93.

Rakow, Lana F. "Gender and Race in the Classroom: Teaching Way Out of Line." *Feminist Teacher* 6 (1991): 10–13.

Rothenberg, Paula. "Integrating the Study of Race, Gender, and Class: Some Preliminary Observations." *Feminist Teacher* 3 (1988): 37–42.

Russell, Diana E. H. *The Secret Trauma: Incest in the Lives of Girls and Women*. New York: Basic Books, 1986.

Ryan, Maureen. "Classroom and Contexts: The Challenge of Feminist Pedagogy." *Feminist Teacher* 4 (1989): 39–42.

Uzzell, Odell, and Wilma Peebles-Wilkins. "Black Spouse Abuse: A Focus on Relational Factors and Intervention Strategies." *The Black Family: Essays and Studies*. Ed. Robert Staples. Belmont, CA: Wadsworth, 1991. 131–38.

Weiler, Kathleen. *Women Teaching for Change: Gender, Class, and Power*. South Hadley, MA: Bergin and Garvey, 1988.

———. "Freire and a Feminist Pedagogy of Difference." *Harvard Educational Review* 61 (1991): 449–74.

CHAPTER TEN

The Shift from Identity Politics to the Politics of Identity: Lesbian Panels in the Women's Studies Classroom

MARY MARGARET FONOW AND DEBIAN MARTY

This chapter discusses the teaching implications of constructionist approaches to the study of sexual identity and evaluates our efforts in implementing these approaches in introductory women's studies classes. Borrowing insights from postmodern feminism, we also offer suggestions for how we teach and theorize about sexual identities. Primary attention is given to an analysis of students' reactions to lesbian panels and to an assessment of the usefulness of these panels in fostering student understanding of sexual identity. Our discussion is based on our own teaching experience, on interviews with other instructors, and on 169 written student responses to lesbian panels. Our primary goal is to examine how the topic of sexual identity is taught to general education students enrolled in the basic women's studies survey course offered by the Center for Women's Studies at the Ohio State University.[1] Students who take this course to fulfill general education requirements usually have little or no knowledge of feminist scholarship and rarely have had the opportunity to study and discuss the topic of sexual identity.

We are aware of the limitations in constructionist arguments and of the existence of tendencies toward essentialism in some important feminist writing on sexuality and sexual identity.[2] Nonetheless, we deliberately chose constructionist approaches for this particular audience because we believe such approaches encourage students to be more self-reflexive about their own sexuality. Constructionist approaches encourage students to think historically and cross-culturally about sexuality and gender and challenge students to examine their own and society's assumptions about the naturalness of both categories. Thus, the use of the lesbian panel as a pedagogical tool is embedded within the general context of how we teach about gender and sexuality.

The readings, films, and exercises we choose help students reconstruct categories of sexual identity and gain a historical understanding of how categories of sexual identity are created, changed over time, and claimed by individuals. These activities also help students to develop an appreciation of diversity within and between categories of sexual identity and to understand the role of homophobia and heterosexism in privileging heterosexuality at the expense of all our sexual identities. Students read

Originally published in the Autumn 1991 issue of the *NWSA Journal*.

literary and first person accounts, oral histories, and interviews with in-dividuals who have challenged gender norms and the heterosexual im-perative. Growing-up narratives and coming-out stories, a staple of les-bian and gay culture, encourage students to grasp socialization pressures as well as the joy of self-discovery. Selected readings from this genre help students recognize that, while violations of societal norms are difficult and often painful, such violations are necessary for personal and politi-cal empowerment.[3]

To insure a diverse representation of experience, special care is taken to incorporate the writing of lesbians of color and working-class lesbi-ans.[4] These perspectives help students to comprehend the complexity of multiple identities and the systems of oppression based on differences of race and class. When the experiences of women with multiple marginal-ized identities are validated, several responses are possible. One response, which we see frequently, is that heterosexual students who are marginal-ized in other ways may bridge their resistance to homosexuality through solidarity on the basis of race or class. Students can recognize in the mul-tiplicity of identities the potential for conflict and for common cause. Historical materials are important in this course because they provide students the opportunity to examine the economic and social changes that make it possible for women to claim a lesbian identity. The materi-als also show how lesbians can build communities and politics around their identity. Historical texts also provide concrete examples and illus-trations of changing sexual mores and practices and in this way further undermine the naturalness of sexual categories and reveal the political nature of sexual definitions and categorization.[5]

Through a variety of activities and exercises, students begin to iden-tify and analyze the pressures they have encountered from parents, teachers, clergy, peers, and popular culture to adopt a heterosexual iden-tity. These activities include writing a hypothetical coming-out letter to parents; asking students to locate or create a greeting card for a same-sex lover, lesbian, gay family member, or friend; and participating in role-playing exercises, for example, bringing a lesbian lover to an office party, being a lesbian at a parent-teacher conference, coming out at a family reunion, or holding a lesbian/gay marriage ceremony. But we believe one of the most effective tools in aiding students with the task of deconstruc-tion is the lesbian panel.

Late in the term, usually around the seventh or eighth week, instructors invite a panel of guest speakers to discuss their lesbianism with the stu-dents. Speakers typically share biographical information about coming out or coming to consciousness as lesbians. Most of the students' ques-tions focus on intrapersonal and interpersonal relationships: How do lesbians relate with their families of origin, lovers, friends, coworkers, employers? How do lesbians negotiate the terrain of disapproval? When and how did they know about their lesbianism? Communicating about the lives of lesbians presents a central challenge, since one of the most prevalent student misconceptions is that lesbians are solely defined by their sexual orientation. We ask them, as members of a social group whose membership is determined by sexual criteria, to speak about their experiences in ways that overcome audience stereotypes based on sexual categorization. Meredith Maran, a speaker from the Pacific Center for Sexual Minorities in Berkeley, California, addresses this concern from the panelist's point of view:

> It strikes me then that people we speak to during these engagements—the students and workers and inmates and teachers—know . . . [little] of our lives. That by opening up only the sexual aspect of ourselves for discussion, we are inviting them to see us as one-dimensional sexual beings and simultaneously demanding that they relinquish that stereotype.[6]

While lesbians are struggling to be defined by more than the gender of their sex partners, it is, nonetheless, their sexual attraction to women, and by implication their rejection of heterosexuality, that is at the core of both societal and student opposition. This paradox can constrain the presentation of information about lesbian sexuality and encourage a form of self-censorship. The counterbalance to this impulse toward impression management is the dynamic and spontaneous exchanges that happen in small classroom settings. These exchanges make it hard to maintain the mask and the myriad variables that come into play in the selection of panelists, such as who is available to be a panelist—who is "out."[7]

In order for this exercise to work, students must be willing to see past the comfortable stereotypes that serve important psychological and social functions for them, and instructors must be willing to recognize the emotional and intellectual difficulty of such a project. Throughout the term we ask students to reexamine their most cherished values and assumptions about human nature, gender, and the nature of relations between the sexes. When we succeed, they no longer see gender as a fixed and stable category. Can we say the same for heterosexuality? Though we have carefully woven information about the experiences and contributions of lesbians throughout the course, our best efforts to deconstruct heterosexuality are tested most severely by students' face-to-face confrontations with lesbians.

In addition to a lack of basic knowledge about homosexuality, students bring to the college classroom their own sexual histories, experiences, and insecurities, which have been shaped by their gender, age, race, class, and sexual orientation, and which interact in complex ways with our efforts to teach about sexuality and sexual identity. Side by side, in the same classroom, are lesbian, bisexual, heterosexual, and gay students of various racial and ethnic backgrounds; children and other relatives of gays and lesbians; students questioning their sexual identity; incest and rape survivors; students who are not yet sexually active; and sexually experienced students. This diversity in the classroom is both a challenge and a resource. Students of color frequently draw the parallels between racism and homophobia. A black student, for example, who was outraged when one panelist talked about employment discrimination, dramatically told the class:

> I'm sick of this. What gives people the right to impose their petty prejudices on others? Do you think as a black person I care what you think about me or say about me behind my back? But if you try and take away my livelihood, my education, my job, then you are going to have a fight on your hands.[8]

A white woman who had dated a black man made the following connection:

> The fact that lesbians sometimes have to hide their partners is similar to interracial dating. I was in an interracial relationship for nearly six years and had to hide that from my family. They never even met him, and wouldn't! I guess that "coming out" is important to your happiness in relationships. It hurts to hide the one you love.

Lesbian and gay students have a variety of reactions to the lesbian panels and other efforts to teach about their experiences. These reactions may include pride and self-validation, fear of exposure and embarrassment about overgeneralizations, and anger when other students reveal their homophobia. One woman wrote, "I feel very supported in being a lesbian . . . a sense of camaraderie and positive reinforcement." Another lesbian, concerned about overgeneralizations, wrote, "I feel it is very important to state in the beginning (like one of the women did) that it was her own opinion. She was not representing the opinions of all lesbians, just her own." Family members and friends of gay men and lesbians may also find validation in the gay-affirming classroom. One student volunteered the following: "I've never judged a person based on sexual preference. My fiancé's father is a homosexual, and he has been living with his partner ever since his divorce twelve years ago. Homosexual couples can also raise children in an open-minded and moralistic way."

Among heterosexual students, only a small number of written reactions to the lesbian panels could be clearly labeled hostile. These remarks included "makes me feel sick," "uncomfortable and disgusted," "sinful," and "gross." Most, while awkward and sometimes ambivalent, indicate some degree of acceptance or understanding of the experiences, feelings, or rights of the lesbian panelists. The majority of students report they felt more comfortable with gays and lesbians or with homosexuality after the panel. Typical responses were "Gay people aren't as scary to me anymore"; "I feel more open minded because of being confronted face to face with homosexuals"; "The stereotypes I had were really shattered. . . . I feel more of an understanding."

Ethical considerations demand careful attention to the creation of a safe environment in which all participants can discuss sensitive topics. Gay students and instructors will be exposed to the homophobic reactions of nongay students, who need to have the freedom to reveal their prejudices and lack of knowledge in order to have them challenged. For real learning to occur, confrontations with students about their homophobia must be dealt with directly, in a way that does not shame or humiliate the offending student and at the same time repairs the damage done to the self-respect of gay, lesbian, and bisexual students. It is important not to reproduce in the classroom the racism, class privilege, sexism, and heterosexism found in society. To foster a positive environment in which students can acquire an understanding of diversity, including sexual diversity, some instructors distribute a set of guidelines developed by Lynn Weber Cannon that lays the ground rules for classroom discussions of social and cultural diversity.[9] Early in the course we talk about the power of words to coerce and silence as well as to liberate, and we insist that students use language that honors diversity.

"I" statements encourage accurate placement of responsibility for students' feelings. Students, for example, can look to themselves for the reasons they are homophobic, rather than projecting their reasons onto lesbians. We also find it useful to disclose our own struggles with racism, sexism, heterosexism, and class biases.[10]

It is evident from our experience that, in an effort to transcend descriptive categorization, lesbianism must first be reclaimed from dominant stereotyping and presented as a total human experience. Within the process of naming and defining their own lives, speakers repair and validate an experiential, as opposed to an ideological, lesbian identity. As students hear the speakers talk about their aspirations, needs, desires, and practical day-to-day living, many students respond by recognizing how "normal" lesbians are. One student wrote, "Homosexuals have the same human desires as heterosexuals, only towards the same sex. They want love, respect, knowledge, etc. In fact, they're probably a lot more human and honest than most heterosexuals I know." Other students have written, "It [the panel] makes a lesbian more human, like myself, instead of being someone weird"; and "The panel made me realize even more that there is no difference between heterosexuals and homosexuals, both lead the same types of lives, both have feelings and both put their pants on the same way."

Beyond humanizing the topic, panelists identify homophobia as the culprit responsible for distorting lesbian lives. When speakers reveal homophobia as the ideological barrier keeping lesbian and gay people from the common roundtable of humanity, they simultaneously make it evident that there is nothing inherently deviant or inhuman in being a lesbian. As a result, many students relocate their understanding of responsibility for stigma from lesbians to homophobic beliefs and practices. As instructors make it explicit that lesbianism and homophobia are different but overlapping social constructs, students, many of whom freely acknowledge their homophobia, have an opportunity to clarify that homophobia is a problem for heterosexuals and homosexuals in different ways. We hope that as students recognize how homophobia limits them but is not all that they are, so too homophobia limits but does not define lesbians. One student wrote, "It is not a problem that lesbians are lesbians, it is the problem of prejudice on the part of others." Another reported, "The panel made me feel pity for people who are homophobic because everyone is different and should be accepted by others for who they are and not their sexual orientation."

Students sometimes make painful connections with their own homophobia, as did the student who wrote, "On the first day of class I opened my big mouth and said I am very prejudice against homosexuals. I feel now I am more open." Another student reported, "It made me feel bad about how I've made gay/lesbian jokes in the past, but the panel made me see for myself that they are real people with real feelings." This process of relocating responsibility for homophobic attitudes often occurs in discussions of lesbian parenting. Students frequently cite society's prejudice as a reason that gay people should not parent and exhibit concern about the anxiety gays' children must inevitably suffer because of their parents' nonconformity. Helping students to recognize homophobia as the problem, and not lesbian mothers, validates lesbians' experiences and choices. This recognition parallels the parenting responsibilities of lesbians with those of other parents from oppressed groups and legitimates the feelings and concerns of the children of gays and lesbians, some of whom are in the class.

Once audience members recognize the "normalcy" of lesbian humanity, heterosexual identity cannot remain unproblematic. After all, if lesbians are "normal" people, then the heterosexual claim to exclusive normality is dispelled. To facilitate student exploration of heterosexism, several women's studies instructors have initiated heterosexual guest panels. Instructors frequently use a "heterosexual questionnaire," which inverts many of the questions typically asked of lesbian panelists, such as, "When did you first know you were a heterosexual?" or "Since the overwhelming majority of child molesters are heterosexual males, should heterosexual men work at daycare centers or as elementary school teachers?" What becomes most evident during heterosexual panels is the unquestioned power of heterosexual identity. Problems reside not with heterosexual acts or heterosexual actors but with the construction of an identity dependent on diminishing other sexual acts and actors in order to appear as the sole socially acceptable choice. Once heterosexism is challenged, a space is created that allows students to think more reflexively about their own sexual orientation.

Evidence that both types of panels promote self-reflexivity was revealed when one heterosexual student wrote, "I have homosexual friends, lesbians, whom I've talked with about why they are the way they are, but never before have I examined so much the question, why I am the way I am." Another student responded,

> In total honesty, the lesbian panel made me think about my reasons for being a heterosexual and whether I have made the right decision. I'm not sure if I am just curious as to what it is like to be a lesbian or if, maybe, I might have some tendencies towards being a lesbian—I'm just not sure now—and this forces me to really think about it.

A third student wrote, "I am disappointed in myself that I am fearful of being labeled lesbian if I associate with lesbian women—same with my boyfriend and his gay friend—shows a lack of self-esteem."

Speakers, activities, and supportive readings not only undermine the heterosexist-homophobic hegemony that distorts gay and lesbian experiences but also reveal the distortion of heterosexual experiences as well. This function is characterized in Hortense Spillers's assertion that racial categories and definitions developed by the dominant group "tell us little or nothing about the subject buried beneath them, but a great deal more concerning the psychic and cultural reflexes that invent and invoke them."[11] Heterosexist and homophobic descriptions of lesbians are more often expressions of what heterosexuals are not supposed to be, rather than what lesbians are. Branding lesbians as man haters, for example, does not describe the experiences of most lesbians but rather serves as a warning to all women not to step out of line.[12]

This form of negative socialization explains the confusion some students report between sexual behavior and sexual identification and contributes to their inability to recognize personal feelings that do not fit into the norm. To define oneself in terms of not being like some devalued "other" forces a heterosexual to deny any of the qualities or characteristics she or he may have in common with homosexuals. Any recognition of commonality almost always seems to us to come by way of the back door: "Homosexuals are just like us" but never "We are just like homosexuals." Making explicit the interdependence of heterosexual and lesbian identities, by exposing their common yet differently distorted experiences, creates the possibility for relationships and moves classroom participants beyond a superficial exploration of difference.

We demonstrate homophobia and heterosexism as culturally debilitating ideas for everyone. By reframing the normative relationships between homosexuals and heterosexuals, we establish the grounds for a relational politics that can break down hierarchical oppositions inherent in the modern construction of sexual identities. In the process of cultivating an explicit interconnectedness, panelists and students find common ground. Panelists draw on the standard of fairness, rhetorically offered to all people through the dominant discourse on democratic ideals, as their leverage for criticizing the failure of our democracy to extend equal rights to lesbians.[13] Students generally respond affirmatively to appeals to the rights of life, liberty, and the pursuit of happiness. One student wrote, "Lesbians aren't asking for special rights or privileges just the opportunity to live within mainstream society without being harassed or discriminated against solely because of their sexual orientation."

Yet other students affirm individual choice while denouncing homosexuality. Typical remarks of this position are "No I don't agree/identify with it, but I don't condemn those who do. I believe in freedom of choice in any situation." Another student wrote, "I do not condone homosexuality—that has not changed; however, I feel even more strongly that their rights should be protected. I don't feel I have to support what they do, but I do feel a responsibility to make sure I do not discriminate against them." This contradiction reflects an implicit hazard in holding the dominant ideology accountable for its promises. When efforts to change stereotypical conceptions occur on hegemonic terrain, lesbians will experience assimilation pressures in order to be recognized as "normal" and "human" and, therefore, entitled to basic human rights.

Often, lesbian speakers are acutely aware of editing their personal narratives in order to build emotional bridges between themselves and resistant audiences. Maran relates her frustration with the pressure to sanitize:

> As we speak in measured, reasonable tones, another voice begins to speak— and then to yell—inside me. This voice knows half-truths are lies. This voice won't joke or equivocate or prettify; it won't tell "fairy tales" with politically correct endings; it wants the truth to be known.[14]

Once again, the tension of validating the lesbian identity as fully human while repairing and rebutting stereotypes can promote defensive protectionism on the part of speakers. Allowing lesbian experiences to be evaluated by dominant perceptions of normality and happiness is a risky undertaking; consequently, many lesbian and gay speakers, scholars, and activists insist upon deconstructing compulsory heterosexuality first.[15]

In sum, teaching about sexuality humanely and holistically through the use of lesbian and heterosexual panels, coming-out stories, oral histories, role playing, and films provides a useful opportunity to excavate social contradictions in the construction of sexual identities.[16] Our analysis leads us to believe that several important outcomes are possible with this approach. Lesbians come to be seen as total human beings; the costs of homophobia and heterosexism are identified for everyone; definitions of sexuality that privilege some at the expense of others are challenged; and the notion of normality is problematized.

At the same time we are aware of the potential such a project has for undermining the rationale some lesbians and gay men may feel for a political movement based on sexual identity. A similar paradox exists for women and has been expressed by Linda Alcoff when she asks social constructionists, "How do we ground a feminist politics that deconstructs the female subject?"[17] We could similarly ask, How do we ground a sexual politics that deconstructs sexual identity? And how do we ground a sexual politics that incorporates the interests of those with multiple marginalized identities? Our conceptualization of individuals within their historical and social contexts is enhanced when we understand people in relationship to one another, rather than exclusively in relationship to a distorted meaning imposed on their bodies.[18] As the lesbian and heterosexual panels illustrate, these intrapersonal and interpersonal considerations are paramount in creating meaning in our lives and should also be paramount in our teaching, politics, and scholarship. Placing people in the context of their community allows for multiple constellations of interactive meanings, including disparities in power. Our experiences in the introductory classroom leads us to believe that we should shift the emphasis from identity politics, for example, fitting everyone into the center, to the politics of identity or the questioning of why the center should be privileged.

Despite its debatable usefulness, it would be impractical to abandon the concept of identity politics.[19] The inequitable exercise of power based on ranking social differences creates material, psychological, and social oppression that cannot be ignored. Rather, it is imperative that teachers reject the dominant discourse on sexual identities and instead create a space where students may explore how they name themselves. We must offer students both resistance and relationally based strategies for engaging in personal and social change—resistance against rigid categorization and a simultaneous sense of community with the diversity inherent in humanity.[20]

Notes

Portions of this paper were published under the title "Teaching College Students about Sexual Identity from a Feminist Perspective," in *Sexuality and the Curriculum*, ed. James T. Sears (New York: Teachers College Press, 1992).

1. The course enrolls about fifteen hundred students a year, one-fourth of whom are men, and 12 percent of whom are students of color. The authors frequently have taught the course at the Ohio State University.

2. For a fuller discussion of these issues, see Carole S. Vance, "Social Construction Theory: Problems in the History of Sexuality," in *Homosexuality, Which Homosexuality?*, ed. Dennis Altman (London: GMP Publisher, 1989), 13–34; Steven Epstein, "Gay Politics, Ethnic Identity: The Limits of Social Constructionism," *Socialist Review* 17 (May-August 1987): 9–54; Scott Bravmann, "Invented Traditions: Take One on the Lesbian and Gay Past," *NWSA Journal* 3 (Winter 1991): 81–92. We are particularly aware of feminist concerns about the political paralysis associated with constructionist arguments and the universalizing tendencies of essentialism.

3. Ruth Baetz, *Lesbian Crossroads: Personal Stories of Lesbian Struggles and Triumphs* (New York: Morrow, 1980); Martha Barron Barret, *Invisible Lives: The Truth about Millions of Women Loving Women* (New York: Morrow, 1989); Margaret Cruikshank, *The Lesbian Path* (Tallahassee, FL.: Naiad Press, 1980), and *Lesbian Studies* (New York: Feminist Press, 1982); Loralee MacPike, *There's Something I've Been Meaning To Tell You* (Tallahassee, FL.: Naiad Press, 1989); Julia Penelope and Sarah Valentine, *Finding the Lesbians: Personal Accounts from around the World* (Freedom, CA.: Crossing Press, 1990).

4. Audre Lorde, *Sister Outsider* (Freedom, CA.: Crossing Press, 1984); Gloria Anzaldúa, ed., *Making Face, Making Soul Haciendo Caras: Creative and Critical Perspectives of Women of Color* (San Francisco: Aunt Lute Foundation, 1990); Barbara Smith, ed., *Home Girls: A Black Feminist Anthology* (New York: Kitchen Table Press, 1983); Cherríe Moraga and Anzaldúa, eds. *This Bridge Called My Back: Writings by Radical Women of Color* (Watertown, MA.: Persephone Press, 1981); Faith Conlon, Rachel da Silva, and Barbara Wilson, *The Things that Divide Us* (Seattle: Seal Press, 1986); Janet Zandy, *Calling Home: Working-Class Women's Writings* (New Brunswick, NJ.: Rutgers University Press, 1990).

5. Carroll Smith-Rosenberg, "The Female World of Love and Ritual: Relations between Women in Nineteenth-Century America, *Signs* 1 (Winter 1975): 1–29; John D'Emilio, "Capitalism and Gay Identity," in *Powers of Desire: The Politics of Sexuality*, ed. Ann Snitow, Christine Stansell, and Sharon Thompson (New York: Monthly Review, 1984), 101–13; Lillian Faderman, *Surpassing the Love of Men: Romantic Friendship and Love between Women from the Renaissance to the Present* (New York: William Morrow, 1981); Martin Duberman, Martha Vicinus, and George Chauncey, eds., *Hidden from History: Reclaiming the Gay and Lesbian Past* (New York: Meridian Press, 1989).

6. Meredith Maran, "Ten for Bravery, Zero for Common Sense: Confessions of a Speakers Bureau Speaker," *Outlook* 7 (Winter 1990): 70.

7. Panelists are not professional speakers or activists. Most are former students, friends, or relatives of instructors. The emphasis is on selecting panelists who represent cultural and social diversity, not a particular political perspective. This diversity affords students the opportunity to compare feminist analyses of sexuality with lived experience.

8. Quotations in this essay are from students who were enrolled in the course, Introduction to Women's Studies, spring quarter 1990 at the Ohio State University, Columbus, Ohio.

9. Lynn Weber Cannon, "Fostering Positive Race, Class, and Gender Dynamics in the Classroom," *Women's Studies Quarterly* 18 (Spring-Summer 1990): 126–34.

10. For other discussions on homophobia in the classroom, see Allison Berg, Jean Kowaleski, Caroline LeGuin, Ellen Weinauer, and Eric Wolfe, "Breaking the Silence: Sexual Preference in the Composition Classroom," *Feminist Teacher* 4 (Fall 1989): 29–32; David Bleich, "Homophobia and Sexism as Popular Values," *Feminist Teacher* 4 (Fall 1989): 21–28; Laurie Crumpacker and Eleanor M. Vander Haegen, "Pedagogy and Prejudice: Strategies for Confronting Homophobia in the Classroom," *Women's Studies Quarterly* 15 (Fall-Winter 1987): 65–73.

11. Hortense J. Spillers, "Notes on an Alternative Model—Neither/Nor," in *The Difference Within: Feminism and Critical Theory*, ed. Elizabeth Meese and Alice Parker (Philadelphia: John Benjamins, 1989), 166.

12. Suzanne Pharr, *Homophobia: A Weapon of Sexism* (Little Rock, AK.: Chardon Press, 1988).

13. For discussions of social change through the standards of dominant discourse, see Joan Scott, "Deconstructing Equality-Versus-Difference: Or, the Uses of Poststructuralist Theory for Feminism," *Feminist Studies* 14 (Spring 1988): 33–59; and E. Frances White, "Africa on My Mind: Gender, Counter Discourse and African-American Nationalism," *Journal of Women's History* 2 (Spring 1990): 73–97.

14. Maran, "Ten for Bravery," 71.

15. Mariana Valverde, "Beyond Gender Dangers and Private Pleasures: Theory and Ethics in the Sex Debates," *Feminist Studies* 15 (Summer 1989): 237–54; Jonathan Ned Katz, "The Invention of Heterosexuality," *Socialist Review* 20 (January-March 1990): 7–34.

16. There are a number of important journals that regularly publish scholarly articles and book reviews about gays and lesbians. These include *Journal of the History of Sexuality*, a new journal located at Bard College; *Journal of*

Gay and Lesbian Psychotherapy; Journal of Homosexuality; NWSA Journal; Signs; Lesbian Ethics; Conditions; Common Lives/Lesbian Lives; Sinister Wisdom; Socialist Review; and the *Women's Review of Books.* In addition, there are two multipurpose publications that serve as resources for gay and lesbian studies: *Empathy: An Interdisciplinary Journal for Persons Working to End Oppression on the Basis of Sexual Identity* and *Matrices: Lesbian Feminist Resource Network,* published by the Department of Women's Studies at the University of Minnesota. The last two contain archival reports; dissertation summaries; research reports; book, film, and video reviews; bibliographies for resource materials; creative products; conference calls; curricular and workshop guides; and reports from lesbian and gay research centers. Most professional associations now have gay and lesbian caucuses that publish newsletters, conduct research on the status of gays and lesbians in the professions, and organize sessions at professional meetings. These groups can also be a valuable resource.

17. Linda Alcoff, "Cultural Feminism vs. Post Structuralism: The Identity Crisis in Feminist Theory," *Signs* 13 (Spring 1988): 405–36.

18. John De Cecco and Michael G. Shively, "From Sexual Identity to Sexual Relationships: A Contextual Shift," *Journal of Homosexuality* 9 (1984): 1–26.

19. L.A. Kauffman, "The Anti-Politics of Identity," *Socialist Review* 20 (1990): 67–80.

20. Dale M. Bauer, "The Other 'F' Word: The Feminist in the Classroom," *College English* 52, no. 4 (1990): 385–96.

CHAPTER ELEVEN

The Protest as a Teaching Technique for Promoting Feminist Activism

SUZANNA ROSE

Women's studies courses have been hugely successful at facilitating the personal growth of students, including changing attitudes about gender roles, enhancing feelings of personal worth, increasing career goals, and developing an awareness of women's common oppression.[1] A major challenge, however, that feminist faculty continue to face even in established women's studies programs is how to motivate students to strive for social, as well as personal, change. A raised consciousness does not automatically lead to rabble-rousing. Feminist faculty more than ever need to develop classroom techniques that specifically promote activism, particularly because women's studies now provides a safe haven for feminists on many campuses, making it less necessary for students (and faculty!) to agitate for social change in the university and community. In addition, even students dedicated to feminist goals may lack the experience and skills required to translate their commitment into action. The future of feminism will be affected, in part, by our ability to help students become activists and leaders.

How might advocacy and action be encouraged in the women's studies classroom? At the suggestion of Joyce Trebilcot from Washington University, I decided to make a "protest" part of the requirement for my upper-level course, Theories of Feminism. I chose an upper-level course for this experiment because many students in lower-level courses are being exposed to feminist thought for the first time and have not undergone the personal growth that precedes action. Seven of the eight students enrolled held women's studies certificates, and all had taken at least one women's studies course. A range of characteristics was represented in the group: five students (two black, three white) were heterosexual women in their twenties; three were white lesbians (one in her twenties and two in their forties). All labeled themselves as feminists.

The assignment was to "Protest sexism, racism, homophobia, or any other 'ism' related to feminist thought in one situation." The protest could be done by writing a letter of complaint to the perpetrator or one "to the editor," by confronting the institution or person directly, by organizing a picket or leafleting or letter-writing campaign, or by any other creative means. Students were to discuss their ideas for a protest with the class and to write a two-page paper describing the action and their

Originally published in the Spring 1989 issue of the *NWSA Journal*.

feelings about it. Fulfillment of the protest requirement was worth 10 percent of the student's grade. Full credit was given for completion of the assignment in any form. "Quality" of the protest was not assessed in order to keep the assignment as nonthreatening as possible and to encourage nonhierarchical student-teacher relations.

Overall, the protest assignment was highly successful. On entering the class, six students had never been involved in any social action. They had never written a letter of complaint or verbally protested sexism, racism, or homophobia, and none had ever been invoved in a collective protest action. By the end of the semester, five of the novice activists had taken a stand on an issue they cared about deeply (or at least, moderately), as had the two experienced lesbian activists.

The protests ranged from those in the time-honored traditions of marching and petitioning to letter-writing. One novice protester, a young black woman, got heavily involved in the campaign to stop Robert Bork, the right-wing ideologue, from being appointed to the Supreme Court. She learned of Bork's racism and sexism in class discussions and began her protest by asking all her friends and neighbors to sign and mail anti-Bork postcards to their legislators. Enraged by the continued support of Bork by the conservative Republican senators from Missouri, she drew her mother into her protest, and they wrote additional letters of complaint to the Missouri senators. This student also helped the National Abortion Rights Action League (NARAL) in a petition-signing drive to defeat Bork. Over the course of the semester, she became more knowledgeable about the importance of Supreme Court appointments, more identified with the anti-Bork campaign, and more comfortable being in the midst of a battle. Most important, she expressed a sense of personal victory with the defeat of the Bork nomination, writing in her paper, "Many people say it is impossible to beat the system and most of the time it is. But every now and then you can win. I'm lucky. I've won my first fight, and I hope to win many more."

Other protests included organizing picketing to protest a court decision that denied custody to a lesbian mother, participating in the 1987 Gay and Lesbian March on Washington aimed at repealing sodomy laws, complaining to networks about sexist television programming, protesting the handling by local police of a youth gang's attack on a student's car, challenging the institutionalized pressure to date and marry at a Christian university, and protesting a "sexy legs" contest held on campus. Two students also wrote letters of praise, one to Working Assets, an investment company, for promoting socially responsible investing, and one to a local news station, which had broadcast an excellent weeklong segment on battered women.

A few students made the decision to get more involved when their initial protests were ineffective or received an unsatisfactory response; for example, the young white woman angered about the sexy legs contest decided to investigate the decision-making process and funding for these events. When she learned it was not a campus-sponsored activity, she nonetheless pressured student and faculty representatives of the University Senate to challenge Student Affairs for not censuring the event. She also wrote an article for the women's studies newsletter about the contest and resolved to get involved the following year in the Student Affairs committee that reviews such events. Likewise, the white student who protested police unwillingness to file a report on gang violence and who complained about racist comments the police made about the youths, refused to withdraw her complaint against the officer despite pressure and a visit from the police to her home. She eventually was sent a letter of apology from the police captain indicating that new procedures for dealing with similar incidents were now in effect.

Only one student had considerable difficulty with the assignment and did not complete it as originally defined. She cared about feminist issues but could not think of a target for protest. The group shared their experiences and tried to help her pinpoint an issue, but she floundered until the very end of the semester. The idea of complaining made her anxious; she often missed class. Finally, I proposed that she initiate a positive action if she could not develop a protest and urged her to speak out in praise of an event or institution she viewed as particularly egalitarian or nonsexist. Even this was hard for her to do, but she at last wrote a very substantive letter of praise to a local news station for their series on battered women.

The merits of using the protest as an assignment in women's studies classes, based on this one trial, are threefold. First, it helped students translate vague dissatisfactions about "the way things are" into specific issues and targets. One effect women's studies courses have had is to make students aware of how pervasive sexism is; however, this outcome also often depresses motivation for action. By encouraging students to identify a concrete target of sexism and to act against it, the chinks in the structure become visible.

Second, planning a protest, even if it is only letter writing, teaches students political strategy. Students considered and discussed who was responsible for a specific oppression, where the best outlets were for their messages, and what issues and strategies made the best use of their energy. Should the protest be aimed at the television station manager or the advertisers or both? Should complaints be addressed to the police captain or the mayor? Was there enough community support for leafleting or picketing? Many ideas were discarded after discussion or were started and then abandoned; for example, one black woman considered protesting a local automotive-supply store where her boyfriend shopped because pictures of nude women were hanging all over the store. After the group discussed this idea, she decided to reject it because not enough women shopped at the store for her protest to appeal to them; she also thought any public protest might give the store free publicity and improve its business. Another student, a white woman on an athletic scholarship, began investigating why women's sports were so poorly funded by the university. She was unable to get access to budget information and was stonewalled by the coaches and athletic director, so she eventually gave up on the idea. These "failures" were learning experiences in themselves, helping the women evaluate initial ideas, carefully strategize, and prepare to cope with frustration.

The third advantage of the protest assignment was its effect on students' feelings of efficacy. Even when a student did not achieve the outcome she desired or did not receive any response to her actions, the act of protesting was empowering. The peer-group norm that was created supported each woman's right to be annoyed, disgusted, or outraged at oppression and to do something about it. The peer support was crucial, particularly for students with friends, family, or boyfriends who ridiculed or discouraged their anger.

Two problems associated with the protest assignment did arise, however, that require faculty preparation. First, even after teaching women's studies courses for more than ten years, I was surprised by the anxiety and uncertainty the assignment generated among students. I was well aware of how difficult it is to get students (or anyone) involved in social action but still could not comprehend what obstacles prevented some students from focusing on an issue, given the availability of countless worthy causes. I was frustrated by their unspoken desire for me to tell them what to do. In using this teaching technique, one should be prepared to give suggestions but also to avoid making decisions for students.

The second problem concerned the need for me, as teacher, to gauge the consequences of the protest for both the student and myself. Inexperienced students frequently are unaware of the depths of misogyny in our society and are personally devastated by an antifeminist backlash.

In addition, not all students have the emotional strength to be nonconformists; for example, the student who protested the sexy legs contest was very upset when a hostile male student's response to her was published. She also was quite distraught about a negative personal ad someone placed in the paper about her. She wanted to respond by picketing the event. Her distress concerning the backlash alarmed me, however, and I discouraged her from picketing when she could not arouse sufficient support for the action from other students. In my judgment, she was not able by herself to handle the hostility picketing would generate. In class, other strategies were suggested, which she later pursued. Thus, it is crucial that the teacher encourage students to anticipate all possible personal consequences of a protest and to evaluate their ability to accept those consequences. If necessary, the teacher should discourage a student from a protest that might be too costly for him or her.

Likewise, I had to consider whether I was prepared to accept the responsibility for the outcome of this assignment. I had no idea where students' imaginations would lead them in terms of identifying an injustice but was aware they could select issues that were potentially embarrassing to the university or my department. I was willing to back my students on any worthy cause because I have tenure and knew that negative sanctions would be social, not economic. I was ready to live with social disapproval, if necessary; however, untenured faculty would be at greater risk in terms of job security and should honestly evaluate what costs they can sustain.

In conclusion, the protest was a highly effective teaching technique for promoting feminist activism, particularly in an upper-level women's studies class. The technique probably also could be adapted for lower-level courses, if made an option for earning course credit. The protest taught students how to speak out when their rights or values were violated. Making the protest a course requirement legitimized political action as a form of "scholarship" and provided opportunities for putting theory into action. It also had the added advantage of rewarding students already active in the movement by valuing and giving credit for their ongoing activities. If "passivity is the dragon each woman must slay in her quest for independence," as Jill Johnston claimed in the 1970s, then the protest is truly the teaching technique that can make that happen.

Notes

This paper was presented at the National Women's Studies Association conference, Minneapolis, Minn., June 1988.

1. Barbara W. Bennett and George S. Grosser, "Movement Toward Androgyny in College Females Through Experiential Education," *Journal of Psychology* 107 (March 1981): 177–83; Jayne E. Stake and Margaret A. Gerner, "The Women's Studies Experience: Personal and Professional Gains for Women and Men," *Psychology of Women Quarterly* 11 (September 1987): 277–84.

Women's Studies on Television? It's Time for Distance Learning

ANNIS H. HOPKINS

Standing in line at Wendy's, my daughter nudges me in the ribs. "That guy keeps looking at us," she whispers.

"What guy?"

"That one over there. The one who looks like my grandpa."

Our food in hand, we head for an empty table in the corner. The elderly gentleman's eyes follow our progress, and as we near him, he raises his hand, tentatively, like a student unsure of his ground.

"Are you . . . aren't you . . . the lady that teaches on the TV?"

I stop. "I might be, yes; I *do*."

"You see there, Martha. I told you it was her." His head swivels. "I told her it was you. And this must be your daughter." Swivels again. "She talks about you all the time. Oh, don't worry. It's all good." Swivel. "It's her daughter, Martha. See, I told you." Back to me. "I've been watching your class for two years and I just love it. Don't I Martha? Don't I tell you about it all the time? Don't I?"

It happens all the time—at Wendy's, at the grocery store, the mall, the bookstore. My students lovingly call our time together "The Annis Winfrey Show," and we have a cadre of faithful viewers that let me know they haven't gotten tired yet of hearing about "women in contemporary American society," even though they watch the "same old class" semester after semester. Some of them are channel surfers who've caught our curl, some have actually gone looking for "the educational channel," and some are even former students checking up on me, but they all come together on Tuesday and Thursday afternoons (or set their VCRs) to hear and see what the issue of the day will be.

Of course, there are registered students watching, too, about ninety each semester, most of them full-time workers who videotape "the show" and then invite me into their living rooms in the evening or on Sunday afternoon, with husband, wife, kids, and neighbors buzzing through to comment and argue with what "that crazy lady is saying this time."

For the past five years, I've been teaching the only live-cablecast introductory women's studies survey course in my region, and, in light of my research, perhaps the only course of its kind in the United States and Canada.

Originally published in the Summer 1996 issue of the *NWSA Journal*.

Why am I the only one? I have some ideas about the reasons. Equipment needs, lack of vision on the part of distance-learning departments, resistance to women's studies, and women's studies programs' own reluctance to participate may be obstacles that must be overcome. Concerns grounded in feminist pedagogy about conducting courses in a lecture format without direct interaction are valid but not insurmountable. In this chapter I offer some strategies that have been working in my class in the hope that more women's studies faculty will take the plunge. A course containing a balance of theory with personal narrative offered by the teacher, a selection of exciting guest speakers, and the students themselves raises consciousness and leads students into analysis and skills that will permanently enhance their lives, whether they are in a traditional classroom or not.

Distance-Learning Methods and Programs

Typically, distance-learning technology forms a part of a university's extended-education program.[1] Technologies such as cable television, public television, radio broadcast, satellite transmission, computer conferencing, audio- and videocassette, audio and audiographic conferencing, interactive audio and video, teleconferencing, and electronic mail

> serve adult students for whom distance is just one of several barriers to education, along with limited time, work and family commitments, and constrained financial resources. Distance education affords students greater control over where they study, and often, how long they take to complete a course. (*The Electronic University* 1993, xiii)

My students fit this national profile of students who can't get to campus. For example, nearly every semester, I have at least one brand-new mom who is homebound by health or by choice; I can't imagine a better way to start life than by having a budding feminist for a mom!

Women's Studies via Distance Learning

Current Courses

Very few women's studies classes are currently being offered via distance learning.[2] The standard distance-learning guides list only four.[3] In May 1995, I posted a request for more information to the Internet via the Women's Studies List and the Distance Learning List sponsored by the Western Interstate Commission for Higher Education Telecommunications Cooperative. My e-mail respondents referred to electronic discussion groups, teleconferencing, Internet lists, video, and compressed-video courses rather than live courses like mine.

I received only two responses about current video women's studies courses. Muriel Oaks, Director, Extended University Services, reports that Washington State University offers "two video courses W St/Pol S 305, Gender and Politics (3 cr) and W St/Mgt 315, Women in Management (3 cr)."[4] Ellen Rose, Women's Studies, University of Nevada, Las Vegas, has "just completed the first-ever distance-education women's studies course in Nevada, a course in feminist theories, [which she taught] . . . via compressed video, to a small group of students [there] and another small group of students at University of Nevada, Reno." Evidently, while some of us are experimenting with the newer technologies, women's studies by distance learning is still in its infancy.

Obstacles to Distance Learning for Women's Studies

First, only about three hundred colleges and universities in the United States are now offering distance education; of these, fewer than one hundred have women's studies programs.[5] Thus it might not be possible to take women's studies immediately onto live TV everywhere, but most institutions do have the equipment to begin using video and audio technologies, even without the support of a formal distance-learning component. All it takes is a pioneer willing to be taped and to modify an existing course.

Second, most current distance-learning course work focuses on technology itself, rather than on meeting general-education requirements, especially where funding limits choices in the range of offerings to a particular audience. Many technology courses are offered primarily because local employers set up "universities" within their own systems. For example, here at Arizona State University (ASU) Main in Tempe, far more distance courses are offered by the College of Engineering and Applied Sciences than by other colleges, and many of them go directly to major corporate centers, such as Motorola. However, distance learning pays for itself by expanding its services, and proposals are welcomed. Besides, heads of industry are finally beginning to notice that more of their workers are women. Might they not be interested in learning about contemporary American women, especially if their personnel could attend classes right in their employees' break room?

Third, women's studies continues to experience resistance on many campuses. Students still come into my classes fresh from the usual barrage of comments from friends who hear they're taking women's studies: "They're all a bunch of lesbians over there, you know." "Oh, when did you become a radical feminist?" "Why isn't there a men's studies class?" Wary administrators may not wish to have the college or university openly represented by what they identify as our theoretical stances. Televised courses are one of the most visible outreach vehicles available to a university, and cautious decision makers are careful to tailor the image portrayed to the expectations of those to whom they must answer, such as appropriations committees and alumni organizations. I think it is time for women's studies advocates to defuse such concerns by inviting administrators and politicians to visit our programs and classrooms, so that they may see exactly what goes on. Do we really gain anything by continuing to allow the popular media to define us in the minds of potential allies? Further, at ASU, the administration places a high priority on building links with the surrounding community; our president tells us this is a trend sweeping higher education. Women's studies programs can link with other units on campus in these efforts, increasing our visibility and making friends outside the academic realm. With or without distance learning, these are connections women's studies programs need to be making.

WST 300: Women in Contemporary American Society

The purpose of Women in Contemporary American Society is to introduce junior-level, general-studies students to the women's studies curriculum—specifically, to a feminist analysis of U.S. institutions in terms of the status and roles of women since World War II. I encourage students to conceptualize and experience social theory in ways that will lead them to become active participants in the task of challenging women's oppression, in other words, we work on consciousness-raising that will lead to action.[6] On cable, I must also effectively introduce our curriculum to the unidentifiable audience tuning in on any given day; thus each segment must both conceptualize and concretize its own theoretical frameworks, being more or less self-contained while maintaining the integrity and flow of the course.

Teaching WST 300 on Television

WST 300 originates in a studio on ASU's Tempe campus, where sixty-two students attend two seventy-five-minute classes a week. The studio is a large lecture hall with a lectern in a pit at the bottom of tiers of immovable student tables and chairs. Viewers see the lecturer and students in the classroom, and students must use microphones on their desks so that the TV audience can hear them; this daily exercise keeps in-studio class members acutely aware of their "absent" classmates. A computer system makes the use of various graphics and other "presentation" programming possible, adding a colorful high-tech feel where appropriate. Pink and yellow graphs don't make women's income figures any less appalling, but they are more eye-catching than enlarged newspaper print.

There are three cameras positioned around the room, one directly in front of the lectern (for the speaker), one over the speaker's desk (for use as an overhead projector), and one in the right rear corner of the room (to provide a wide shot of the entire classroom). The cameras are in fixed positions and are operated remotely from a tech room located behind a one-way window to the speaker's left. The technician can manipulate the cameras to provide close-ups of individual students when they are talking, so that we are all engaged by a full-face picture on the four monitors that show us the same picture home viewers are seeing.

While the setup may seem intimidating, teaching in this situation is not as different from teaching in the regular classroom as one might expect. There are no teleprompters and no stopwatches, although I do have to make that final point before the clock ticks and the camera is turned off. A novice might want to practice a few lectures on video before going on live, although it isn't really necessary. The essential ingredients are enthusiasm, a firm grasp of the material, and a willingness to take the risk.

To my continuing dismay, however, a format primarily based on lectures does work best in this setting, although some degree of general discussion is possible, provided one response is given at a time; the format accommodates only extremely brief small-group discussion. We have no choice but to forgo many of the teaching techniques and tools that have become part of the feminist pedagogical array, including a low student-teacher ratio. Another difficulty is that here I cannot "wander," except with a very wide shot of the classroom; and students must remain seated. This structure is especially hard for me, since I prefer to roam around a classroom talking one-on-one with students.

Also, video clips that I might use in a regular classroom usually cannot be shown due to copyright restrictions and the limited availability and expense of broadcast-quality tape. It *is* possible to secure some permissions, if you start early enough and have the necessary funding.

Small-group discussion and in-class team projects are also problematic. For one thing, live television demands that "something" be happening at a focal point at all times, so extended "dead air space" is unacceptable. In a class whose material makes people want to talk, the broadcast medium's demand for "action" can be intimidating, even frustrating at times. To meet this challenge, we frequently have exercises in which all students quietly discuss the topic at hand in small groups, with a camera trained on only one pair or triad, whose mike is activated. While the din in the background is distracting, cable students report positive reactions to being included in such "private" conversations between classmates. The conscious intention of the on-mike students to draw in and include the otherwise isolated viewer matters too.

A related difficulty concerns the fact that the cablecast is live; therefore anyone who speaks must be rather careful. Not only do FCC rules prohibit some language that might be appropriate in a nontelevised classroom, but also speakers must be aware that everything they say is being cablecast and taped, without any possibility of editing.

On the positive side, live television encourages a level of preparation that might otherwise not occur. When I'm paying close attention to everything that comes out of my mouth, I tend to stick more closely to my outline and cover the material more completely than I do in some other situations. Even when I throw in personal anecdotes or get involved in a heated exchange with students, I take more care than I otherwise might, to everyone's benefit.

One last issue, the large class size, is familiar to all women's studies programs that provide "service courses" at a large university; the televised section is not significantly different from my usual class size. Even for those accustomed to small numbers, a class of 150 loses some of its negative impact when it is reframed and welcomed as an opportunity to reach more people with the messages and analyses of society so important to women's studies. After all, if what we want to do is change the world, what better place to start than in people's own living rooms?

Answering Pedagogical Objections to Distance Learning as a Tool for Women's Studies

Two significant objections to presenting a women's studies curriculum via live cable television still need to be addressed more fully: the resistance to a primarily lecture-only format and the lack of direct interactivity with students not in the classroom.

Lecture-Format Issues

The lecture as a teaching technique has been identified by some critics as part and parcel of the "traditional approach" to education that excluded both women and information about women from the learning process. Many feminist teachers have worked to eliminate the lecture as a primary teaching tool; in fact, at my university, lectures given by the instructor take up less than half the time in the average women's studies survey course. Frances Maher and Mary Tetreault (1994) observe that

> in traditional approaches, the scholarly expert, having distilled "the truth" from the best minds in the field, transmits it to students. Students learn either through lectures, or by engaging with the professor in a form of so-called "Socratic" dialogue, in which the professor elicits, through a series of probing

questions, the right or appropriate answers to the problem posed. Learning is equated to understanding the material in the terms put forward by the scholarly authorities. (8)

When we resort to giving lectures, we may feel that we have somehow "gone back on" ourselves, but this need not be the case. To be successful in the distance-learning mode, lectures must and can be reconceptualized and restructured to eliminate the authoritarianism that gave rise to these critiques. As Maher and Tetreault point out, it is not the method so much as the motivation that matters. The aim of the pedagogy is key:

> Feminist and liberatory pedagogies aim to encourage the students, particularly women, working-class students, and members of underrepresented ethnic groups, to gain an education that would be relevant to their concerns, to create their own meanings, and to find their own voices in relation to the material. Just as the disciplines are evolving toward multifocal and constructivist forms of knowledge, based on the experiences and viewpoints of all groups in society and not just the most powerful, so does the enactment of these new epistemologies in the classroom draw upon the viewpoints and experiences of students and teachers in new ways. (9–10)

My cable course embraces most aspects of Maher's and Tetreault's recommendations. My students regularly include reentry women and men, working-class students, and members of underrepresented ethnic groups who might otherwise not be in college at all. The class also draws a large percentage of more familiar college students; this diversity contributes immeasurably to the character of the learning environment.

In addition, the guest speakers who visit the class bring unique voices that create a space in which nontraditional students can find their own voices as well. When one of the first female underground miners in Kentucky spoke about sexual harassment and assault by male coworkers, for example, at least five other reentry women in the studio shared similar experiences they had had in the local fire department, at the airport, and in construction work and thus helped to answer the questions of less-experienced students in ways I could never have done on my own. Cable students also reported both personal experiences and new understandings that grew out of the theoretical discussions that surrounded the speaker's presentation.

Our guests have included some quite remarkable speakers, such as Gretchen Bataille[7] and Siera Russell,[8] sharing the past and present patterns of oppression experienced by Native American women in the United States; two lesbian couples, explaining the effects of external and internalized homophobia; a sixty-five-year-old woman Mexican American mayor; and a Bosnian American woman who had just spent a year in the camps where Bosnian Muslim women who have been raped by Serbian Christian soldiers come for assistance.

Guests' personal narratives help students to confront oppression as real, not theoretical, as lived, not imagined. Examining the speakers' victories over oppression both highlights the oppression and discourages labeling the guests as victims. Survivors of oppression are inspiring role models for all of us. In the context of the feminist theoretical framework, they challenge students to look beyond preconceptions about the oppression of women. As one of my distance-learning students wrote:

> I must admit that before I enrolled in this course, I believed that most of the discrimination against women was a thing of the past. However, I soon began to speak with my family and friends concerning this issue and found that many of them believed that men were fundamentally superior to women. As a result, they felt that women did not deserve equal treatment. I was dismayed that so many people I had known for years had these beliefs. . . . I now believe that an enormous amount of oppression continues to exist in our society. . . . My first reaction was anger. I found it outrageous that so many people felt that I was in some way inferior to males. I had several arguments with friends concerning this issue, which only increased my anger. My second reaction was one of fear. I found it extremely frightening that so many people considered women second-class citizens. My final and current reaction to the acceptance of this information is one of action. I now feel that I am able to offer more accurate advice to my friends when they are in situations where oppression occurs. In addition, I can identify oppression in my own life more easily and react accordingly. Although ignorance concerning the existence of oppression appears to make life simpler, I feel very fortunate to have had the opportunity to learn of this oppression so that I can take further appropriate actions.[9]

This response from a cable student who watched the course on tape shows that, even without live participation, theoretical frameworks brought to life by the experiences of real people change students' attitudes and inspire activism.

During these visits, we in the studio actively engage the guest lecturers. When students see themselves playing a role in analysis, either actually or vicariously, they see their opinions as critical to the dialogue. As a result of such conversations, however brief, students learn not to blindly accept everything people say, including everything their instructors say. I remind them on an almost daily basis that their responsibility is to develop their own social theory, to collect as many different perspectives as they can, and then decide for themselves on an ongoing basis which are most likely to get them what they want in their lives. Students often articulate these learning processes quite clearly:

> I completely accept the proposition that oppression must be challenged. . . . In order to obtain social justice, people must fight oppressive structures. This course has taught me many ways to combat oppression. People must acknowledge that oppression exists. We must survive in spite of it. People need

to educate themselves and others about oppression. We must question authority even though our culture opposes it. We must learn to say no to uncomfortable situations and refuse to participate in the cycle of oppression. People need to set goals and meet them. This is important because ending oppression begins small with individuals.

Thus I have found that lectures can be combined with brief discussions in ways completely consistent with feminist pedagogy to successfully present our material.

Interactivity Issues

Classroom interactivity has long been accepted as a positive characteristic by contemporary educators, including members of the collaborative-learning movement and those advocating feminist pedagogy. In *The Feminist Classroom* Maher and Tetreault point out that

> what has made feminist pedagogy unique . . . has been its attention to the particular needs of women students and its grounding in feminist theory as the basis for its multidimensional and positional view of the construction of classroom knowledge. As Maher puts it in one article, "we need an interactive pedagogy, a pedagogy which integrates student contributions into the subject matter, just as the subject matter integrates the new material on women."
>
> One mark of this pedagogy is that learning proceeds at least partly from the questions of the students themselves and/or from the everyday experiences of ordinary people. (9)

When, after five years in the regular women's studies classroom, I was initially invited to conduct a women's studies survey course via cable television, I struggled with the problem of reduced interactivity. Some direct interaction with cable students *is* possible. Registered cable students may call a restricted-access telephone number during the cablecast to participate in discussion. Callers bring a fresh voice to the room and in-studio students perk up to listen, perhaps more carefully than to what goes on in the room. In-studio responses are most often welcoming and delighted, making the caller feel that she or he is a vital part of the class; students who cannot or choose not to call nevertheless report feeling welcomed into the discussion.

However, the majority of students taking the course on cable videotape the class for later viewing, because they work full-time or take other courses during the live cablecast. Thus our in-depth written communications serve as the primary link between classroom, teacher, and student. Cable students and teacher interact weekly through journaling (called learning evaluation), study questions that bring together readings and lectures, and formal essay assignments.

The amount of written work generated in this way is, quite frankly, mountainous. With a work-study student or TA available only for checking off graded assignments, I devote considerable time to reading and responding to student materials. I believe this commitment is necessary if my teaching is to remain consistent with my feminist ideology.

Lack of direct interactivity is a legitimate concern. However, studies on interactivity in distance-learning situations suggest that actual individual interactions with an instructor or with other students may not be as essential as sometimes thought. Shuqiang Zhang and Catherine Fulford (1994) "examined relationships between student perceptions of classroom interaction and the actual amount of time allocated for interaction in a 10-session interactive television course with an enrollment of 260 students" (58). They found that "students' assessment of overall interactivity was found to be largely based upon their observation of peer participation rather than overt personal involvement" (58). In fact, they concluded that

> vicarious interaction—interaction that is observed but involves no direct and overt participation of the observing student—consistently contributes more to a person's assessment of overall interactivity than his or her own observable participation in interaction. . . . This provides an empirical basis for a claim that student perception of overall interactivity is shaped more by the participatory behaviors of the peers than by his or her own share of the action. (62)

Written comments from students in my televised course affirm these findings. Many report that they feel free to express opinions and to debate the material, even though they may never have actually participated live in such activity. In fact, some of the liveliest debates in the class develop on paper moving between cable students and me.

Students report that both the theoretical and the physical structures of the televised course are quite effective in overcoming issues of reduced interactivity and meeting the stated goals of women's studies. A portion of a student's answer to a final exam question serves as a representative response:

> The main reason why I accepted most of the material was the course structure. This is the first class that I have taken at ASU that requires you to look into your own self. . . . This class has enabled me to dig deep into my thoughts, to evaluate my own social theory, and to open my eyes to many problems that exist. . . . [The structure] put the responsibility back onto the students to look at themselves and apply the material . . . to our own lives. This was accomplished in a number of ways. . . . Instead of placing emphasis on standardized tests, you place emphasis on hands-on learning. The weekly study questions and learning evaluations have required me to focus more on what I put into the class. The method of . . . lecture pulls in students to comment and participate. . . . Although I have not been in the classroom, but rather in the comfort of my own

home, the message conveyed made me feel there. My wife has also learned from
being there as I watch the tapes of your class. Yes, the class has liberated me.

These comments from a young man whom I have never met or spoken to
are similar to those of many other students. A balance of theory and personal narrative draws students into the women's studies curriculum,
even when they encounter it via television.

It must be noted as well, however, that there's more going on here than
content. I know that my personality helps. Elsewhere in his essay, the
student just quoted makes it clear that a large part of "the method of lecture" is my manner, my ease with the subject matter, and my consistent
unflappability. It is true that neither teaching women's studies nor teaching on television is for the seriously faint of heart, but it's well worth the
effort.

There are other benefits to learning about women's studies at home,
especially on videotape, beyond the obvious advantage to the homebound or working student of class availability. Further research to find
out which of these benefits are consistent, and whether they actually
outweigh any disadvantages individual students may encounter is in
order, but what I have already observed has convinced me of the positive
impact of the course materials when students use videotaped class
sessions.

One benefit is that whereas students taking women's studies in a normal classroom must take notes and experience their reactions to the
material "as it goes by," students watching on video may stop the tape,
rewind, listen again, and pick up details they missed the first time. This
means that rather than "missing out," they actually get significantly
more of the course material than students in the classroom. All students
in this class are required to hand in notes covering each class session as
evidence of "attendance." While there is great variation in the compre-
hensiveness of student note taking, it is possible to tell from a cursory
examination which notes were taken on a single run-through of the
material—either in class or viewed live—and which were the result of a
more reflective viewing of the taped broadcast. The physical distance
entailed in the format actually provides more space for meaningful con-
templation than can usually be afforded in-class students.

When a guest speaker presents highly emotional material, physical
distance becomes crucial. For example, an incest survivor who regularly
visits during the unit on violence against women provides such an intense experience that most "live" students take very few notes; they
later wish they had, but the opportunity is gone. In contrast, students
who view a taped version of the session usually submit detailed notes,
often interspersed with personal comments; their learning-evaluation
comments also reveal greater depth of analysis.

Again, whereas "live" students may be constrained in their reactions by the presence and perceived expectations of other students, most of whom they do not know well, students watching the class in the privacy of their own homes report they feel free to laugh, cry, express anger, shout, argue with the speaker, and discuss the material with family members or friends. At home there is no need for the false bravado that students often resort to in the classroom; at home, they are more able to "claim" their own reactions to the material. Powerful reactions show up more clearly in cable students' written work than in that of studio students. Like the young man quoted above, many students report important familial interactions that might not have happened had their entire experience of the class taken place in a regular classroom, especially not in front of three television cameras.

Writing assignments that are designed to create dialogue between me and the students provide another key form of interaction. Most text assignments are the subject of study questions that ask for both factual answers and personal responses. The study questions are graded closely for both content and presentation. In addition, each week students are asked to evaluate their learning; in these entries, students are to identify at least one area of disagreement with material they have encountered in the class and one area of positive learning. They must explain how they intend to use something from the week's work to bring their lives more in line with what they would like them to be. In other words, they must address, in a journal-like form, the ways in which course information has affected their personal social theory.

Students undertake two independent projects: a written critical analysis of course-appropriate outside reading and an in-person investigation of a local agency that serves women, followed by an essay. Thus each student must do more than repeat theoretical information on a test in order to pass the course.

Women in Contemporary American Society ends with an essay-format final exam that asks students to examine their individual areas of acceptance and rejection of course material (using Patti Lather's [1991] model)[10] and to articulate their own social theories. The final exam is the only written assignment of the semester on which students do not receive some form of direct teacher response to their ideas.[11]

Through the exchange of written materials, especially those that offer personal opinion—mine as well as theirs—I become acquainted with many students as individuals; from their perspective, students routinely report that they feel well acquainted with me, since they are, after all, visiting with me in their own living rooms on a regular basis. My seemingly personal presence in their homes provides a level of bodily proximity and eye contact (however illusory) rarely available in any regular classroom. Such a "perception" of interaction, as described above, goes a long way toward making students feel a part of the class.

Other Benefits of Teaching Women's Studies on Television

The resources and outreach provided by this class to the women's studies program, the university, and the community make it well worth the investment of energy and time required to offer women's studies on television.

Each class session is videotaped in our Video Resources Center, and copies remain available for student use for two weeks after each class. Thus it is possible to require "attendance"; students who miss class must go to the lab and make up the session within that time. The availability of classes on tape allows every student a kind of guaranteed continuity that cannot be achieved in a regular classroom. Further, I request a copy of each session for the women's studies program video collection (at women's studies' expense); the university retains copyright to the videos, but the women's studies program has permission to use them in its classes at our own discretion. Since the sessions are relatively self-contained, they can be used by other instructors in the event of an illness or other absence. Video also makes it possible for unusual or difficult-to-schedule guests—like a former state secretary of Public Instruction, one of the local founders of the Gray Panthers, or the head of the Governor's Office for Women—to be "reused" in other classes.

Finally, we now offer an Independent Study by Correspondence WST 300 package, which uses a set of the TV tapes, available to students anywhere the mail goes. This course is much like the ones offered at Washington State University and the University of Nevada at Reno and at Las Vegas.

Women's studies stands to benefit profoundly from having our classes on television. If our mission is to "change the world"—and I tell my students from the very first day that that is *my* goal—should we not consider seriously a medium that takes our message beyond the walls of our classrooms? Not only does a well-conducted course enhance the reputation of women's studies as a discipline by systematically refuting the objections put forth in the popular press, but it also makes people who might otherwise not know of its existence aware of women's studies. Whereas not everyone will come to the university to take our classes, nearly every home now has a television set. Televising courses breaks barriers of class and gender in uniquely powerful ways. Increasing our visibility allows people to see what we are really doing in our programs, replacing myth with firsthand experience. Offering our curriculum on television both brings us students and encourages feminist analysis in the lives of viewers we will never meet. Most important, it actually makes our curriculum available to the public in ways that make us more activists than simply the academic arm of the feminist movement.

The university benefits as well in terms of visibility and enhanced goodwill in the community. The contemporary, personal nature of our material appeals to a wide audience. We can help to represent the university as a thoughtful, caring, inviting place. Thus the program, the university, and the community benefit from the visibility of Women in Contemporary American Society on local television.

Conclusion

Making the case for using television and other distance-learning technologies in women's studies has brought me insights that will become a part of all my teaching in the future. It would be good for all of us to examine "how we do things" regularly. We should ask ourselves, What is it that we wish to achieve in our courses, particularly in the large survey sections that serve the university by meeting general-studies requirements for graduation? What evidence do we have that our methods are effective? Although certain aspects of these questions deserve a great deal more research, my experience has revealed that it is possible to bridge even the actual physical distance between my podium and a student's living room. As one reentry woman student commented,

> This material has enriched my life and taught me to think in new and different ways. It has led me to be concerned with social justice for everyone. It has provided me with a chance to express my feelings and opinions about society and human nature. The information has taught me to be more open-minded. . . . It has also inspired me to take action. I am very angry that society is full of oppressive structures. . . . We must take action.

Other students focus more on their personal growth:

> This class . . . has taught me to think differently and to look at things from a different perspective. But what I have found most enlightening is a greater understanding of myself as an individual. This class came to me at a perfect time in my life. Because of this class, I now have a better sense of who I am, what I am about, and what my goals are for the future.

I am convinced that a mix of feminist theory and personal narrative not only works to overcome the initial resistance of students and nonregistered viewers to the women's studies curriculum but also leads them to examine their lives as they have never done before. They learn that parts of their society are ugly, but they also learn that they can commit to not being ugly to each other. They learn that as caring, thinking human beings, they can contribute to the amelioration of the human condition.

I urge women's studies teachers, whatever their fears, to make our transformative curriculum available through distance learning. If framed appropriately, the material speaks for itself. It's time to move beyond the confines of our classrooms into the technology of the twenty-first century.

Notes

1. Extended education includes evening and weekend classes both on and off campus, adult continuing-education programs, and correspondence study, as well as distance learning using technologies. While the 298 universities, colleges, community colleges, consortiums, public-broadcasting stations, and statewide telecommunications services listed in Oryx Press's 1994 *Guide to Distance Learning* by William Burgess (1994) offer a wide variety of course work, six subject areas predominate: accounting, business administration, computer science, engineering, nursing, and teacher education. Counted as one area, liberal arts forms a seventh category with myriad courses.

2. Written reports are scarce. A relevant article with an excellent Canadian-emphasis bibliography is "Tele-communication: Women's Studies through Distance Education" by Helen Lenskyj (1991), who teaches at the Ontario Institute for Studies in Education and writes about Canadian efforts to reach women living in remote areas. Lenskyj cites several other sources. One of my respondents, Janet Baldwin, a graduate student in Adult and Continuing Education at the University of Saskatchewan, is conducting research there, with a special interest in compressed video.

3. *The Electronic University* has none, and the Oryx guide identifies these: Introduction to Women's Studies (University of Nevada, Reno—audio- and videocassette); Northern Minnesota Women: Myths and Realities (University of Minnesota—audiocassette); and Women in Western Culture and Women in Judaism (University of Arizona—live broadcast). According to U of A Video Services, their two courses were taught only once, and the tapes were not retained.

4. "They include 15 video lessons, an extensive course guide with readings and lessons, and interaction via voice mail and/or e-mail with the instructor" (e-mail from Muriel Oaks).

5. This number was obtained by cross-referencing the distance-learning guidebooks with the National Women's Studies Association's 1990 directory; the

overlap has likely increased somewhat with the proliferation of distance-learning technologies.

6. We define social theory as follows: a set of statements about how the world is, how it got to be that way, and how it ought to be changed, from a particular perspective, with a particular focus.

7. Gretchen Bataille's relevant texts include *American Indian Women: A Guide to Research* (New York: Garland, 1991), *American Indian Women: Telling Their Lives* (1984 Lincoln: University of Nebraska Press,), and *Native American Women: A Biographical Dictionary* (New York: Garland, 1993).

8. Siera Russell is a Yavapai-Apache attorney working in the Indian Legal Program, College of Law, Arizona State University.

9. All of the anonymous student comments cited here are taken from written materials submitted by students in the spring 1995 cablecast WST 300 section.

10. In her chapter entitled "Staying Dumb? Student Resistance to Liberatory Curriculum," Lather (1991) explains that students either accept or reject oppositional information (information that is different from what they already accept as true, information that challenges their belief systems). She further describes acceptance as taking several possible directions: it can be burdensome, leading to hopelessness and fear, it can lead to anger, or it can be liberating, leading to action. For this final exam, students are asked to choose specific areas of "oppositional information" and place themselves in Lather's schema (127).

11. Paper exchanges are conducted in two ways. First, students who are on campus regularly may drop off and pick up assignments in the women's studies program office where the staff maintains a confidential file. Students who do not come to campus, perhaps a third of those registered via cable, mail assignments weekly. Mailing my responses back to them is the major expense the distance-learning format presents to the women's studies program.

Works Cited

Burgess, William E. *The Oryx Guide to Distance Learning.* Phoenix: Oryx P, 1994.

The Electronic University: A Guide to Distance Learning. Princeton. NJ: Peterson's Guides, 1993.

Lather, Patti. *Getting Smart: Feminist Research and Pedagogy with/in the Postmodern.* New York: Routledge, 1991.

Lenskyj, Helen. "Tele-communication: Women's Studies through Distance Education." *Resources for Feminist Research* 20 (1991): 11–12.

Maher, Frances, and Mary Kay Thompson Tetreault. *The Feminist Classroom: An Inside Look at How Professors and Students Are Transforming Higher Education for a Diverse Society.* New York: HarperCollins, 1994.

NWSA Directory of Women's Studies Programs, Women's Centers, and Women's Research Centers. College Park: University of Maryland Press, 1990.

Zhang, Shuqiang, and Catherine P. Fulford. "Are Interaction Time and Psychological Interactivity the Same Thing in the Distance Learning Television Classroom?" *Educational Technology,* July–Aug. 1994: 58–64.

CHAPTER THIRTEEN

"I Was [So] Busy Fighting Racism That I Didn't Even Know I Was Being Oppressed as a Woman!"
Challenges, Changes, and Empowerment
in Teaching about Women of Color

LILI M. KIM

Women's Studies as a discipline has undergone tremendous changes since its beginning in the 1970s, and it continues to transform in innovative ways. According to the 1999 National Women's Studies Association (NWSA) Task Force, the issue of diversifying faculty and course offerings continues to be at the heart of the new initiatives of women's studies programs and departments across the country: "Women's Studies has developed its theory base by examining the interconnected effects of race, class, sexuality, physical ability, region, and ethnicity on women's lives, and attracts a diverse range of students. Therefore, including as part of the core curriculum courses that bring racism, classism, homophobia, and other vectors of women's oppression into focus continues to hold priority in program development nationally" (1999).

Critical race theory (CRT) has both broadened and sharpened feminist thought by diversifying women's studies curricula. CRT began with several important premises that profoundly altered feminist understanding of social reality: that racism is the norm, not the exception, in American society; that our current cultural construction of reality must be challenged with antiracist rhetoric and agenda; and, lastly, that liberalism must be critiqued for it may have done more good for whites than people of color (Delgado 1995). How all of these translate into feminist pedagogy and thought is complex, but one of the most significant analytical results is the development of the "intersectionality" of different identities as a central site for examining the lives of women of color (Crenshaw 1997). As Angela P. Harris has argued, in a world where "gender essentialism" and "racial essentialism" exist, "black women's experience will always be forcibly fragmented before being subjected to analysis, as those who are 'only interested in race' and those who are 'only interested in gender' take their separate slices of our lives" (1995, 255). In other words, race and gender studied separately renders an incomplete understanding of the realities of women of color. Furthermore, those who maintain that there is a monolithic "feminist voice" or "women's experience" in the end only promote and embrace *white* women's voice and experience as the dominant narrative (Harris 1995, 256).

Originally published in the summer 2001 issue of the *NWSA Journal*.

Moving away from a monolithic women's voice and experience, scholars have begun to examine the interconnection of race, class, gender, ethnicity, region, and sexuality as an intellectual and analytical tool to diversify women's studies curricula. Women of Color and the American Experience, the course I taught for three semesters, is one of the tangible examples of such a move toward embracing diversity and interconnectedness of different vectors in the lives of women of color.

The goal of this article is to share what I have learned from teaching Women of Color and the American Experience, to discuss particular challenges I faced as a teacher, and to explore the reasons why we still need courses like this one devoted specifically to women of color. I am offering my experience as one example of how women's studies can embrace the experience of women of color and not dismiss the important identities of race, class, and sexuality, along with gender, as part of the broader dialogue already taking place within women's studies departments and programs.

The title of my chapter comes from an actual statement made by one of my students the first time I taught the course. Subsequently, teaching the course two more times, I have had a chance to reflect on the statement, which I found very striking. But even as I knew and somehow felt that the statement captured the realities and experiences of the majority of my students, I did not quite know how to assess the statement or what to make of it in relation to the goals and end results I hoped to accomplish through the course. Together with my students from this past semester, I tried to critically explore the meaning behind the statement. What did it mean for a woman of color to experience racism primarily and other forms of oppression secondarily? Was this truly the case—or just how we perceived our realities? Should we embrace such a statement, or try to rethink it in terms of how we can best achieve social justice as feminists? I hope to provide some insights into these questions as my students and I tried to wrestle with them. I thank my students who willingly and openly pondered these questions with me and gave me permission to quote from their papers.

My Vantage Points and Feminist Pedagogy

First, I want to delineate my perspectives. I am a young, relatively novice teacher and an Asian American woman. I teach at a large state university where students are fairly diverse in their cultural, racial, and economic backgrounds. Most of the students in these classes were first-generation college students. A good many of them had small children, several talked freely about growing up in "the housing projects," and most were motivated about their future and took their education very seriously. A good number of the students in my class also juggled multiple responsibilities as working moms and held nearly full-time jobs. These particularities of the environment in which I taught and the kinds of students who took my course affected the experience I had as an instructor.

I strongly subscribe to the philosophy of feminist pedagogy as a political tool. Scholars have long pointed out the patriarchal practice of university learning, which persistently and systematically ignores women's experiences and perspectives (Freeman and Jones 1980). Feminist pedagogy, then, as Kelly Coate Bignell has argued, is a conscious act of restructuring the power dynamics in the university "to favor women and is specifically concerned with empowering female students" (1996, 316). It is similar to Paulo Freire's "pedagogy of the oppressed, . . . a pedagogy which must be forged *with*, not *for*, the oppressed (whether individual or peoples) in the incessant struggle to regain their humanity" (1994, 30). To fully practice feminist pedagogy, the teacher becomes an authority *with* the students, not *over* them. This kind of classroom dynamic is in itself a departure from the traditional learning experience. As bell hooks has long argued, for education to become the practice of freedom, the first and foremost step is to deconstruct the authority of the professor and distribute the power and responsibilities to the students as well (1994, 8).

Another important aspect of feminist pedagogy is the use and importance of personal experience. Proponents of feminist pedagogy strongly advocate that students in women's studies courses learn to make connections between their personal lives and course materials. This approach furthers the goal of consciousness-raising and social awareness (Humm 1991). This pedagogical goal and its implementation are not without critics. Opponents argue that validating personal experiences in the classroom only leads to "therapeutic pedagogy" and that serious inquiry and scholarship are lost in the drama (Patai and Koertge 1994; Sommers 1994). While we cannot have the class be a personal confession or a counseling session, we certainly cannot dismiss each individual experience as isolated and unimportant when appropriate connections are indeed warranted and made. The goal here is not simply to have students air their anger, opinions, and personal experiences but to have also them critically analyze their experience in the context of the existing gender, class, and racial hierarchies. Scholars have termed this skill of bridging our personal experience and academic scholarship "connected knowing," or "the ability to put the perspectives and voices of 'experts' in dialogue with one's own and others' voices and experiences" (Belenky et al. 1986, 101–103). Such skills, these critics maintain, help students to develop critical thinking and analytical skills (Hoffmann and Stake 1998,

79–98; Belenky et al. 1986). Furthermore, we must ensure that students learn that while knowledge is power, knowing is not enough. Students must understand that our new knowledge must accompany action for social change.

The Course and the Students

I advertised the course as a critical examination of the experiences of women of color in the context of American history, culture, and politics. The course focused on the effects of institutionalized racism, sexism, classism, and homophobia in the experiences of women of color, as well as the autonomy that women of color enjoy and strive to maintain in their lives. The course was consciously about empowerment, not victimization. I was not as interested in my students learning a specific body of knowledge in this course as I was in helping them see the world through the multiple analytical lenses of gender, race, ethnicity, class, and sexuality. We sought to find ways in which women of color and white women could be allies in our united fight against sexism, racism, classism, homophobia, and our quest for effective social change. Topics of discussion included family relationships, the workforce and labor market, immigration, public policy, social welfare systems, higher education and professions, sexuality, media representation, affirmative action, and feminism.

This course was one of the rare classes in which the majority of the students were women of color. In one semester, for example, I had a total of twenty-one students. Most of them were African American women. There were a few Caribbean African women, a handful of Latinas, two Native American women, one Asian American woman, three white women, and one Puerto Rican man. Occasionally, I have had a few white male students who varied in their level of awareness of the impact of these issues in people's lives and in American society. These class demographics meant that I usually had a group of students whose understanding of racism, in particular, was much more sophisticated than students in my other classes. For many students this course was one of the few classes where, as women of color and the majority, they felt more comfortable expressing their opinions. For them, this was the first time they were not asked or expected to speak as a numerical minority for the rest of their race.

I used three anthologies that complement each other quite well. I assigned *Race, Class, and Gender*, a text familiar to the readers of the *NWSA Journal* (Anderson and Collins 1998). To provide theoretical bases for issues concerning women of color, I used *Critical Race Feminism* (Wing 1997). I also assigned essays from the early anthology with the telling title, *All the Women Are White, All the Blacks Are Men, But Some of Us Are Brave* (Hull, Scott, and Smith 1982). Published almost two decades ago, this pioneering anthology for black women's studies provided a context from which women of color began focusing on issues important to them within the field. It also provided us a site for measuring the progress of Women's Studies by comparing the challenges the editors and contributors faced then, to the issues women of color currently encounter within Women's Studies. In addition, I put together a collection of essays and articles as a course packet.[1]

The course ended with Audre Lorde's *Sister Outsider* (1984). For me, Audre Lorde embodies the strength and power of a woman of color who engaged in the important challenge of fighting for social justice in special unapologetic ways that empower us even today. She publicly fought her private battles of being a black socialist lesbian, thereby bettering not only her personal life, but also the lives of other women of color. Each semester, students responded to her essays very strongly, in both positive and negative ways. Most found her writing inspirational and powerful, some found her style intimidating and confrontational, and yet others thought they would really like her and would have a lot to tell her if they met. Whatever their personal feelings towards her approach and style, no one walked away from Lorde's writing without being profoundly affected by the messages.

One of my assignments was what I called "current event days." Students brought in recent newspaper or magazine articles on women of color and discussed contemporary issues that affected the lives of women of color. Almost always, this assignment turned out to be a very interesting exercise in both how much of the news concerns the lives of women of color, and also how little attention women of color receive from the media. The topics brought in by students ranged from interracial dating, to breast cancer and women of color, to a lack of juicy roles for African American women in Hollywood, to an article about a black woman tennis player that focused, not on her athleticism, but on the kind of uniform she wore during the match. These articles generated heated discussions, allowing us to connect issues we read about to everyday happenings around us.

The oral history assignment was designed specifically to reach back into our histories and find valuable resources. Students were required to interview a woman of color; this gave my students a chance to learn from and become empowered by the experience of the woman they interviewed. Most often, my students interviewed their mothers or other female relatives. While they thought they already knew everything about their own mothers, they came back surprised to find out how much they did not know. The formal set up of the interview assignment allowed my students to ask their mothers more personal questions that before they had avoided asking. These women told powerful stories of struggle and survival, but most important they exemplified the power of inner strength and unconditional belief in themselves and in those who loved and supported them. In turn, their mothers were my students' source of inspiration. Through this assignment, empowerment occurred on a very personal, private level which then connected to the public and political. Of course, I did not grade the project on the content of the story their interviewee told; I evaluated each paper on the level of the student's engagement with the interviewee, as evidenced by the follow-up questions and commentary, and on the *analysis* of the story their interviewee told.

My students themselves had incredible stories. When we read Gloria Yamato's "Something About the Subject Makes It Hard to Name," students had some shocking examples from their own experience of the four different types of racism Yamato calls to our attention: 1) aware/blatant racism, 2) aware/covert racism, 3) unaware/unintentional racism, and 4) unaware/self-righteous racism (1998, 93). If we in the United States have made any progress in fighting racism, it is in the fact that blatant racism has become unfashionable or unacceptable, at least publicly. But the incidents of aware/blatant racism the students shared with the class were a reminder that the fight against racism is very far from being over.

One of my students worked as a manager in a clothing store in Buffalo, New York. When an angry customer asked for the manager and the student came to the counter, the customer became even more irate and said, "I don't want to deal with a nigger" and left. Another student faced a neighbor who sold t-shirts that read "100% cotton" on the front and, "And you niggers picked it" on the back. My students take these situations at face value. They did not let these racist incidents degrade them, even though they were hurtful. My student involved in the store incident said this about the overt racism her customer displayed, "This was the first time that any person had used that term in the tone she used with intended hostility. Naturally, my first reaction was anger, but it was only fleeting. I made a joke of it and would tell people that I would have been really mad if she had called me a *Spic*." This is not to say that the student dismissed the seriousness of the customer's racism; she simply chose her battle wisely and devoted her energy to articulating the incident without shame rather than hiding it in silence.

Yamato's article also warns us not to internalize racism, which is a very important point all women of color should take care to remember. Yamato writes:

> Internalized racism is what really gets in my way as a Black woman. It influences the way I see or don't see myself, limits what I expect of myself or others like me. It results in my acceptance of mistreatment, leads me to believe that being treated with less than absolute respect, at least this once, is to be

expected because I am Black, because I am not white. Because I am *(you fill in the color)* you think, "life is going to be hard." The fact is life may be hard, but the color of your skin is not the cause of the hardship. The color of your skin may be used as an excuse to mistreat you. . . . If it seems that your color is the reason, if it seems that your ethnic heritage is the cause of the woe, it's because you've been deliberately beaten down by agents of a greedy system until you swallowed the garbage. That is the internalization of racism. (91)

My students often told me, "I know I have to work doubly hard to succeed." Though I used to commend such determination because I thought it showed that they were driven and motivated, I realized that I was guilty of encouraging and condoning the internalized racism that Yamato warns us about. As women of color we are conditioned to accept these subtle things; we do not even question why it is that "we have to work doubly hard to succeed." Therefore, our heightened awareness of these subtle forms of racism helps us resist and combat all types of racism. The ability to recognize and resist racism in all of its ugly disguises is precisely the kind of empowerment with which I wanted my students to walk away.

Challenges

I encountered some specific challenges while teaching the course where, again, my particular circumstances came into play. First, I had to fight my students' perception that as an Asian American woman I was not really a woman of color. Many of my students admitted that they came into the class thinking that women of color really meant African American women, and they were surprised to see an Asian American woman instructor as well as to find readings on the syllabus which dealt with issues concerning Native American women, Latinas, and Asian American women. Perhaps this explains why a relatively small number of Latinas, Native American women, and Asian American women took the course.

One of the unintended consequences of not having other Asian American women in class was that, as an Asian American woman, I was sometimes put in the position of having to speak for my race. Gradually accepting that Asian American women were a racial minority who faced racism and sexism similar to that faced by African American women, students expected me in some ways to be the Asian American spokesperson. This had been a familiar situation for me as a student, and here I was facing the same burden, only this time as a teacher.

I reluctantly but purposefully embraced the role of being the lone Asian American woman in the class for the sake of contributing another voice, another perspective; I served the role of the staunch *educator*, correcting the stereotypes of Asian Americans some of my students held in their mind. I did so in the spirit of embracing women's studies as a site for a more democratic, less authoritative learning. I willingly replayed the role as a representative of my race hoping that in doing so I could accomplish the important goal of dispelling some stereotypes about Asian American women. Tellingly, the notion of Asian Americans as a recent, model immigrant at best, and a permanent foreigner at worst, had a strong foothold in my students' consciousness. Despite the history of Asian immigrants' presence that dates back to the 1850s, Asian Americans were still not legitimate Americans in their mind. Trying to fight that stereotype was particularly difficult as a teacher for, in many ways, such a view of me as a permanent foreigner undermined my legitimacy as an instructor teaching a course on women of color and the American experience. But again, I embraced this challenge as an opportunity for an important lesson in collective learning and democratic classroom dynamics. I did not outwardly resent students' misperception of Asian Americans and, by extension myself, and hoped that my actions would eventually provide them with a counterexample of the stereotypes of Asian American women as foreign, exotic, and submissive.[2]

Another challenge was that some students, even those who identified themselves as self-proclaimed feminists, objected to talking about homosexuality and reading articles by and about lesbians. On the first day of the class last semester, I had one student ask why there were so many articles and essays by and about lesbians, including Audre Lorde's *Sister Outsider*. She wanted to know what homosexuality had to do with a course on women of color. Wasn't this after all a course about race and gender? I tried to answer this student's objection by referring to the points made by Cherríe Moraga in her article "La Guera," in *Race, Class, and Gender*. Moraga, given her light complexion, could *pass* as white, but she faced a tremendous amount of discrimination based on her homosexuality. The source of her oppression was not her minority status as a Chicana but her sexuality as a lesbian (1998, 26–33). The interconnectedness of all forms of oppression was a concept that this student was never able to fully embrace.

Given the nature of the course and the fact that class discussion intimately involved our own identities, I faced the challenge of trying not to alienate anyone, in particular the white women students. Most of the white female students were willing to discuss racism and its impact, as long as they were not included among those who benefited from racism or were themselves considered racists. Invariably, even the most vocal ones, at some point, withdrew from class participation as a result of worrying about sounding or appearing racist and feeling like they had to defend and speak for the entire white race. Their resentment seemed to subside when we read Peggy McIntosh's article, "White Privilege and Male Privilege: A Personal Account of Coming to See Correspondences Through Work in Women's Studies" (1998, 94–105). This personal essay helped the white students realize that even if they were not racists, they still benefitted from the white privileges which they sometimes took for granted. Also, McIntosh's comparison of white privilege to male privilege helped students to understand their complicity in keeping the racist system intact by not actively speaking out against institutional and structural racism.

By far my biggest challenge in the course was the statement that makes up the title of this chapter: "I was [so] busy fighting racism that I didn't even know I was being oppressed as a woman." In many ways, I was not surprised. How could they not make such a statement given their everyday encounter with the most blatant forms of racism? It was a telling statement, indeed, underscoring the importance of race in the lives and experiences of women of color. As feminist theorist bell hooks pointed out, "Feminist thoughts and practice were fundamentally altered when radical women of color and white women allies began to rigorously challenge the notion that gender was the primary factor determining a woman's fate." She reflects on her own coming-of-age:

> I can still recall how it upset everyone in the first women's studies class I attended—a class where everyone except me was white and female and mostly from privileged class backgrounds—when I interrupted a discussion about the origins of domination in which it was argued that when a child is coming out of the womb the factor deemed most important is gender. I stated that when the child of two black parents is coming out of the womb the factor that is considered first is skin color, then gender, because race and gender will determine that child's fate. Looking at the interlocking nature of gender, race, and class was the perspective that changed the direction of feminist thought. (2000, xi–xii)

Indeed, for too long, white bourgeois feminists have neglected the needs and realities of women of color and poor women.

The statement, "I was [so] busy fighting racism that I didn't even know I was being oppressed as a woman," reflects both revelation and lament. The student who made this statement correctly recognized the urgency of a particular form of oppression in her life, but she also realized the multiplicity of her oppression and lamented having been previously blind to it. Trying to separate what is a result of racism and what is a result of sexism is an impossible, as well as ineffective exercise. The focus of our attention in the course was the interconnectedness of racism, sexism, classism, and homophobia, or what feminist scholars call "a matrix of domination, which posits multiple, interlocking levels of domination that stem from the societal configuration of race, class, and gender relations"

(Anderson and Collins 1998, 5). So while race may be the most urgent and pressing form of oppression for women of color, this awareness of the racism that is built into the very fabric of our society must not come at the expense of ignoring the interconnectedness of oppressions and the overlapping of our multiple identities at work.

I also found the statement to be a challenge, because to me feminism, in addition to fighting sexism, is about more than fighting racism, or even achieving racial, gender, and class equality. Like hooks and other feminists, I believe that feminism is *the* radical movement that will successfully challenge the current power structures in a transformative way. "The fight against sexist oppression is of grave political significance—it is not for women only. Feminist movement is vital both in its power to liberate us from the terrible bonds of sexist oppression and in its potential to radicalize and renew other liberation struggles" (hooks 2000, 42). She reminds us to look beyond our own immediate fight for freedom from oppression toward the end goal of systematic, structural, social changes.

The third time I taught this course I asked my students to ponder the statement, "I was [so] busy fighting racism that I didn't even know I was being oppressed as a woman." How did they feel about such a statement? If they were women of color, did they feel that racism was indeed the biggest, most pressing source of oppression in their lives? I asked them to write honestly and reflectively, drawing upon the discussions and readings from the semester. I have received permission to share some of their responses.

> Race and sex for black women are so intertwined that it is almost impossible to pull the two apart when the situation does not state blatantly on what grounds we are being judged. I believe that women who do not see sexism and only see racism are those women who refuse to recognize the fact that they are tied in together. (Angela)

> "I was [so] busy fighting racism that I didn't even know I was being oppressed as a woman" is a very true statement. Like many women of color I am taught to recognize racism before sexism. Since racism is a more universal issue or problem that all people face, I am trained to realize when I am being discriminated against by my skin color, but not my gender. By taking this class, I know I will be more aware of this in the future. (Monique)

> I am a twenty-year-old woman whose mother is Polish and whose father is black. Most often, racially, I would be defined as mulatto. Visually, the majority of people I encounter assume that I am Hispanic. I have a skin tone that is a lighter shade of tan and long brown hair that is worn very straight, but naturally has a very loose curl. The characteristics are not considered as typical of a black person so it is very rare that I am discriminated against because I am black. . . . I find myself fortunate to be racially mixed. Visually, it allows me a type of racial androgyny. It is hard to oppress someone without being able to define the basis on which to oppress them. I think that is why I haven't been

exposed to as many instances of racism that other women of color have been subjected to. Sexism, on the other hand, is completely different. (Eve)

Until I took this class, I did not know that I was being oppressed as a woman just as much as I was being oppressed for my race. It scared me to a certain extent, because I was ignorant and ignorance is not good. Through reading the different articles and understanding the different situations that many women have overcome, I can now say that I am proud to be both African American and a woman. Being a woman of color, I believe that my race has held me back, more than being a woman. . . . Race, class, and gender all play hand in hand in oppressing individuals. However what people must realize is that each issue must be tackled in the urgency that it affects the person. You cannot get a hungry man to fight against racism until he has eaten. (Malika)

All of these answers reflected their sophisticated understanding of how the interconnectedness of different forms of oppression affects their own lives as women of color. They also understood that the pervasiveness of the racism that they cannot escape is in many ways the easiest to identify. But as bell hooks said, "Racism is fundamentally a feminist issue because it is so interconnected with sexist oppression" (2000, 53). Both Angela's and Monique's comments reflect that understanding. Eve found that the racial ambiguity resulting from her biracial background offered her a measure of protection from racism. Malika, who began by saying, "I did not know I was being oppressed as a woman, just as much as I was being oppressed for my race," later concluded that, "[b]eing a woman of color, my race has held me back more than being a woman." This underscores the continued saliency of race in the lives of women of color. Along the same line, Malika also made a very profound point when she said, "you cannot get a hungry man to fight against racism until he has eaten." Indeed, one has to deal with the most urgent issue facing one at any given moment. If it is ending hunger, the fight against racism or sexism becomes secondary and almost impossible. Similarly, I take Malika's example of hunger in both the literal and metaphorical sense. If we are not nurtured and empowered to find strength and pride in ourselves, or if we are mentally hungry or emotionally depleted, we are in no shape to engage in the feminist movement to bring about transformative changes in society.

Our racial, gender, sexual, and class identities are enmeshed in such a way that we cannot neatly separate them. Moreover, our experience is intertwined with other people's experiences. For example, as Anderson and Collins point out, white Americans do not fit in "either/or" categories—either as oppressive or as oppressed (1998, 5). Isolating white Americans as if their experiences stand alone ignores how white experience is intertwined with that of other groups; more complexity needs to be given to how white Americans are framed in our dialogues. Relational

thinking that probes the multiplicity of our identities helps us to redefine and reconceptualize how our racial, gender, class, and sexual identities and their intersections continue to matter.

Courses devoted specifically to the experience and lives of women of
color are needed so that we do not succumb to the "culture of silence" by
having our voices and needs go unheard and unrecognized in women's
studies departments, programs, and organizations (Freire 1995). Audre
Lorde said, "To imply . . . that all women suffer the same oppression simply because we are women is to lose sight of the many varied tools of
patriarchy. It is to ignore how those tools are used by women without
awareness against each other" (1984, 67). Or, as one scholar of African
American Women's Studies put it at the last annual meeting of NWSA,
the silencing of the voices and needs of women of color in Women's Studies is essentially "patriarchy with a vagina."[3]

, The goal of diversity in our own community of women's studies scholars and activists must go beyond lip service and have a transformative
impact on the structure and foundations of our field. Women of Color
and the American Experience is an attempt to ensure that the feminist
consciousness of women's studies students comes *with* their racial, sexual, and class awareness, and not at the *expense* of such awareness. We
should encourage our students of color to embrace their racial identity,
along with their gender identity as women, and empower them to fight
discrimination stemming from their race, class, and/or sexuality. But
feminists must take on the fight not just against racism but also against
all forms of oppression related and connected to racism. The end goal
must be the transformation of society, not merely escape from oppressive
circumstances. As feminists, we want all of our sisters of color as well as
our white sisters—and our male allies—united in battling this demon.

Acknowledgments

An earlier version of this essay was delivered at the Twenty-First Annual Meeting of the National Women's Studies Association at Simmons College, Boston,
Massachusetts, June 2000. I thank the audience for their helpful questions and
comments. I also gratefully acknowledge the financial assistance of the National
Women's Studies Association's Travel Scholarship, which made my attendance
possible. I wish to thank Pat Washington for inviting me to submit the essay and
for giving me abundant encouragement and support along the way, and the
anonymous NWSA Journal referees for their astute criticism and constructive
feedback that greatly improved this essay from its original form. Finally, I thank
the students in Women of Color and the American Experience in Spring 2000
who wrestled with important questions and gave me permission to quote from
their papers.

Notes

1. I varied the readings the second time I taught the course by assigning a number of articles from *Women Transforming Politics: An Alternative Reader* (Cohen et al. 1997).

2. The second time I taught the course, I showed an excellent video, *Slaying the Dragon* (Gee 1987), which effectively critiques Hollywood's images of stereotypical Asian and Asian American women.

3. Personal conversation with author, Boston, MA, 17 June 2000.

References

Anderson, Margaret L., and Patricia Hill Collins, eds. 1998. *Race, Class, and Gender: An Anthology.* New York: Wadsworth.

Belenky, Mary F., Blythe M. Clinchy, Nancy R. Goldberger, and Jill M. Tarule. 1986. *Women's Ways of Knowing: The Development of Self, Voice, and Mind.* New York: Basic.

Bignell, Kelly Coate. 1996. "Building Feminist Praxis Out of Feminist Pedagogy: The Importance of Students' Perspectives." *Women's Studies International Forum* 9:315–25.

Cohen, Cathy J., Kathleen B. Jones, and Joan C. Tronto, eds. 1997. *Women Transforming Politics: An Alternative Reader.* New York: New York University Press.

Crenshaw, Kimberlé. 1997. "Beyond Racism and Misogyny: Black Feminism and 2 Live Crew. In *Women Transforming Politics*, eds. Cathy J. Cohen, Kathleen B. Jones, and Joan C. Tronto, 549–68. New York: New York University Press.

———. 1991. "Demarginalizing the Intersection of Race and Sex: A Black Feminist Critique of Antidiscrimination Doctrine, Feminist Theory and Antiracist Politics." In *Feminist Legal Theory*, eds. K.I. Bartlett and R. Kennedy, 57–80. Boulder, CO: Westview.

Delgado, Richard. 1995. *Critical Race Theory: The Cutting Edge.* Philadelphia: Temple University Press.

Freeman, Helen, and Alison Jones. 1980. "For Women Only?" *Women's Studies International Quarterly* 3(4):429–40.

Freire, Paulo. 1994. *Pedagogy of the Oppressed.* New York: Continuum.

Harris, Angela P. 1995. "Race and Essentialism in Feminist Legal Theory." In *Critical Race Theory: The Cutting Edge*, ed. Richard Delgado, 253–66. Philadelphia, Temple University Press.

Hoffman, Frances L., and Jayne E. Stake. 1998. "Feminist Pedagogy in Theory and Practice: An Empirical Investigation." *NWSA Journal* 10(1):79–98.

hooks, bell. 2000. *Feminist Theory: From Margin to Center.* 2nd ed. Cambridge, MA: South End Press.

————. 1994. *Teaching to Transgress: Education as the Practice of Freedom.* New York: Routledge Press.

Hull, Gloria T., Patricia Bell Scott, and Barbara Smith, eds. 1982. *All the Women Are White, All the Blacks Are Men, But Some of Us Are Brave.* New York: Feminist Press.

Humm, Maggie. 1991. "'Thinking of Things In Themselves': Theory, Experience, Women's Studies." In *Out of the Margins: Women's Studies in the Nineties,* eds. Jane Aaron and Sylvia Walby, 49–62. London: Falmer Press.

Gee, Deborah. 1987. *Slaying the Dragon.* San Francisco, CA: National Asian American Telecommunications Association, Cross Current Media. Video tape.

Lorde, Audre. 1984. *Sister Outsider: Essays and Speeches By Audre Lorde.* Freedom, CA: Crossing Press.

McIntosh, Peggy. 1998. "White Privilege and Male Privilege: A Personal Account of Coming to See Correspondences Through Work in Women's Studies." In *Race, Class and Gender,* eds. Margaret L. Anderson and Patricia Hill Collins, 94–105. New York: Wadsworth.

Moraga, Cherríe. 1998. "La Guera." In *Race, Class, and Gender,* eds. Margaret L. Anderson and Patricia Hill Collins, 26–33. New York: Wadsworth.

NWSA Task Force. 1999. "Defining Women's Scholarship: A Statement of the National Women's Studies Association Task Force on Faculty Roles and Rewards." Online. Available at http://www.nwsa.org/taskforce.htm.

Patai, Daphne, and Noretta Koertge. 1994. *Professing Feminism: Cautionary Tales from the Strange World of Women's Studies.* New York: Basic Books.

Sommers, Christina Hoff. 1994. *Who Stole Feminism? How Women Have Betrayed Women.* New York: Simon & Schuster.

Wing, Adrien Katherine, ed. 1997. *Critical Race Feminism: A Reader.* New York: New York University Press.

Yamato, Gloria. 1998. "Something About the Subject Makes It Hard to Name." In *Race, Class, and Gender,* eds. Margaret L. Anderson and Patricia Hill Collins, 89–93. New York: Wadsworth.

CHAPTER FOURTEEN

Negotiating Tensions: Teaching about Race Issues in Graduate Feminist Classrooms

ANNE DONADEY

As more and more feminists in academia engage in an analysis of multiple forms of oppression and bring our research into the classroom, we are faced with new scholarly, ethical, and pedagogical challenges. Several scholars have discussed the power differentials involved in multicultural scholarship and have pointed to the risks of neocolonial cultural appropriation inherent in the interpretation of non-Western cultural practices from the perspective of a Western intellectual framework (Spivak 1991; Mohanty 1991; Patai 1991; Rose 1992). Such ethical issues in scholarly research also arise when curricula become more integrated and multicultural.

As women's studies curricula become more integrated, and as our understanding of male supremacy comes to intersect with an analysis of white supremacy, imperialism, heterosexism, and capitalism, some white female students who have become comfortable with a theoretical paradigm placing them at the center may resist theories that unsettle their assumptions. Instructors experience attitudes of denial from students, especially when questions of racism and colonialism arise in the feminist classroom. The revolution in thinking demanded of feminists, from a monist view of oppression as gender-based only to a multiple consciousness model taking into account the interlocking force of race, class, and gender, comes from the repeated calls of womanists and feminists of color, not only in academic women's studies programs and in theoretical writings, but in the broader frame of the women's movement (King 1990; Sandoval 1991). Issues of student resistance in the feminist classroom must thus be understood in a more general context and seen as related to monist versus intersectional theories of oppression in women's studies and to the broader problem of racism in the women's movement in a society that still has to rid itself of its white supremacist ideology (Davis 1981). Like most feminist organizations inside as well as outside academia, the NWSA itself has experienced these struggles over different visions of feminism firsthand (Sandoval 1990). It is particularly important to its future that its members confront these issues pedagogically as well as institutionally. Texts such as Audre Lorde's *Sister Outsider* (1984), Gloria Anzaldúa's *Making Face, Making Soul* (1990), Chandra Mohanty, Ann Russo, and Lourdes Torres's *Third World Women and the Politics of*

Originally published in the Spring 2002 issue of the *NWSA Journal*.

Feminism (1991), and bell hooks's *Teaching to Transgress* (1994), which I regularly teach in my feminist criticism classes, form the intellectual backbone on which my interpretation rests.

Before developing my argument, I begin by defining some of the terms used in this chapter. *Feminist pedagogy,* as characterized by women's studies practitioners, highlights "feminist process" in classroom interactions: it focuses on "consensual, collaborative, non-hierarchical processes of learning/teaching" (Kenway and Modra 1992, 149). Crucial tenets of feminist pedagogy include the need to value experiential knowledge (Hartsock 1983; hooks 1994), the question of the female teacher's authority in the classroom (Friedman 1985; Rakow 1991; Kenway and Modra 1992; Nnaemeka 1994), the classroom as a safe space (Ellsworth 1989; Lewis 1990; hooks 1994; Nnaemeka 1994), the use of democratic dialogue (Ellsworth 1989; Kenway and Modra 1992), and empowering student voice (Ellsworth 1989; Mohanty 1989–1990; hooks 1994). These notions reflect feminist pedagogy's engagement with the liberatory pedagogy of Paulo Freire and others (Kenway and Modra 1992). Two of the concepts on which I focus my analysis are safe space and student voice. For the purposes of this chapter, safe space is defined as "a discursive arena that enables women to talk about issues that are too dangerous to discuss in other contexts" (Kozol 1999, 10). One of the ways to create a safe space is for the instructor to value, recognize, and encourage each student's voice (hooks 1994). The desire to help students come to voice is related to a view of students as active participants in the learning process (hooks 1994) and to a feminist belief that women's silencing can be redressed in the feminist classroom. Until the late 1980s and early 1990s, the consensus in feminist pedagogy tended to be that feminist faculty should downplay their authority in the classroom and make classrooms safe spaces in which students could be empowered to come to voice through the use of democratic dialogue and sharing their own experiences of oppression. Elizabeth Ellsworth's (1989) critique of the limitations of these concepts ushered in an era of reevaluating the main tenets of feminist pedagogy such as empowerment (Lewis 1990; Gore 1992), safe space (Kozol 1999), and student voice (Orner 1992; hooks 1994) by asking teachers to take into account power differentials within and outside the classroom.

Finally, the definition of racism that I use in this essay is much broader than the common understanding. It places individual attitudes and practices within the broader framework of institutional, systemic racism (Mohanty 1989–1990; Ng 1993) and includes white solipsism, or the view of dominant white, commonsense ideology as normative (Rich 1979; Ng 1993). I follow Gloria Yamato (1990), who makes a useful distinction between four kinds of racism: aware/blatant racism (the tip of the iceberg), aware/covert racism (the racism people think they can get away with), unaware/unintentional racism (the bulk of the iceberg), and unaware/self-righteous racism (when white people tell people of color what their issues should be and how to handle them). I would add the component of racism by omission to unaware/unintentional racism. In the context of the feminist classroom, for example, this would mean not putting works by women of color on the syllabus, by only tokenizing a few such texts at the end of the semester, or by discussing only the gender implications of works by writers such as Zora Neale Hurston or Toni Morrison.

It is becoming more and more urgent for instructors who bring an analysis of multiple forms of oppression in the classroom to examine the following crucial issues that arise in our teaching: How are people silenced in the classroom? Is the feminist concept of "safe space" always an empowering one? How long should teachers let a "conversation" continue once it has clearly become circular? Should the instructor silence racist talk or attempt to reason with it? What are the limits of the liberal concepts of free speech and pluralistic conversation? What are the consequences of racist comments on students, especially on students of color? Where does the instructor's responsibility lie? Do we play into the racist's hands by responding to her arguments on her own terms? How does the instructor enlist the help of students in the process of dealing with racism in the classroom? How should racism be named and exposed? What is so threatening about theorizing race and gender as interlocking systems of domination that it would cause some (white) feminists to reject the entire concept? These issues crystallized for me the first time I taught a graduate course in feminist criticism at the University of Iowa.

The class, a broad overview of contemporary feminist criticism, aimed to expose students to the richness of feminism's multiple discourses and to explore some of its contested terrains. The idea was to examine a variety of feminist and womanist texts that theorize the connections between forms of oppression such as homophobia, classism, colonialism, sexism, and racism. Readings were multicultural, and topics covered included historicizing feminisms, French feminisms, postmodernism and feminism, race/gender/sexuality, identity politics, masculinities, reproductive technologies, feminism and science, feminism and the law, international feminism, and rape. The class was run as a seminar and mainly consisted of a discussion of the readings after a short student presentation on the day's readings. There were thirteen graduate students in the class, mostly from the English department. It soon became clear that two or three students consistently refused to engage issues of race and racism and tried to steer the class discussion back to a monist, gender-only focus.

They clearly felt that the feminist classroom was one that could accommodate discussions of race only insofar as these discussions did not disrupt their assumption of the primacy of gender in feminist analysis, and they refused any redefinition of gender-based oppression as interlocked with racial oppression. They did not completely reject a model taking multiple oppressions into account, as they were perfectly happy to include sexuality and class into their analysis. Their refusal to engage multiple oppressions was limited to race and, to a lesser extent, colonialism. Considering the history of race relations in the United States in general, and the unfortunate history of institutional racism in the women's movement since the nineteenth century in particular, it is not surprising that race issues should remain a contested terrain in the field. I realize that terming the reluctance to address race issues racism may seem controversial to some. Following Adrienne Rich, I contend that white solipsism, the focus on a white middle-class experience rendered as universal, is part of racism because it narrows feminist vision and erases the existence and experiences of other women (1979). It also serves to bolster white, upper-middle-class dominance by providing theoretical justification for women of the dominant strata of society to view themselves only as oppressed people. While I expected that most of the tensions that might arise in the class would most likely be around questions of race and racism, given my previous experience teaching Introduction to Women's Studies at Northwestern University, I was not quite prepared for the high level of resistance I encountered. I have since taught the graduate feminist criticism class with much better results, due in part to the strategies I implemented (which I present in the third section).

This chapter represents and continues my process of reflecting on this painful experience through research and discussion with some of the students involved as well as with antiracism activist colleagues.[1] My comments in this chapter do not constitute a pedagogy per se. Since many colleagues (professors and graduate students) struggle with similar issues in their classes semester after semester, I present these reflections and strategies hoping that this work may be as useful to others as it has been to me. This chapter's blind spots are my sole responsibility. To address the question of what happens when the tenets of feminist and critical pedagogy clash with antiracist work, I first interrogate the concepts of coming to voice and creating safe spaces by discussing some of the problematic implications of voicing resistance in the classroom. I then propose an overview and analysis of the literature on the causes of student resistance, and conclude by offering strategies I have used in subsequent versions of my graduate feminist criticism class to challenge student resistance and negotiate tensions more effectively.

Implications of Voicing Resistance

Before teaching this graduate class, I knew that many women of color have more difficult and mixed experiences with—and ambivalent feelings toward—feminism than white women. Reasons for this include the historical legacy of racism in the women's movement and the continuing predominance of monist frameworks in feminist theory produced by white women. Because of this, I did expect fraught class dynamics around the intersection of race and gender issues (see Smith 1990; Zinn et al. 1990; Uttal 1990). Therefore, one of my main concerns from the start was to avoid making the class an oppressive experience for what I knew would be very few students of color, to avoid perpetuating a situation where they would find themselves silenced, objectified, and discounted. In Uma Narayan's words, I wanted to avoid a situation "in which dialogue between people who share and people who do not share the experience of a certain form of oppression can be damaged because the emotions, and hence the sense of self, of the members of the oppressed group are *unintentionally* violated by non-members of the oppressed group who participate in the dialogue" (1988, 31). Therefore, it is my *responsibility* as a teacher and especially as a white person in a racist society, to be proactive against racism and to always respond firmly to racist comments whenever I catch them. I agree with Sonnenschein that "to maintain within the classroom an environment free of bigotry and conducive to learning for all students . . . [r]acist remarks . . . should never go unchallenged. Students should recognize that the teacher considers expressions of prejudice unacceptable and that they too are expected to regard such expressions as unacceptable" (1988, 265). I certainly did not want the burden of responding to such remarks to be placed on the students of color. I was also hoping to model pedagogical practices that could be helpful to graduate students who, as rhetoric and literature teaching assistants, do encounter blatant forms of racism in their own classrooms (one of the resisting students was ironically very concerned about her own students' racism).

Although the two students of color in the class appreciated my efforts, and often responded to the problematic comments made by some of the other students, they also felt that I was not "pointing these issues out as racist and dealing with them as such." I certainly was not as direct as I should have been in my class responses and most likely was not aware of all of the racist implications either. It was clear to these two students that class discussions of race and colonization operated in such a way that, as one of them wrote, "my questions and comments were refigured and (re)presented in ways that silenced the issues I was trying to bring up . . . the authors were whitewashed/decolored/rendered as speaking to a universal (in the U.S., this is white) experience." Obioma Nnaemeka sees this problematic practice on the part of some feminists as a way to rename struggles by misnaming them (1995, 81). It took several out-of-class discussions with the two students of color (who initiated these visits together) for me to realize toward the end of the semester that by constantly responding to the resisters' arguments on the terms that they were setting up, I inadvertently perpetuated the silencing of students of color.

As a consequence of my feminist pedagogy assumption that students should be encouraged to voice all of their arguments so they could be debated, one of the students of color wrote that her subjectivity and feelings were being negated in the class. Although there is an extensive body of scholarship dealing with student and classroom resistance, only one of the essays I read discusses the negative consequences experienced by students from nondominant backgrounds when other students voice resistance, especially in a context in which the former are already marginalized several times over (Ellsworth 1989; in her case, a graduate feminist classroom in an historically white Midwestern university located in a rural area—a situation quite similar to my own). Like Ellsworth, I have reservations regarding such tenets of feminist pedagogy as student empowerment, student voice, and the classroom as safe space. Until I taught this graduate feminist criticism class, such notions had always appeared to me to be lofty goals that I had made my own. Ellsworth points out that these concepts become dangerous when applied to classrooms with the underlying assumption of homogeneity. In an egalitarian world, these goals would be attainable. In a world structured by systemic inequalities such as our own, trying to reach for these goals can sometimes serve to reinforce oppressive classroom practices (Ng 1995; Kozol 1999). In Ellsworth's words, "[a]cting as if our classrooms were a safe space in which democratic dialogue was possible and happening did not make it so" (1989, 315).

In a redefinition of the concept of the public sphere that is relevant to the view of classrooms as safe spaces encouraging participatory democracy, Nancy Fraser points out that the main flaw of "the bourgeois conception of the public sphere [is that it] requires bracketing inequalities of status" so that "interlocutors . . . speak to one another as if they were social and economic peers" (1992, 118). She points out that "such bracketing usually works to the advantage of dominant groups in society and to the disadvantage of subordinates" and that it would be much more effective to "explicitly thematiz[e]," rather than bracket, such inequalities and differences (120). It is ironic that radical feminist pedagogy tends to replicate the assumptions of the bourgeois concept of the public sphere with respect to the belief that the classroom can be a safe space in which power differences are downplayed in the interest of every individual coming to voice (hooks 1994). Fraser concludes that true democracy would require the abolition of societal inequalities (1992). In the context of the classroom, Roxana Ng similarly notes that it is important to begin by acknowledging that "[t]he university classroom is *not*, by definition, a democratic place. To pretend it can be is to deny that hierarchy and institutional power exist" (1995, 140).

The concept of voice becomes particularly problematic in two specific instances: "when the student of color finds a voice and then gets told repeatedly that that voice distracts from the issues," and when the voice white students find is a racist one (or more generally one that reproduces ideologies of dominance).[2] When a "reconstructed racist"—that is, someone who has been made aware of her/his racist assumptions but refuses to question them—monopolizes class time, thereby reinforcing domination, is it not the teacher's responsibility to stop this process? A "pedagogy of the oppressed" (Freire 1993, 30), created for the purposes of nurturing revolutionary consciousness among peasant and working-class people, should probably not be applied wholesale to the context of American universities preparing students to maintain or achieve middle-class status.

There are at least two positions that differ from my own with respect to the question of instructor responsibility. Some scholars refuse to engage in this type of antiracism work in the classroom because they feel it is too hard for students of color to deal with or because it is too difficult and draining for instructors (Garcia 1994). They attempt to avoid having students' emotions erupt in the classroom and try to maintain distance from emotions in the learning process. I do not view this position as realistic because emotionally fraught class dynamics usually occur in classes with a majority of white students whenever multicultural readings are assigned and because keeping silent about unnamed classroom tensions is ultimately unproductive. As Chickasaw scholar Jodi Byrd argues, students of color are at least as hurt by unchallenged racist comments as they can be by a discussion putting these comments into question. It is the instructor's job to challenge racist remarks, not that of students of color.[3]

Another response to the question of instructor responsibility is the issue of free speech in the classroom. Whereas liberal pluralists, relativists, and civil libertarians may view a classroom discussion of both racist and antiracist positions as an example of a successful, democratic learning process, Ian Barnard's point (made in the context of antihomophobic pedagogy) resonates with my discussion of antiracism pedagogy. Barnard disagrees with the common practice of "inviting students to argue 'both' sides" of an issue: "*these kinds of topics and discussions have the effect of privileging dominant power relations* and of further silencing our queer students. For example, if we ask our students to debate whether homosexuality is 'wrong' or not, we are expecting our queer students to justify their very existences in the classroom. . . . Queer students have a right to expect not to be wounded in this way in the classroom" (1994, 27, my emphasis). While free speech is vital for a healthy and balanced society, it is also crucial that an understanding of the concept be linked to an assessment of the structural inequalities built into U.S. democracy. In other words, we need to ask the question of *whose* freedom of speech is being protected. Although the theoretical concept guarantees free speech for all, in practice the free speech argument is often invoked to guarantee the speech of the dominant, even in its most excessive forms.[4] It is important to always weigh the question of free speech against that of freedom from harassment. The concept of free speech is legally circumscribed: for example, speech that poses a clear and imminent danger to others can be restricted. Likewise, legal definitions of sexual harassment, for example, involve not simply direct sexual threats but also the creation of a climate contributing to a hostile environment (Stein 1995b). Just as feminist teachers have learned to respond effectively to sexist comments in our classes, we can translate this knowledge to the issue of racist comments. Repeated racist remarks in the classroom contribute to creating a hostile environment for students of color. Consequences of such "epistemic violence" include silencing, thus threatening these students' access to free speech (Spivak 1991, 804). When the instructor does not question racist remarks, the message sent to all students is that the instructor either is oblivious to racism or agrees with the comments being made. In either case, the racist message is reinforced for the entire class, and education as the practice of freedom is replaced by education into the dominant ideology.

Understanding Student Resistance

Several scholars have discussed the causes of student resistance (Rothenberg 1988; Tatum 1992). Paula Rothenberg proposes that students of all genders, class positions, and racial heritages may have invested a lot in "the American Dream/Myth of Success" (1988, 38). She rightly links this investment to the dominant colorblind ideology of "contemporary conservatism," one of whose consequences is that "today's students confuse failing to notice race and gender with the absence of racism and sexism" (38). As Nancy Hartsock points out, the dominant vision is marked by both its partiality and perversity, which allow it to ideologically manipulate reality so as to reverse it (1983). When power differentials between groups are taken into account in an analysis of oppression, the issue of privilege becomes salient. Students from dominant groups tend to feel threatened because such analyses "point a finger at those whose interests are served" by racism and sexism (Rothenberg 1988, 38). As Paulo Freire observes, at some point, "participants begin to realize that if their analysis of the situation goes any deeper they will either have to divest themselves of their myths, or reaffirm them" (1993, 138). Resistance is a way to reaffirm the myths that justify one's dominance. Bohmer and Briggs insist that an analysis of oppression will also need to generate an examination of privilege in order to be effective. It has been my experience that this is one of the hardest things to do (1991). The normative status bestowed on whiteness, maleness, middle-/-upper-class status, and heterosexuality in our culture makes it easier to deny the privileges associated with these characteristics. It seems to be easier to get in touch with one's experience as victim of a specific form of oppression than it is to take responsibility for the ways in which we benefit from the oppression of other groups or peoples. We generally do not experience our own privilege as intensely as we do injustices done to us on the basis of group belonging (McIntosh 1992).

Moreover, there may be a resistance to self-identifying as *the norm* in classrooms where the norm is shown to be an ideological construct used to perpetuate systemic inequalities (Lorde 1984). Many emotions enter into play: guilt, anger, shame, defensiveness, and denial. Often, student resistance takes the form of resentment and accusations of guilt building: "refusal or failure to initiate changes creates guilt and dissonance between their actions and their self-images as just and thoughtful people" (Aiken et al. 1987, 262–3). Guilt can become a paralyzing emotion that paradoxically allows one not to initiate social changes, as feeling bad about a situation and wallowing in guilt become substitutes for action.[5]

These problems can be related to the continued dominance of monist frameworks of analysis in the women's studies classroom (King 1990). White, middle-/-upper-class female students in the graduate feminist criticism classroom are not only aware of the oppression they have experienced as women, they have also theorized that oppression, analyzed and interpreted their often painful experiences from a gender-based perspective. They have sometimes invested a lot in terms of their own personal survival in a sense of identity as victims of male violence and male domination. When the feminist parameters with which students have been provided prove to be monist (gender-only), students will tend to resist the use of more complex parameters that take race and class into account. When the curriculum is integrated from the start, as it is with the undergraduate Introduction to Women's Studies class taught by my colleague Jael Silliman at the University of Iowa, students are much more willing to engage in feminist discussions of race and class. The undergraduate students who took my Feminist Theory and Feminist Criticism classes after the introduction class tended to be more open to intersectional perspectives than graduate students who were previously trained with monist models. For Rothenberg, curriculum integration will be the key to lowering student resistance: "The majority of students will continue to resist dealing with issues of race, class, and gender as long as those issues are raised in a few isolated courses" (1988, 42).

Resistance is linked to very powerful emotions aroused in students by complex subject matter. The resistance against complicating the parameters of analysis on the part of white, middle-/upper-class female graduate students is due in part to the fact that they may have become comfortable with a "victimized woman" stance (see Butler 1985, 235). The generalization "women are oppressed" gives these students a theoretical position from which to deny the threatening fact that, as white people, as U.S. citizens, and as (future) members of the upper/middle/professorial class, they occupy the location that they usually assign to men: that of perpetrator or dominator. This desire to deny (and therefore protect) privilege is a crucial reason for resistance. A related reason has to do with the assumption of innocence and moral superiority of the victim, which can lead to a dangerously comfortable position, and one that may be difficult to give up. There is remarkable resistance to acknowledging that based on group belonging, most of us stand on *both* the target/receiving end of some oppressions *and* on the perpetrator side of other oppressions. Denying the importance of one form of oppression can become a way to disavow one's position as a member of a dominant group by focusing on one's position as morally pure victim.[6] This denial is facilitated by the pervasive U.S. ideology of individualism, which makes it harder to consider group belonging in any analysis (see Eisenstein in Mohanty 1989–1990, 205).

Student resistance is often linked to feelings of defensiveness in the face of a perceived personal attack. The partiality and perversity of the dominant vision (Hartsock 1983) make it possible to operate what I call an ideological reversal of reality whereby the person who objects to racist comments is construed as the assailant. Antiracism activists are often perceived as rude, offensive, or pathological people disrupting polite society by stirring up unwarranted trouble.[7] This allows the person making racist comments to discount the entire point and to retire to a position of hurt dignity (Essed 1991). Essed concludes that as a result, "[t]he problem is reversed: Racism is not the problem; people 'who go around accusing' others of racism are the problem" (275). As one of the two resisting students in my class pointed out, she was sick and tired of the "current hatred for white women." This sounds eerily reminiscent of white men (and some women) complaining of male bashing in the feminist classroom. Rakow's analysis of "white males who most object to being decentered in the classroom" applies to some white female students as well

(1991, 11).[8] As in the case Rakow discusses, students who attempt "to recenter themselves through the assertion of the dominant discourse . . . [tend] to feel themselves silenced because they learn their discourse will not pass uncritiqued" (12). The ideological discourse that passes off the dominant as victim is a very powerful weapon of the dominant: so-called reverse racism/sexism and reverse discrimination are concepts that must be exposed for what they are: ideological weapons used to enforce continued dominance.[9] As Memmi argues, *"guilt is one of the most powerful moving forces behind racist mechanisms. Racism certainly is one way to fight . . . remorse. This is why privilege and oppression call so strongly for racism.* If there is oppression, there must be a guilty party, and if the oppressor himself will not plead guilty, which would soon be unbearable, then the oppressed must be guilty. In short, *racism is what allows the victim to be charged with the crimes . . . of the racist"* (1994, 150, my translation). Resistance can thus be interpreted as a symptom of a refusal to give up the privileges one has just begun to acknowledge as one's own. The fear of losing one set of privileges when one experiences oppression on another level may be a reason for refusing to take responsibility for fighting all oppressions (see hooks 1994, 116). In the context of graduate women's studies classes more specifically, I view the students' resistance as being based on three closely related fears:

1. The fear that women's issues (narrowly defined through the lens of gender) are being subsumed under other issues gaining prominence (see hooks 1994, 113; Butler 1985, 236).
2. The fear that white women's experience of oppression, which had so far been validated by feminist theory and praxis, is losing its centrality.
3. The fear of losing the one safe space for women who experience gender as the main category of oppression in academia.

Unexamined territorial feelings about feminist criticism were being threatened in my class. As Bernice Johnson Reagon (1983) eloquently argues, the concept of home is double-edged in that one's safe space can very quickly become exclusionary and alienating to others (see also hooks 1994, 113; Nnaemeka 1994, 302). While some white female students came to the feminist graduate classroom expecting a safe space, a home place, one of the students of color in the class wrote to me that she "knew to some degree that taking a feminist theory class at U of I would be an agonizing experience." One of the most painful things for me about the class has been the extent to which I was unable to prevent her foreboding from coming true.

Because of the fears outlined above, some white female students in my class became increasingly unwilling to share the power to define women's issues. They expressed more and more resistance against being challenged to go beyond any matter that had not been part of their own experience as white, middle-class women, especially with respect to race and racism.[10] They refused to acknowledge the power issues involved in who gets to decide what counts as women's issues and which women's concerns are being represented at any given time (see Johnson-Odim 1991). Yet this is precisely one of the main challenges feminism must rise to if it is to heed the call of feminists of color: fighting against the oppression of *all* women (Smith 1990). Otherwise, the risk is that feminism itself becomes an oppressive discourse for women who are the targets of other oppressions beside gender (King 1990; Jaimes and Halsey 1992; Rose 1992; Mohanty 1991).

Finally, several scholars point out that student resistance may be linked to a struggle for authority in a context where the teacher is not a mature white male and s/he tries to implement less authoritarian pedagogical models (Rakow 1991; Friedman 1985). Even though in the feminist classroom students would probably be initially suspicious of a male feminist teacher (who would have to *earn* the students' trust by proving he is an ally), unconscious mechanisms and expectations of women as nurturing may still work to undermine a female teacher's position of authority. When the teacher is not white, and especially if s/he is "teaching to transgress" (hooks 1994, 1), students may feel empowered to contest or deny his or her authority (Ng 1993; Nnaemeka 1994). Even in a feminist classroom, resistance may become an unconscious way to deny women a position of authority more easily granted to men (Rakow 1991; Friedman 1985). Although it is possible that some of this might have been operating in my class, by no means do I wish to imply that I was victimized by students since I was obviously the one in the position of power in the classroom. I suspect that some of the white students might have been experiencing feelings of betrayal by a white feminist teacher questioning gender as *the* primary category of analysis in a feminist criticism class.

To summarize, there are at least nine possible ways to account for student resistance to intersectional approaches: students' personal investment in dominant paradigms; their denial of privilege; the continued dominance of monist frameworks of analysis in feminist classrooms; a focus on one's position as morally pure victim; emotions such as defensiveness, guilt, anger; fear of seeing one's issues subsumed under larger ones; fear of losing one's home turf; refusal to share the power of definition; and finally, resistance to female authority. Obioma Nnaemeka notes that these nine possible causes are all facets of one central fear, that of losing power.[11] The last section of this chapter proposes some strategies that can be useful to address the problems I have been analyzing in the first two sections.

Strategies to Challenge Student Resistance

It is perhaps easier to define student resistance and its nefarious effects on learning and on classroom dynamics than it is to find effective pedagogical responses to it. In what follows, I outline five possible strategies that have been developed and used by myself and others.

1. *Anticipate resistance.* Discussions of issues of oppression, especially in multicultural classrooms, are bound to generate tensions, which the instructor should be prepared to negotiate. I now begin each new graduate class with essays discussing ethical issues in feminist scholarship and research (hooks 1989; Patai 1991; Mohanty 1991), the role of emotions in epistemology (Narayan 1988), models of racial identity-formation and student resistance (Tatum 1992; Hardiman and Jackson 1992), and classroom dynamics (Rothenberg 1988; Rakow 1991). The essay by Beverly Daniel Tatum is especially helpful (although she only deals with models developed for black and white people). Providing students with models of black and white racial identity development allows students to put their feelings and those of others in a larger psychosocial context so they realize that they are going through a general process, which may in turn reduce anxiety and resistance.[12]

Several instructors provide a list of ground rules for productive cross-cultural class interaction at the beginning of the semester (Weinstein and Obear 1992). The list may include confidentiality, respect, honesty, speaking for oneself only, using "I" messages (e.g., "I feel angry about what you said" rather than "you're wrong"), listening to each other without interrupting, and being aware of one's feelings. Finally, a few instructors have included community-based service learning in their courses, providing opportunities for students to work with social agencies serving various marginalized populations and to reflect on these experiences. One of the results of including such a component is that it helps reduce student resistance. Because the students are confronted directly with other groups' marginalization, this helps open their minds to experiences different from their own (Washington 2000). In a theory class, such an approach may also help bridge students' perceived gap between academia and activism.

2. *"Make the interaction part of the discourse of the classroom,"* keeping in mind that discussing class dynamics will not always work to resolve them (Rakow 1991, 11; see also Lewis 1990; Butler 1985, 236). One way to increase the effectiveness of this strategy is to avoid remaining at an abstract, intellectual level (sometimes a tall order in a graduate criticism class!). Mohanty reminds us that radical pedagogy "involves taking responsibility for the material effects of these very pedagogical practices on students" (1989–1990, 192). A truly radical pedagogy would integrate emotions in the epistemological model rather than attempt to

circumvent them (Narayan 1988). For Tatum, "[i]nforming students at the beginning of the semester that these feelings may be part of the learning process is ethically necessary (in the sense of informed consent) and helps to normalize the students' experience" (1992, 19). It is important that the instructor be emotionally and pedagogically prepared to deal with students' anger against her/him. Culley reminds us that if the teacher "initiates a process challenging the world view and the view of self of her students, she will surely—if she is doing her job—become the object of some students' unexamined anger" (quoted in Rakow 1991, 12; see also hooks 1994, 42). Moreover, an instructor of color will run the risk of becoming a target of students' racism (Ng 1993), often couched covertly in accusations of lack of professionalism.[13]

3. *Engage students in one-on-one dialogue outside of class* as soon as tensions develop. Brainstorm strategies with students committed to antiracist action and foster alliances with them. Try to defuse the anger of resisting students, engaging them one-on-one in nonthreatening ways but make it clear to them that racist comments (like sexist ones) are not acceptable in your class.

4. *Resist the urge to identify with or protect the resisting students.*[14] Learn to shift your concerns toward the progressive students (as we have already learned to do with respect to gendered classroom dynamics). This is a crucial issue, especially for teachers involved in multicultural education in predominantly white settings. We expect resistance and are often tempted to focus our efforts primarily on the students exhibiting such attitudes. Hoping that their resistance is a function of ignorance that can be overcome through education, we focus on *their* education to the detriment of the education of the other students, who find themselves objectified and their very existence discounted in the process.

5. *Refuse to engage recurring racist arguments* when the second strategy fails. I used to believe that it was better to have students voice their prejudices rather than hypocritically repress them. I felt that repression would only lead to a stronger resurgence of those prejudices later on. In spite of the fact that the two students of color in the class explicitly disagreed with me on this point, I kept on approaching the problem in this way throughout the semester. I operated under the naive and misguided assumption that once prejudice was expressed, it could be logically reasoned away. This strategy was unsuccessful because racism is an emotionally based, self-interested belief rationalized after the fact by supposedly logical arguments. That the logic be exposed as faulty does not change the racist feelings that called for the creation of justificatory arguments in the first place (Memmi 1994). Not only did I find that the students' resistance became stronger and more vocal as they felt more and more authorized to voice it, but the actual consequence of this position was a privileging of the problem students' subjectivity and a nega-

tion of the subjectivity of the students of color. Class discussion was stuck on two students' repeated rejection of nonmonist approaches, preventing the class as a whole from moving beyond Racism 101 and thereby blocking the education process. With the knowledge gained from reflecting on this experience, I now respond to the resistance arguments the first few times, which is usually enough for many students to begin questioning their assumptions and delve honestly into these complex issues and the feelings they arouse in them (this did happen in the class for some students). However, I would now refuse to engage resistance in class if I felt it was turning into stalling tactics.[15]

Cognitive dissonance (the destabilizing experience of having one's core beliefs questioned) can result in two main responses: one can wrestle with it, learning and growing in the process, or one can repeatedly deny and resist it. In the terms of Janet Helms's 1990 model of white racial identity development (as outlined in Tatum's 1992 essay), white people who become aware of institutional racism and white privilege may react to the discomforting nature of this newly found awareness either by taking on an antiracist position or by refusing this new knowledge and "reshaping [their] belief system to be more congruent with an acceptance of racism," transforming their guilt feelings into anger directed against people of color (Tatum 1992, 15). This reintegration stage is expressed in the women's studies classroom when students consistently refuse to let go of their monist parameters even after being shown many times that they are oppressive to women of color. It is only in this case that refusal to engage resistance within the classroom should be considered.

When the class becomes divided, and oppressive processes of dominance are being reproduced in the feminist classroom, it is everyone's responsibility, but especially the instructor's (as the one who does hold final authority whether we want it or not, whether we feel we do or not) to find ways to stop these processes and to keep on challenging the reproduction of *all* systems of dominance in our classrooms (Lewis 1990; Manicom 1992). It is crucial that we not give up, nor stop integrating courses because this work is too hard, or too divisive, or too uncomfortable. This work is a tremendous opportunity for us and our students to grow, learn from each other, facilitate social change, and create hard-won, long lasting alliances.

Notes

1. I especially thank Obioma Nnaemeka and Jodi Byrd for their remarkable insights on this issue. This essay is part of our continuing dialogue. Thanks also go to Jael Silliman, the members of the Women Against Racism Committee, and anonymous reviewers for the *NWSA Journal.*

2. Jodi Byrd, personal communication, 1996.

3. Personal conversation, 1995.

4. For an excellent discussion of the use of the free speech argument to justify artistic/religious imperialistic appropriations of Native cultures, see Wendy Rose (1992). For a discussion of how free speech in K–12 schools is applied differentially according to gender, see Nan Stein (1995a). Stein reminds us that "there is no First Amendment right to sexually harass" (1995a, 625), to which I would add, or to harass others based on their race/ethnicity, class, religion, sexual orientation, ability, age, etc. See also Matsuda et al. (1993) and Roof (1999).

5. Jodi Byrd, personal conversation, 1995.

6. That resistance to discussions of the United States' continued colonialism against Native nations also occurs in antiracism groups shows that resistance to an analysis of privilege is not limited to race and racism issues. Peggy McIntosh (1992) also draws links between males' and whites' denial of privilege.

7. For a parallel analysis in the British context, see Gilroy (1994, 409–10).

8. In my class, the two male graduate students tended to be responsive to the discussion, without ever monopolizing it.

9. This process is best exemplified in anti-affirmative action rhetoric. The reality is that affirmative action does not unfairly tip the scales in favor of people of color and women. Rather, it attempts, in a very small and imperfect way, to tilt the rigged scales ever so slightly into a less unequal position. What this means for the groups that were traditionally used to being in a position of privilege is that some of their privileges have been chipped away. But these groups are not being discriminated against. There is a world of difference between loss of privilege and discrimination. The purpose of the rhetoric of so-called reverse discrimination is to ensure that the dominant groups retain all of their privileges, which is done by blaming the real victims of the system of dominance for their victimization. This perverse logic can only work if the reality of structural power imbalances between groups is hidden and erased.

10. This, incidentally, points to one of the main limitations of theorizing from experience (see Manicom 1992).

11. Personal communication, 1996.

12. For example, Tatum points out that at one stage of the model, students are often tempted to withdraw from the class, through absenteeism or not turn-

ing in assignments (both happened in my class). Alerting students to this possibility seems to reduce its incidence (1992, 6–7).

13. Obioma Nnaemeka, personal communication, 1996.

14. Jodi Byrd, personal conversation, 1995.

15. I am suggesting that instructors silence only recurring, aware racist attitudes and remarks and respond to the unaware kinds with varying degrees of strength depending on the context.

Works Cited

Aiken, Susan Hardy, Karen Anderson, Myra Dinnerstein, Judy Lensink, and Patricia Mac Corquodale. 1987. "Trying Transformations: Curriculum Integration and the Problem of Resistance." *Signs: Journal of Women in Culture and Society* 12(2):255–75.

Andersen, Margaret, and Patricia Hill Collins, eds. 1992. *Race, Class and Gender: An Anthology.* Belmont, CA: Wadsworth.

Anzaldúa, Gloria, ed. 1990. *Making Face, Making Soul. Haciendo Caras: Creative and Critical Perspectives by Feminists of Color.* San Francisco: Aunt Lute Books.

Barnard, Ian. 1994. "Anti-Homophobic Pedagogy: Some Suggestions for Teachers." *Radical Teacher* 45:26–8.

Bohmer, Suzanne, and Joyce L. Briggs. 1991. "Teaching Privileged Students About Gender, Race, and Class Oppression." *Teaching Sociology* 19(2):154–63.

Butler, Johnnella E. 1985. "Toward a Pedagogy of Everywoman's Studies." In *Gendered Subjects: The Dynamics of Feminist Teaching*, ed. Margo Culley and Catherine Portuges, 230–39. Boston: Routledge and Kegan Paul.

Calhoun, Craig, ed. 1992. *Habermas and the Public Sphere.* Cambridge, MA: MIT Press.

Culley, Margo, and Catherine Portuges, eds. 1985. *Gendered Subjects: The Dynamics of Feminist Teaching.* Boston: Routledge and Kegan Paul.

Davis, Angela Y. 1981. *Women, Race and Class.* New York: Random House.

Ellsworth, Elizabeth. 1989. "Why Doesn't This Feel Empowering? Working Through the Repressive Myths of Critical Pedagogy." *Harvard Educational Review* 59(3):297–324.

Essed, Philomena. 1991. *Understanding Everyday Racism: An Interdisciplinary Theory.* Newbury Park, CA: Sage Publications.

Fraser, Nancy. 1992. "Rethinking the Public Sphere: A Contribution to the Critique of Actually Existing Democracy." In *Habermas and the Public Sphere*, ed. Craig Calhoun, 109–42. Cambridge, MA: MIT Press.

Freire, Paulo. (1970) 1993. *Pedagogy of the Oppressed.* Trans. Myra Bergman Ramos. New York: Continuum.

Friedman, Susan Stanford. 1985. "Authority in the Feminist Classroom: A Contradiction in Terms?" In *Gendered Subjects: The Dynamics of Feminist*

Teaching, eds. Margo Culley and Catherine Portuges, 203–208. Boston: Routledge and Kegan Paul.

Garcia, Claire Oberon. 1994. "Emotional Baggage in a Course on Black Writers." *Chronicle of Higher Education* (27 July):B1–B3.

Gilroy, Paul. 1994. "Urban Social Movements, 'Race' and Community." In *Colonial Discourse and Postcolonial Theory: A Reader*, ed. Patrick Williams and Laura Chrisman, 404–20. New York: Columbia University Press.

Gluck, Sherna Berger, and Daphne Patai, eds. 1991. *Women's Words: The Feminist Practice of Oral History*. New York: Routledge.

Gore, Jennifer. 1992. "What We Can Do for You! What *Can* 'We' Do for 'You'? Struggling Over Empowerment in Critical and Feminist Pedagogy." In *Feminisms and Critical Pedagogy*, ed. Carmen Luke and Jennifer Gore, 54–73. New York: Routledge.

Hardiman, Rita, and Bailey W. Jackson. 1992. "Racial Identity Development: Understanding Racial Dynamics in College Classrooms and on Campus." *New Directions for Teaching and Learning* 52(Winter):21–37.

Harding, Sandra, and Merrill B. Hintikka, eds. 1983. *Discovering Reality: Feminist Perspectives on Epistemology, Metaphysics, Methodology, and Philosophy of Science*. Boston: D. Reidel.

Hartsock, Nancy C. M. 1983. "The Feminist Standpoint: Developing the Ground for a Specifically Feminist Historical Materialism." In *Discovering Reality: Feminist Perspectives on Epistemology, Metaphysics, Methodology, and Philosophy of Science*, ed. Sandra Harding and Merrill B. Hintikka, 283–310. Boston: D. Reidel.

Higonnet, Margaret R., ed. 1994. *Borderwork: Feminist Engagements with Comparative Literature*. Ithaca, NY: Cornell University Press.

hooks, bell. 1994. *Teaching to Transgress: Education as the Practice of Freedom*. New York: Routledge.

———. 1989. "Feminist Scholarship: Ethical Issues." In her *Talking Back: Thinking Feminist, Thinking Black*, 42–8. Boston: South End Press.

Jaimes, M. Annette, ed. 1992. *The State of Native America: Genocide, Colonization, and Resistance*. Boston: South End Press.

Jaimes, M. Annette, with Theresa Halsey. 1992. "American Indian Women: At the Center of Indigenous Resistance in Contemporary North America." In *The State of Native America: Genocide, Colonization, and Resistance*, ed. M. Annette Jaimes, 311–44. Boston: South End Press.

Johnson-Odim, Cheryl. 1991. "Common Themes, Different Contexts: Third World Women and Feminism." In *Third World Women and the Politics of Feminism*, ed. Chandra Talpade Mohanty, Ann Russo, and Lourdes Torres, 314–27. Bloomington: Indiana University Press.

Kenway, Jane, and Helen Modra. 1992. "Feminist Pedagogy and Emancipatory Possibilities." In *Feminisms and Critical Pedagogy*, ed. Carmen Luke and Jennifer Gore, 138–66. New York: Routledge.

King, Deborah K. (1988) 1990. "Multiple Jeopardy, Multiple Consciousness: The Context of a Black Feminist Ideology." In *Feminist Theory in Practice and Process*, ed. Micheline R. Malson, Jean F. O'Barr, Sarah Westphal-Wihl, and Mary Wyer, 75–105. Chicago: University of Chicago Press.

Kozol, Wendy. 1999. "Can Feminist Pedagogy Find a Safe Space? White Defensiveness and the Politics of Silence." *Concerns* 26(1–2):10–20.

Lewis, Magda. 1990. "Interrupting Patriarchy: Politics, Resistance, and Transformation in the Feminist Classroom." *Harvard Educational Review* 60(4): 467–88.

Lorde, Audre. 1984. "Age, Race, Class, and Sex: Women Redefining Difference." In her *Sister Outsider*, 114–23. Freedom, CA: Crossing Press.

Luke, Carmen, and Jennifer Gore, eds. 1992. *Feminisms and Critical Pedagogy*. New York: Routledge.

Malson, Micheline R., Jean F. O'Barr, Sarah Westphal-Wihl, and Mary Wyer, eds. 1990. *Feminist Theory in Practice and Process*. Chicago: University of Chicago Press.

Manicom, Ann. 1992. "Feminist Pedagogy: Transformations, Standpoints, and Politics." *Canadian Journal of Education* 17(3):365–89.

Matsuda, Mari J., Charles Lawrence III, Richard Delgado, and Kimberlè W. Crenshaw. 1993. *Words That Wound: Critical Race Theory, Assaultive Speech, and the First Amendment*. Boulder, CO: Westview Press.

McIntosh, Peggy. (1988) 1992. "White Privilege and Male Privilege: A Personal Account of Coming to See Correspondences Through Work in Women's Studies." In *Race, Class, and Gender: An Anthology*, ed. Margaret Andersen and Patricia Hill Collins, 70–81. Belmont, CA: Wadsworth.

Memmi, Albert. (1982) 1994. *Le Racisme: Description, définitions, traitement*. Paris: Gallimard.

Mohanty, Chandra Talpade. 1991. "Under Western Eyes." In *Third World Women and the Politics of Feminism*, ed. Chandra Talpade Mohanty, Ann Russo, and Lourdes Torres, 51–80. Bloomington: Indiana University Press.

———. 1989–90. "On Race and Voice: Challenges for Liberal Education in the 1990s." *Cultural Critique* 14:179–208.

Mohanty, Chandra Talpade, Ann Russo, and Lourdes Torres, eds. 1991. *Third World Women and the Politics of Feminism*. Bloomington: Indiana University Press.

Narayan, Uma. 1988. "Working Together Across Difference: Some Considerations on Emotions and Political Practice." *Hypatia* 3(2):31–47.

Ng, Roxana. 1995. "Teaching Against the Grain: Contradictions and Possibilities." In *Anti-Racism, Feminism, and Critical Approaches to Education*, eds. Roxana Ng, Pat Staton, and Joyce Scane, 129–52. Wesport, CT: Bergin and Garvey.

———. 1993. "'A Woman Out of Control': Deconstructing Sexism and Racism in the University." *Canadian Journal of Education* 18(3):189–205.

Ng, Roxana, Pat Staton, and Joyce Scane, eds. 1995. *Anti-Racism, Feminism, and Critical Approaches to Education*. Wesport, CT: Bergin and Garvey.

Nnaemeka, Obioma. 1995. "Feminism, Rebellious Women, and Cultural Boundaries: Rereading Flora Nwapa and Her Compatriots." *Research in African Literatures* 26(2):81–113.

———. 1994. "Bringing African Women into the Classroom: Rethinking Pedagogy and Epistemology." In *Borderwork: Feminist Engagements with Comparative Literature*, ed. Margaret R. Higonnet, 301–18. Ithaca, NY: Cornell University Press.

Orner, Mimi. 1992. "Interrupting the Calls for Student Voice in 'Liberatory' Education: A Feminist Poststructuralist Perspective." In *Feminisms and Critical Pedagogy*, eds. Carmen Luke and Jennifer Gore, 74–89. New York: Routledge.

Patai, Daphne. 1991. "U.S. Academics and Third World Women: Is Ethical Research Possible?" In *Women's Words: The Feminist Practice of Oral History*, ed. Sherna Berger Gluck and Daphne Patai, 137–53. New York: Routledge.

Rakow, Lana F. 1991. "Gender and Race in the Classroom: Teaching Way Out of Line." *Feminist Teacher* 6(1):10–13.

Reagon, Bernice Johnson. 1983. "Coalition Politics: Turning the Century." In *Home Girls: A Black Feminist Anthology*, ed. Barbara Smith, 356–68. New York: Kitchen Table Press.

Rich, Adrienne. (1978) 1979. "Disloyal to Civilization: Feminism, Racism, Gynephobia." In her *On Lies, Secrets, and Silence. Selected Prose 1966–1978*, 275–310. New York: Norton.

Roof, Judith. 1999. "The Truth About Disclosure, or Revoking a First Amendment License to Hate." *Concerns* 26(1–2):42–54.

Rose, Wendy. 1992. "The Great Pretenders." In *The State of Native America: Genocide, Colonization, and Resistance*, ed. M. Annette Jaimes, 403–21. Boston: South End Press.

Rothenberg, Paula. 1988. "Integrating the Study of Race, Gender, and Class: Some Preliminary Observations." *Feminist Teacher* 3(3):37–42.

Sandoval, Chela. 1991. "U.S. Third World Feminism: The Theory and Method of Oppositional Consciousness in the Postmodern World." *Genders* 10:1–24.

———. (1982) 1990. "Feminism and Racism: A Report on the 1981 National Women's Studies Association Conference." In *Making Face, Making Soul. Haciendo Caras: Creative and Critical Perspectives by Feminists of Color*, ed. Gloria Anzaldúa, 55–71. San Francisco: Aunt Lute Books.

Smith, Barbara. (1982) 1990. "Racism and Women's Studies." In *Making Face, Making Soul. Haciendo Caras: Creative and Critical Perspectives by Feminists of Color*, ed. Gloria Anzaldúa, 25–28. San Francisco: Aunt Lute Books.

———, ed. 1983. *"Home Girls: A Black Feminist Anthology*. New York: Kitchen Table Press.

Sonnenschein, Frances M. 1988. "Countering Prejudiced Beliefs and Behaviors: The Role of the Social Studies Professional." *Social Education* (April/May): 264–66.

Spivak, Gayatri Chakravorty. 1991. "Three Women's Texts and a Critique of Imperialism." In *Feminisms: An Anthology of Literary Theory and Criticism*, ed. Robyn R. Warhol and Diane Price Herndl, 798–814. New Brunswick, NJ: Rutgers University Press.

Stein, Nan. 1995a. "Is It Sexually Charged, Sexually Hostile, or the Constitution? Sexual Harassment in K–12 Schools." *West's Education Law Reporter* (1 June): 621–31.

———. 1995b. "Sexual Harassment in School: The Public Performance of Gendered Violence." *Harvard Educational Review* 65(2):145–62.

Tatum, Beverly Daniel. 1992. "Talking About Race, Learning About Racism: The Application of Racial Identity Development Theory in the Classroom." *Harvard Educational Review* 62(1):1–24.

Uttal, Lynet. 1990. "Inclusion Without Influence: The Continuing Tokenism of Women of Color." In *Making Face, Making Soul. Haciendo Caras: Creative and Critical Perspectives by Feminists of Color*, ed. Gloria Anzaldúa, 42–45. San Francisco: Aunt Lute Books.

Warhol, Robyn R., and Diane Price Herndl, eds. 1991. *Feminisms: An Anthology of Literary Theory and Criticism*. New Brunswick, NJ: Rutgers University Press.

Washington, Patricia Ann. 2000. "From College Classroom to Community Action." *Feminist Teacher* 13(1):12–34.

Weinstein, Gerald, and Kathy Obear. 1992. "Bias Issues in the Classroom: Encounters with the Teaching Self." New *Directions for Teaching and Learning* 52(Winter):39–50.

Williams, Patrick, and Laura Chrisman, eds. 1994. *Colonial Discourse and Postcolonial Theory: A Reader*. New York: Columbia University Press.

Yamato, Gloria. (1987) 1990. "Something About the Subject Makes It Hard to Name." In *Making Face, Making Soul. Haciendo Caras: Creative and Critical Perspectives by Feminists of Color*, ed. Gloria Anzaldúa, 20–24. San Francisco: Aunt Lute Books.

Zinn, Maxine Baca, Lynn Weber Cannon, Elizabeth Higginbotham, and Bonnie Thornton Dill. (1986) 1990. "The Costs of Exclusionary Practices in Women's Studies." In *Making Face, Making Soul. Haciendo Caras: Creative and Critical Perspectives by Feminists of Color*, ed. Gloria Anzaldúa, 29–41. San Francisco: Aunt Lute Books.

PART IV   **Bibliographies**

CHAPTER FIFTEEN

Feminist Pedagogy: A Selective Annotated Bibliography

LORI A. GOETSCH

This bibliography represents, for the most part, material published since 1986 and is intended to augment Carolyn M. Shrewsbury, "Feminist Pedagogy: A Bibliography," *Women's Studies Quarterly* 15 (Fall/Winter 1987): 116–24. It is also limited to items that are most readily available in university libraries or that present a perspective that is unique in the literature. As with Shrewsbury's bibliography, many of the items listed demonstrate the continued interest in classroom dynamics, strategies, and techniques. There is also still considerable attention being given to the theoretical formulation of a feminist pedagogy and an examination of its relationship to other theories such as liberation education and post-modernism. Finally, an attempt was made to provide a balance of sources from women's studies journals as well as the professional literature of the disciplines, particularly education.

In addition to these citations, there are four major texts that are repeatedly cited in the literature and should be considered in any examination of this topic: Mary F. Belenky, Blythe McVicker Clinchy, Nancy Rule Goldberger, Jill Mattuck Tarule, *Women's Ways of Knowing: The Development of Self, Voice, and Mind* (New York: Basic Books, 1986); Charlotte Bunch and Sandra Pollack, *Learning Our Way: Essays in Feminist Education* (Trumansburg, NY: The Crossing Press, 1983); Margo Culley and Catherine Portuges, eds., *Gendered Subjects: The Dynamics of Feminist Teaching* (New York: Routledge and Kegan Paul, 1985); and Kathleen Weiler, *Women Teaching for Change: Gender, Class, and Power* (South Hadley, MA: Bergin and Garvey, 1988).

Adler, Emily Stier. " 'It Happened to Me': How Faculty Handle Student Reactions to Class Material" and responses. *Feminist Teacher* 3 (Fall–Winter 1987): 22–26. Describes the experiences with students' personal reactions to sex and gender materials and suggests strategies for addressing self-disclosure. Includes two responses from Joanne Belknap, who relates experiences teaching a course on sexual assault, and Nancy Brooks, who presents the perspective of a sexual assault counselor.

Allen, Katherine R. "Integrating a Feminist Perspective into Family Studies Courses." *Family Relations* 37 (January 1988): 29–35. Provides overview of women's studies and feminist pedagogy and offers strategies for curriculum integration.

Originally published in the Autumn 1991 issue of the *NWSA Journal.*

Boyle, Christine. "Teaching Law as if Women Really Mattered, or, What about the Washrooms?" *Canadian Journal of Women and the Law* 2, no. 1 (1986): 96–112. Discusses the "hidden curriculum" in legal education as it relates to women and reports on a small survey of the author's colleagues regarding the inclusion of course materials on women and a feminist perspective on law. Concludes with the author's perspective on fears faculty have when contemplating a feminist pedagogical approach to teaching law.

Bricker-Jenkins, Mary, and Nancy Hooyman. "Feminist Pedagogy in Education for Social Change." *Feminist Teacher* 2, no. 2 (1987): 36–42. Identifies and discusses major themes in feminist research that make up a feminist ideology (for example, end patriarchy, empowerment, process) and their implications for teaching, course design, educational organization and administration.

Brookes, Anne-Louise, and Ursula A. Kelly. "Writing Pedagogy: A Dialogue of Hope." *Journal of Education* 171 (Spring 1989): 117–31. Presents a series of letters between the two authors critiquing critical pedagogy, particularly the work of Paulo Freire and Ira Shor, in terms of gender and silencing.

Burack, Cynthia. "Bringing Women's Studies to Political Science: The Handmaid in the Classroom." *NWSA Journal* 1 (Winter 1988–89): 274–83. Describes the assignment of Margaret Atwood's *The Handmaid's Tale* in an undergraduate political science program to address several pedagogical goals and test the writer's personal and professional assumptions about pedagogy and learning.

Caywood, Cynthia L., and Gillian R. Overing. *Teaching Writing: Pedagogy, Gender and Equity.* Albany: State University of New York Press, 1987.

Davis, Barbara Hillyer, ed. *Journal of Thought* 20 (Fall 1985). Special issue on feminist education.

Foss, Sonja K. "Implementing Feminist Pedagogy in the Rhetorical Criticism Course." Paper presented at the annual meeting of the Speech Communication Association, San Francisco, California, 18–21 November 1989. ERIC, ED 316 890. Describes unit design and identifies students' level of commitment to feminism and the instructor's ambivalence about introducing a feminist perspective as two major problems encountered.

Fraiman, Susan. "Against Gendrification Agendas for Feminist Scholarship and Teaching in Women's Studies." *Iris* 23 (Spring–Summer 1990): 5–13. Discusses the inherent interdisciplinary nature of women's studies and the tensions that disciplinary boundaries create in the classroom and in research. Also calls for preserving the integrity of women's or feminist studies as opposed to gender studies.

Gabelnick, Faith, and Carol Pearson. "Finding Their Voices: Two University of Maryland Teachers Use the Myers-Briggs Typology Indicator to Help Students Identify and Understand Diversity." *Feminist Teacher* 1 (Spring 1985): 11–17. Reports results of testing three hundred women's studies students in an introductory course in order to redesign a course with large enrollment to meet the learning needs of all students. Discusses each category or "voice" expressed through the testing as it applies to students' learning and classroom behaviors.

Gardner, Saundra, Cynthia Dean, and Deo McKaig. "Responding to Differences in the Classroom: The Politics of Knowledge, Class, and Sexuality." *Sociology of Education* 62 (January 1989): 64–75. Describes the emergence of hierarchical responses to classroom differences and its detrimental impact on learning and offers suggestions for responding to these conflicts.

Gayle, Barbara Mae. "Implementing Feminist Pedagogy in the Public Speaking Course." Paper presented at the annual meeting of the Speech Communication Association, San Francisco, California, 18–21 November 1989. ERIC, ED 312 724. Presents assignments and an evaluation system that empower students and create a classroom community.

Grumet, Madeleine R. *Bitter Milk: Women and Teaching.* Amherst: University of Massachusetts Press, 1988.

Hayes, Elisabeth. "Insights from Women's Experiences for Teaching and Learning." *New Directions for Continuing Education* 43 (Fall 1989): 44–66. Discusses the principles of feminist pedagogy (for example, teacher-student collaboration, holistic learning) as more effective in addressing women's experience.

Heald, Susan. "The Madwoman in the Attic: Feminist Teaching in the Margins." *Resources for Feminist Research* 18 (December 1989): 22–26. Discusses resistance to the changes that feminist pedagogy demands in both the teacher's and the student's understanding of learning and knowledge by analyzing student course evaluations. Also describes two teaching practices, critical media events, and autobiographical writing, as techniques to help students revise their views of teaching and learning.

Hoffman, Leonore, and Margo Culley, eds. *Women's Personal Narratives: Essays in Criticism and Pedagogy.* New York: Modern Language Association of America, 1985.

Klein, Renate Duelli. "The Dynamics of the Women's Studies Classroom: A Review Essay of the Teaching Practice of Women's Studies in Higher Education." *Women's Studies International Forum* 10, no. 2 (1987): 187–206. Comments on the lack of theoretical literature on classroom practice, reviews the literature on frequently cited teaching techniques in "gynagogy" (for example, consciousness-raising, interactive learning/teaching), and summarizes teaching methodology guidelines and two models for the study of classroom dynamics. Extensive bibliography.

Laird, Susan. "Reforming 'Woman's True Profession': A Case for 'Feminist Pedagogy' in Teacher Education?" *Harvard Educational Review* 58 (November 1989): 449–63. Assesses recent school reform proposals, discusses the concept of teaching as "woman's true profession" from five different but interrelated theses and suggests implications for the role of feminist pedagogy in teacher education.

Lewis, Magda, and Roger I. Simon. "A Discourse Not Intended for Her: Learning and Teaching Within Patriarchy." *Harvard Educational Review* 56 (November 1986): 457–72. Presents alternating accounts from a male teacher and a female student about silencing in a graduate seminar and suggests several elements necessary to creating a "counter-patriarchic pedagogy" for mixed-gender education.

Loring, Katherine, ed. "Feminist Pedagogy and the Learning Climate: Proceedings of the Annual Great Lakes Colleges Association Women's Studies Conference." Ann Arbor, Michigan, 4–6 November 1983. ERIC, ED 252 493. Includes several papers on feminist pedagogy and teaching methods as well as the text of the keynote speech by Barrie Thorne, "Rethinking the Ways We Teach."

Maher, Frances A. "Inquiry Teaching and Feminist Pedagogy." *Social Education* 51 (March 1987): 186–88, 190–92. Describes these two models and compares their approaches to teaching through examples of units from an American history course.

———. "My Introduction to 'Introduction to Women's Studies': The Role of the Teacher's Authority in the Feminist Classroom." *Feminist Teacher* 3 (Fall–Winter 1987): 9–11. Describes the author's experiences applying her research on feminist pedagogy, in particular, testing assumptions about teachers as authorities.

———. "Toward a Richer Theory of Feminist Pedagogy: A Comparison of 'Liberation' and 'Gender' Models for Teaching and Learning." *Journal of Education* 169 (Fall 1987): 91–100. Discusses the contributions of liberation pedagogy and feminist theories of knowledge and learning to the development of a feminist pedagogy and recommends a synthesis of the two in order to achieve a fully developed feminist pedagogy.

——— and Kathleen Dunn. "The Practice of Feminist Teaching: A Case Study of Interactions among Curriculum, Pedagogy, and Female Cognitive Development." Working Paper No. 144. Wellesley, MA: Wellesley College, Center for Research on Women, 1984. Reports results of a case study of two introductory education courses and the influence of course content and teaching methods on women students' self-awareness and self-concept.

——— and Mary Kay Tetrault. "Feminist Teachers, Feminist Researchers, and Knowledge Construction: Examples of Interactive Teaching and Interpretation." Paper presented at the American Educational Research Association annual meeting, San Francisco, CA, 27–31 March 1989.

Mahony, Pat. "Oppressive Pedagogy: The Importance of Process in Women's Studies." *Women's Studies International Forum* 11, no. 2 (1988): 103–8. Identifies and discusses problems that arise in the teaching of women's studies in British universities, where a conventional hierarchical academic model contradicts feminist pedagogy. Describes efforts to apply feminist teaching methods to a course.

Miller, Janet L. "The Sound of Silence Breaking: Feminist Pedagogy and Curriculum Theory." *Journal of Curriculum Theorizing* 4, no. 1 (1982): 4–11. Explores the silences of both teacher and student caused by the separation of classroom experience from everyday life and identifies the development of feminist and curriculum theories as attempts to challenge the silence.

Morgan, Kathryn Pauly. "The Perils and Paradoxes of Feminist Pedagogy." *Resources for Feminist Research* 16 (September 1987): 49–52. Discusses the contradiction between power/authority in the classroom and feminist pedagogy and analyzes three paradoxes concerning the feminist teacher as role model.

Nemiroff, Greta Hoffman. "Beyond 'Talking Heads': Towards an Empowering Pedagogy of Women's Studies." *Atlantis* 15 (Fall 1989): 1–16. Discusses traditional pedagogy as impersonal and authority-based and suggests that the educational philosophies of humanistic education and critical pedagogy (or liberation education) are ones from which feminist educators can draw to develop a feminist pedagogy. Also discusses various techniques for use in the classroom.

Nicholson, Carol. "Postmodernism, Feminism, and Education: The Need for Solidarity." *Educational Theory* 39 (Summer 1989): 197–205. Discusses postmodernist theory, feminist influences and reactions to postmodernism, and the importance of listening to a feminist voice in defining and developing a postmodernist pedagogy.

Penley, Constance. "Teaching in Your Sleep: Feminism and Psychoanalysis," in *Theory in the Classroom*, edited by Cary Nelson, 129–48. Urbana: University of Illinois Press, 1986. Discusses the relationship of feminist pedagogy and psychoanalysis in terms of knowledge and authority.

Peters, Helene. "Feminist Theory and Feminist Pedagogy: The Existential Woman." Paper presented at the National Women's Studies Association Conference, Columbus, Ohio, 26–30 June 1983. ERIC, ED 236 106. Argues existentialism as a theoretical and methodological base for feminist pedagogy.

Piussi, Anna Marie. "Towards a Pedagogy of Sexual Difference: Education and Female Genealogy." *Gender and Education*, 2, no. 1 (1990): 81–90. Suggests that the major problem in society and education is that the existence of two sexes is not recognized. Encourages feminists to develop a pedagogy that reestablishes relationships among women to "create symbolic and social orders . . . that correspond to their female way of being."

Regan, Helen B. "Not for Women Only: School Administration as a Feminist Activity." *Teachers College Record* 91 (Summer 1990): 565–77. Compares feminist pedagogy and feminist school administration on the issues of voice and authority. Traces the author's development as a feminist administrator and reviews the literature on feminist pedagogy as it relates to administration.

Richardson, Nancy. "Feminist Theology/Feminist Pedagogy: An Experimental Program of the Women's Theological Center." *Journal of Feminist Studies in Religion* 1 (Fall 1985): 115–22. Discusses the development and implementation of a "feminist model of theological education" combining field work, feminist theology and theory, and feminist spirituality and praxis.

Ritchie, Joy S. "Confronting the 'Essential' Problem: Reconnecting Feminist Theory and Pedagogy." *Journal of Advanced Composition* 2 (Fall 1990): 249–73.

Rockhill, Kathleen. "The Chaos of Subjectivity in the Ordered Halls of Academe." *Canadian Woman Studies* 8 (Winter 1987): 12–17. Discusses the role of consciousness raising as a means of creating a "feminist space" to confront a number of dichotomies like public/private, emotional/rational, separatism/integration.

Rose, Suzanna. "The Protest as a Teaching Technique for Promoting Feminist Activism." *NWSA Journal* 1 (Spring 1989): 486–90. Describes a "protest assignment" designed to motivate students' interest in and action for social change.

Rosser, Sue V. "Teaching Techniques to Attract Women to Science: Applications of Feminist Theories and Methodologies." *Women's Studies International Forum* 12 (1989): 363–77. Makes several suggestions following the steps of the scientific method for alternative approaches and techniques that can be used in the science classroom to provide a more supportive environment for women.

———. "Warming up the Classroom Climate for Women." *Feminist Teacher* 4 (Spring 1989): 8–12. Describes five exercises that can be used in faculty workshops or in the classroom to raise issues about sexism.

Ryan, Margaret. "Classroom and Contexts: The Challenge of Feminist Pedagogy." *Feminist Teacher* 4 (Fall 1989): 39–42. Discusses the teaching of literature from a feminist perspective in the traditional classroom with particular attention to the perceived role of the female teacher as both mother and authority. Suggests means of maintaining a feminist pedagogical approach in disciplines other than women's studies.

"Sex and Gender" (special issue). *Teaching Sociology* 12, no. 3 (1985). Contents: "Teaching Sex and Gender: A Decade of Experience" by Catherine White Berheide and Marcia Texler Segal; "Teaching about Men and Masculinity: Method and Meaning" by Meredith Gould; "Teaching Sex and Gender in Sociology: Incorporating the Perspective of Women of Color" by Esther Ngan-Ling Chow; "From Gender Seminar to Gender Community" by Laurel Richardson, Mary Margaret Fonow, and Judith A. Cook; "Learning about Gender through Writing: Student Journals in the Undergraduate Classroom" by Robin L. Roth; and "Resistances to Feminist Analysis" by Mary Jo Neitz.

Shapiro, Joan Poliner, and Carroll Smith-Rosenberg. "The 'Other Voices' in Contemporary Ethical Dilemmas: The Value of the New Scholarship on Women in the Teaching of Ethics." *Women's Studies International Forum* 12, no. 2 (1989): 199–211. Describes an alternative ethics course designed to value "the voice of the marginal and the disempowered." Includes student comments on various ethical issues: feminism, homosexuality, abortion, race, and pornography.

Thompson, Martha F. "The Power of No." *Feminist Teacher* 5 (Spring 1990): 24–25.

Torrey, Morrison, Jackie Casey, and Karin Olson. "Teaching Law in a Feminist Manner: A Commentary from Experience." *Harvard Women's Law Journal* 13 (Spring 1990): 87–136.

Treichler, Paula A. "Teaching Feminist Theory," in *Theory in the Classroom*, edited by Cary Nelson, 57–128. Urbana: University of Illinois Press, 1986. Describes seven current "plots" representing feminist theoretical activity and discusses theory's relationship to practice and pedagogy. Argues that feminist theory is not cohesive but diverse and contradictory and suggests the classroom as a forum for exploring these differences. Includes extensive notes and bibliography.

Weedon, Chris. *Feminist Practice and Post-structuralist Theory.* Oxford: Blackwell, 1987.

Whatley, Marianne H. "A Feeling for Science: Female Students and Biology Texts." *Women's Studies International Forum* 12, no. 3 (1989): 355–62. Presents results of a study of eight secondary biology textbooks for their representation of women as scientists as a means of promoting the sciences as a field of study.

Wiss, Katy. "Conflict in the Women's Studies Classroom: Some Ideas for Coping." *Women and Language* 11 (Winter 1987): 14–16. Discusses the causes of conflict in the classroom, reviews the feminist literature on the topic, and offers suggestions for managing or avoiding conflict.

"Women's Studies Enters the 1990s: A Special Section on Feminism in (and out of) the Classroom." *Women's Review of Books* 7 (February 1990): 17–32. Contains twelve articles by feminist scholars, several of which discuss feminist teaching, feminism in the classroom, and the development of feminist pedagogy.

CHAPTER SIXTEEN

Dynamics of the Pluralistic Classroom:
A Selected Bibliography

STEPHANIE RIGER, CARRIE BRECKE,

AND EVE WIEDERHOLD

The feminist movement has heightened awareness of two important phenomena in institutions of higher education today. First, the demographics of the student body have changed in recent years. Women are the "new majority," and different groups of women bring varying educational needs to the classroom. Second, discussion of sensitive issues related to gender and ethnicity, such as abortion or civil rights, may unleash emotions in the classroom that the teacher is often ill-prepared to handle.

Consider these scenarios:

1. "In this class, there will be a free exchange of ideas," the instructor of a teacher education course announces at the first meeting.
   "Yeah, right," Paul, a white male student mutters. "Open discussion doesn't exist—especially if you're a white male. I'm the bad guy. I can't speak my mind." Concerned that Paul feels silenced, the teacher encourages his participation. But Paul frequently makes racist statements. The teacher faces a quandary: can she build Paul's trust and deal responsibly with his racist expressions?

2. Lupe, a recent arrival from Mexico, has been sitting silent in the back row for an entire semester. The teacher has emphasized the importance of verbal participation in this writing class, but attempts to draw Lupe into the discussion have failed. She hardly responds to questions posed to her and conveys discomfort about speaking in public. Her final research paper argues that she should be allowed to uphold cultural traditions from her homeland that respect silence.

3. In a gay and lesbian literature class, students are told to introduce each other by telling one fascinating fact about themselves. One-fourth of the students announce that they are married or involved with a member of the opposite sex. This scenario is repeated in a women's studies course in which sixteen out of twenty women introduce themselves with information about their marriages, while none of the gay or lesbian students mentions a partner because such declarations may be seen as scandalous. How can the teacher use these first-day conversations to raise awareness of heterosexual privilege?

Originally published in the Summer 1995 issue of the *NWSA Journal*.

The Women's Studies Program at the University of Illinois at Chicago began a discussion group in the spring of 1992 to address these and other issues concerning the pluralistic classroom. Some of the topics considered by the discussion group included

- how to overcome the silence of women and minority students in the classroom;
- how to teach about race and racism; are there "appropriate" pedagogical strategies for students from working-class ethnic backgrounds?
- what characterizes a "feminist" pedagogy?
- how can a teacher challenge racist, sexist, or heterosexist statements without squelching free expression?
- how should a teacher respond when students become angry with each other about issues of race, gender, sexual orientation?
- do students from varying ethnic and social class backgrounds have different pedagogical needs? and
- how can a teacher most effectively incorporate issues of diversity into the curriculum?

Background research for the discussion group led us to develop a bibliography on how gender, race, ethnicity, and other social categories that demarcate differential treatment in our society affect classroom interaction. The purpose of this bibliography is to inform educators and others of the diverse needs of students from varying ethnic and social class backgrounds. Many colleges and universities have become aware of the needs of students from various backgrounds and have instituted diversity requirements or in other ways encouraged faculty and students to address issues of multiculturalism in the classroom. Resources are just beginning to appear that will facilitate this task. This bibliography, for example, could be used as a reading list for a faculty seminar on teaching in the multicultural classroom or as the basis for a faculty member's self-education.

Selecting items for this bibliography was a daunting task because each subheading could itself demand a complete bibliography. To limit the scope, we restricted material to that which has been published fairly recently and which is of interest to those in a variety of fields. Consequently, we did not include material that is limited to one discipline, such as publications by disciplinary associations. We have selected material for inclusion in this bibliography that we have found to be both informative and provocative, that is, material that both addresses how the needs of diverse students affect the classroom and considers underlying issues of fairness and equality.

As we worked, we found that organizing this bibliography raised difficult questions of how and whether one should identify the needs of specific groups. For example, does distinguishing "general" questions about sex equity as different from the concern of Asian women contribute to the continued "marginalization" of this ethnic group? The act of naming categories—Native American, African American, and so forth—maintains the structure of margin and center and the resulting gender/racial biases the articles seek to redress. These categories are also fictitious in that they imply that the needs of, for example, all Latinos or lesbians can be lumped together. Paradoxically, then, the desire to recognize difference among groups simultaneously maintains boundaries of sameness within each group.

But not identifying the various needs of different groups is equally disturbing in that it maintains the status quo. A generalized notion of "female student" or "ethnic student" is inadequate in addressing specific problems facing the varying educational needs of the "new majority." The particular issues facing these students will be ignored and/or subordinated if pedagogical strategies are designed for the mythical "universal" student. At the same time, however, we should note that we have not created a "European American" or a "middle class" category. The articles that might fit these categories are instead filed under "general" headings such as "overview." This is an unfortunate consequence of the way the scholarship itself is organized. Researchers do not write articles that explicitly address issues pertinent to "European Americans" or the "middle class." Perhaps this will change as educators become aware of the political overtones of making gender/race/class distinctions. Our overriding concern in arranging this bibliography was that it be easily accessible—and that requires, at this point, that the categories used in the scholarship be maintained.

Although the bibliography as a whole is organized under the general rubric of pedagogy, we have also included "pedagogy" as a subcategory. The articles in this section specifically delineate strategies to be used in the classroom. Some of the authors do not identify themselves as feminists, but they entertain sympathetic philosophies. Further, sometimes the issues addressed by the articles presented in this bibliography overlap. For example, some of the sources listed in the "student-teacher interaction" section contain advice about pedagogical strategies. We determined the primary focus of the articles, regardless of their titles, and categorized them accordingly.

Women in the Academy: Defining the Issues

The following articles and books deal with issues affecting women both inside and outside of the classroom, in public and private arenas. We have divided the works into two categories: those that deal with the educational needs of women in general and those that pertain to women of particular ethnic backgrounds and/or sexual preferences.

Sites of Struggle: Public and Private

Burstyn, J. N. (1993). "Has nothing changed in a hundred years?": The salience of gender to the undergraduate experience. *American Journal of Education* 101, 196–202.

Hafner, A. L. (1989). The "traditional" undergraduate woman in the mid-1980s: A changing profile. In Pearson, C. S., Shavlik, D. L., and Touchton, J. G. (eds.), *Educating the majority: Women challenge tradition in higher education*, 32–46. New York: Collier, Macmillan.

Hall, R. M., and Sandler, B. (1984). *Out of the classroom climate: A chilly one for women?* Washington, DC: Project on the Status and Education of Women, Association of American Colleges.

Heller, J. F., Puff, C. R., and Mills, C. J. (1985). Assessment of the chilly college climate for women. *Journal of Higher Education* 56, 446–61.

Sandler, B. R. (1991). Women faculty at work in the classroom; or, Why it still hurts to be a woman in labor. *Communication Education* 40, 6–15.

Sandler, B., and Hall, R. (1986). *The campus climate revisited: Chilly for women faculty, administrators, and graduate students.* Washington DC: Project on the Status and Education of Women, Association of American Colleges.

Wyche, K. F., and Graves, S. B. (1992). Minority women in academia: Access and barriers to professional participation. *Psychology of Women Quarterly* 16, 429–37.

Sites of Struggle: Issues of Identity within the Academy

African American Women

Carroll, C. M. (1982). Three's a crowd: The dilemma of the black woman in higher education. In Hull, G. T., Scott, P. B., and Smith, B. (eds.), *All the women are white, all the blacks are men, but some of us are brave*, 115–28. New York: Feminist Press.

Coleman-Burns, P. (1989). African-American women—Education for what? *Sex Roles* 21, 145–60.

Collins, P.H. (1989). The social construction of black feminist thought. *Signs: Journal of Women in Culture and Society* 14, 745–73.

Delpit, L. D. (1987). Skills and other dilemmas of a progressive black educator. *Equity and Choice* 3, 9–14.

———. (1988). The silenced dialogue: Power and pedagogy in educating other people's children. *Harvard Educational Review* 58, 208–98.

Edwards, R. (1990). Connecting method and epistemology: A white woman interviewing black women. *Women's Studies International Forum* 13, 477–90.

Elam, J. C. (ed.). (1989). *Blacks in higher education: Overcoming the odds.* New York: University Press of America.

Fleming, J. (1982). Fear of success in black female and male graduate students. *Psychology of Women Quarterly* 6, 327–41.

———. (1983). Black women in black and white college environments: The making of a matriarch. *Journal of Social Issues* 39, 41–54.

Griffin, J. T. (1986). Black women's experience as authority figures in groups. *Women's Studies Quarterly* 14, 7–12.

Guy-Sheftall, B., and Bell-Scott, P. (1989). Finding a way: Black women students and the academy. In Pearson, C. S., Shavlik, D. L., and Touchton, J. G. (eds.), *Educating the majority: Women challenge tradition in higher education.* New York: Collier Macmillan, 47–56.

Moses, Y. T. (1989). *Black women in academe: Issues and strategies.* Washington, DC: Project on the Status of Women, Association of American Colleges.

Pollard, D. S. (1990). Black women, interpersonal support, and institutional change. In Antler, J. and Bilken, S. K. (eds.), *Changing education: Women as radicals and conservators,* 257–76. New York: State University of New York Press.

Russell, M. (1982). Black-eyed blues connections: Teaching black women. In Hull, G. T., Scott, P. B., and Smith, B. (eds.), *All the women are white, all the blacks are men, but some of us are brave.* New York: Feminist Press, 196–207.

Ugbah, S., and Williams, S. A. (1989). The mentor-protégée relationship: Its impact on the academic and career development of blacks in predominantly white institutions. In Elam, J. C., (ed.), *Blacks in higher education: Overcoming the odds.* New York: University Press of America, 29–42.

Washington, M. H. (1985). How racial differences helped us discover our common ground. In Culley, M., and Portuges, C. (eds.), *Gendered subjects: The dynamics of feminist education,* 221–29. Boston: Routledge.

Asian Women

Chai, A. Y. (1985). Toward a holistic paradigm for Asian American women's studies: A synthesis of feminist scholarship and women of color's feminist politics. *Women's Studies International Forum* 8, 59–66.

Crittenden, K. S. (1991). Asian self-effacement or feminine modesty? *Gender and Society* 5, 98–117.

Sue, S., and Zane, N. (1985). Academic achievement and socio-emotional adjustment among Chinese university students. *Journal of Counseling Psychology* 32, 570–79.

Yamauchi, J. S. and Tin-Mala. (1989). Undercurrents, maelstroms, or the mainstream? A profile of Asian Pacific American female students in higher education. In Pearson, C. S., Shavlik, D. L., and Touchton, J. G. (eds.), *Educating the majority: Women challenge tradition in higher education.* New York: Collier Macmillan, 69–79.

Latinas

Cardoza, D. (1991). College attendance and persistence among Hispanic women: An examination of some contributing factors. *Sex Roles* 24, 133–47.

Melendez, S. E., and Petrovich, J. (1989). Hispanic women students in higher education: Meeting the challenge of diversity. In Pearson, C. S., Shavlik, D. L., and Touchton, J. G. (eds.), *Educating the majority: Women challenge tradition in higher education.* New York: Collier Macmillan, 57–68.

Nieves-Squires, S. (1991). *Hispanic women: Making their presence on campus less tenuous.* Washington, DC: Project on the Status and Education of Women, Association of American Colleges.

Rendon, L. I., and Nora, A. (1991). Hispanic women in college and careers: Preparing for success. In Wolfe, L. R. (ed.), *Women, work, and school: Occupational segregation and the role of education,* 117–39. Boulder, CO: Westview.

Suarez-Orozco, M. M. (1989). Hispanics in the United States. In *Central American refugees and U.S. high schools* (pp. 18–48). Stanford: Stanford University Press.

Walsh, C. E. (1987). Schooling and the civic exclusion of Latinos: Toward a discourse of dissonance. *Journal of Education* 169, 115–31.

Zavella, P. (1989). The problematic relationship of feminism and Chicana studies. *Women's Studies* 17, 25–36.

Zinn, M. B.(1982). Mexican-American women in the social sciences. *Signs: Journal of Women in Culture and Society* 8, 259–72.

Lesbians

Chamberlain, P. (1990). Homophobia in the schools; or, What we don't know will hurt us. In O'Malley, S. G., Rosen, R., and Vogt, L. (eds.), *Politics of education: Essays from* Radical Teacher, 302–11. New York: State University of New York Press.

Crumpacker, L., and Vander Haegen, E. M. (1987). Pedagogy and prejudice: Strategies for confronting homophobia in the classroom. *Women's Studies Quarterly* 15, 65–73.

———. (1990). Valuing diversity: Teaching about sexual preference in a radical/conserving curriculum. In Antler, J., and Bilken, S. K. (eds.), *Changing education: Women as radicals and conservators.* New York: State University of New York Press, 201–15.

Gaard, G. (1991). Opening up the canon: The importance of teaching of lesbian and gay literatures. *Feminist Teacher* 6, 30–33.

Gordon, L. (1983). What do we say when we hear "faggot"? *Interracial Books for Children Bulletin* 14, 25–27.

McNaron, T.A.H. (1989). Mapping a country: What lesbian students want. In Pearson, C. S., Shavlik, D. L., and Touchton, J. G. (eds.), *Educating the majority: Women challenge tradition in higher education.* New York: Collier Macmillan, 102–13.

Raymond, J. G. (1989). Putting the politics back in lesbianism. *Women's Studies International Forum* 12, 149–56.

Van Kirk, C. (1990). Sarah Lucia Hoagland's *Lesbian Ethics:* Toward new value and ablemindism. *Hypatia* 5, 145–52.

Zimmerman, B. (1990). Lesbianism 101. In O'Malley, S. G., Rosen, R., and Vogt L. (eds.), *Politics of education: Essays from* Radical Teacher. New York: State University of New York Press, 22–33.

Native American Women

Ferron, R. (1989). American Indian women in higher education: Common threads and diverse experiences. In Pearson, C. S., Shavlik, D. L., and Touchton, J. G.

(eds.), *Educating the majority: Women challenge tradition in higher education.* New York: Collier Macmillan, 80–89.

LaFromboise, T. D., Heyle, A. M., and Ozer, E. J. (1990). Changing and diverse roles of women in American Indian cultures. *Sex Roles* 22, 455–76.

Medicine, B. (1983). Indianwomen: Tribal identity as status quo. In Lowe, M., and Hubbard, R. (eds.), *Woman's nature: Rationalizations of inequality,* 63–73. New York: Pergamon.

Women Reentering the Academy

Chamberlain, M. K. (ed.). (1988). Re-entry women. In *Women in academe: Progress and prospects,* 61–81. New York: Russell Sage Foundation.

Culley, M. (1989). The authority of experience: Adult women in the college classroom. *Equity and Excellence* 24, 67–68.

Karach, A. (1992). The politics of dislocation: Some mature undergraduate women's experiences of higher education. *Women's Studies International Forum* 15, 309–17.

O'Barr, J. (1989). Re-entry women in the academy: The contributions of a feminist perspective. In Pearson, C. S., Shavlik, D. L., and Touchton, J. G. (eds.), *Educating the majority: Women challenge tradition in higher education.* New York: Collier Macmillan, 90–101.

Wolf, M. A. (1993). Mentoring middle-aged women in the classroom. *Adult Learning* 4, 8–9, 22.

Working-Class Women

Gardner, S., Dean, C., and McKaig, D. (1989). Responding to differences in the classroom: The politics of knowledge, class, and sexuality. *Sociology of Education* 62, 64–74.

Karen, D. (1991). The politics of class, race, and gender: Access to higher education in the United States, 1960–1986. *American Journal of Education* 99, 208–37.

Linkon, S., and Mullen, B. (1995) Gender, race, and place: Teaching working-class students in Youngstown. *Radical Teacher* 46, 27–32.

Ryan, J., and Sackrey, C. (1984) *Strangers in paradise: Academics from the working class.* Boston: South End.

Tokarczyk, M. M., and Fay, E. A. (eds.). (1993). *Working class women in the academy: Laborers in the knowledge factory.* Amherst: University of Massachusetts Press.

Issues of Race and Diversity in the Academy

These works emphasize strategies for developing nonracist, nonexclusionary practices in the classroom. Many of the works address the needs of students whose ethnic heritage is not European American.

Overview

Anthony-Perez, B. (1985). Institutional racism and sexism: Refusing the legacy in education. In Treichler, P., Kramarae, C., and Stafford, B. (eds.), *For alma mater: Theory and practice in feminist studies.* Urbana: University of Illinois Press.

Banfield, B. (1991). Honoring cultural diversity and building on its strengths: A case for national action. In Wolfe, L. R. (ed.), *Women, work, and school: Occupational segregation and the role of education.* Boulder, CO: Westview, 77–93.

Brandt, G. (1986). The context of anti-racist education. In *The realization of anti-racist teaching,* 61–109. Philadelphia: Falmer.

Cannon, L. W. (1990). Fostering positive race, class, and gender dynamics in the classroom. *Women's Studies Quarterly* 18, 126–34.

Collins, P.H. (1990). *Black feminist thought: Knowledge, consciousness, and the politics of empowerment.* Boston: Unwin Hyman.

Gordon, V. V. (1990). Multicultural education: Some thoughts from an Afrocentric perspective. *Black Issues in Higher Education* 6 (16 Aug.), 52.

Hughes, E. (1990). Taking responsibility for cultural diversity. *Black Issues in Higher Education* 6 (18 January), 24–27.

Palmer, T. C. (1992). Changes in the neighborhood: Integrating the academy and diversifying the curriculum. *Women's Studies* 20, 217–24.

Pence, E. (1982). Racism—A white issue. In Hull, G. T., Scott, P. B., and Smith, B. (eds.), *All the women are white, all the blacks are men, but some of us are brave.* New York: Feminist Press, 45–47.

Reid, P. T., and Comas-Diaz, L. (1990). Gender and ethnicity: Perspectives on dual status. *Sex Roles* 22, 397–408.

Rothenberg, P. (1988). Integrating the study of race, gender, and class: Some preliminary observations. *Feminist Teacher* 3, 37–42.

———. (1990). Teaching racism and sexism in a changing America. In O'Malley, S. G., Rosen, R., and Vogt L. (eds.), *Politics of education: Essays from Radical Teacher.* New York: State University of New York Press, 35–45.

Tatum, B. D. (1992). Talking about race, learning about racism: The application of racial identity development theory in the classroom. *Harvard Educational Review* 62, 1–24.

Wolverton, T. (1983). Unlearning complicity, remembering resistance: White women's anti-racism education. In Bunch, C., and Pollack, S. (eds.), *Learning our way,* 187–99. Trumansburg, NY: Crossing.

Empowerment through Multicultural Pedagogy

Banks, J. A. (1993). *Multicultural education: Issues and perspectives.* Boston: Allyn and Bacon.

Diaz, C. (ed.). (1992). *Multicultural education for the 21st century.* Washington, DC: National Education Association.

Giczkowski, W. (1992). The influx of older students can revitalize college teaching. *Chronicle of Higher Education,* 25 March, B3–B4.

Martin, R. J. (1991). The power to empower: Multicultural education for student-teachers. In Sleeter, C. (ed.), *Empowerment through multicultural education,* 287–97. New York: State University of New York Press.

Mattai, P. (1992). Rethinking the nature of multicultural education: Has it lost its focus or is it being misused? *Journal of Negro Education* 61, 65–77.

McCormick, T. M. (1994). *Creating the nonsexist classroom: A multicultural approach.* New York: Teachers College.

Rhoades, G. (1991). Dealing with racism in the classroom. *Feminist Teacher* 6, 34–36.

Schoem, D. L., Frankel, L., Zuniga, X., and Lewis, E. A. (eds.). (1993). *Multicultural teaching in the university.* Westport, CT: Praeger.

Sleeter, C. (1991). Multicultural education and empowerment. In Sleeter, C. (ed.), *Empowerment through multicultural education.* New York: State University of New York Press, 1–23.

Takata, S. R. (1991). Who is empowering whom? The social construction of empowerment. In Sleeter, C. (ed.), *Empowerment through multicultural education.* New York: State University of New York Press, 251–71.

Thompson, B. W., and Tyagi, Sangeeta. (1993). *Beyond a dream deferred: Multicultural education and the politics of excellence.* Minneapolis: University of Minnesota Press.

Sex Equity and Women of Color

Bogart, K. (1985). Improving sex equity in postsecondary education. In Klein, S. (ed.), *Handbook for achieving sex equity through education,* 470–88. Baltimore: John Hopkins University Press.

Christian, B. (1989). But who do you really belong to—black studies or women's studies? *Women's Studies* 17, 17–23.

Huratado, A. (1989). Relating to privilege: Seduction and rejection in the subordination of white women and women of color. *Signs: Journal of Women in Culture and Society* 14, 833–55.

Jones, L. H. (1986). Racism and sexism. *Women's Studies Quarterly* 14, 54–55.

Lewis, S., et al. (1985). Achieving sex equity for minority women. In Klein, S. (ed.), *Handbook for achieving sex equity through education.* Baltimore: Johns Hopkins University Press, 365–90.

Mead, M. (1986). The feminist challenge. *Women's Studies Quarterly* 14, 17–18.

Omolade, B. (1987). A black feminist pedagogy. *Women's Studies Quarterly* 15, 32–39.

Pheterson, G. (1988). Alliances between women: Overcoming internalized oppression and internalized domination. In Minnich, E., O'Barr, J., and Rosenfeld, D. (eds.), *Reconstructing the academy: Women's education and women's studies,* 139–53. Chicago: University of Chicago Press.

Pedagogy

The following works focus on what to do in the classroom and why. Some of these sources discuss the theoretical bases of feminist pedagogy, while others offer advice on how to put theory into practice.

Theories of Teaching

Bezucha, R. J. (1985). Feminist pedagogy as a subversive activity. In Culley, M., and Portuges, C. (eds.), *Gendered subjects: The dynamics of feminist education.* Boston: Routledge, 81–95.

Clinchy, B. M., Belenky, M. F., Goldberger, N., and Tarule, J. (1985). Connected education for women. *Journal of Education* 167, 28–45.

Cocks, J. (1985). Suspicious pleasures: On teaching feminist theory. In Culley, M., and Portuges, C. (eds.), *Gendered subjects: The dynamics of feminist education.* Boston: Routledge, 171–182.

Conway, J. K. (1987). Politics, pedagogy, and gender. *Daedalus* 116, 137–52.

Culley, M., Diamond, A., Edwards, L., Lennox, S., and Portuges, C. (1985). The politics of nurturance. In Culley, M., and Portuges, C. (eds.), *Gendered subjects: The dynamics of feminist education.* Boston: Routledge, 11–21.

Feminist pedagogy: An update. (1993). *Women's Studies Quarterly* 21 (3 and 4).

Lather, P. (1991). *Getting smart: Feminist research and pedagogy with/in the postmodern.* New York: Routledge.

Lyons, N. (1990). Visions and competencies: An educational agenda for exploring the ethical and intellectual dimensions of decision-making and conflict negotiation. In Antler, J., and Bilken, S. K. (eds.), *Changing education: Women as radicals and conservators.* New York: State University of New York Press, 277–94.

Maher, F. A. and Tetreault, M. K. T. (1994). *The feminist classroom: An inside look at how professors and students are transforming higher education for a diverse society.* New York: Basic.

Musil, C. M. (1992). *The courage to question: Women's studies and student learning.* Washington, DC: Association of American Colleges.

Rothenberg, P. (1989). The hand that pushes the rock. *Women's Review of Books* 6 February, 18–19.

Scanlon, J. (1993). Keeping our activist selves alive in the classroom: Feminist pedagogy and political activism. *Feminist Teacher* 7, 8–13.

Shor, I. (1980). *Critical teaching and everyday life.* Boston: South End.

Shrewsbury, C. M. (1987). What is feminist pedagogy? *Women's Studies Quarterly* 15, 6–13.

———. (1993). Feminist pedagogy: An updated bibliography. *Women's Studies Quarterly* 21, 148–60.

Statham, A., Richardson, L., and Cook, J. (1991). *Gender and university teaching: A negotiated difference.* Albany: State University of New York Press.

Tompkins, J. (1990). Pedagogy of the distressed. *College English* 52, 653–60.

Pedagogical Strategies

Banks, J. (1991). A curriculum for empowerment, action, and change. In Sleeter, C. (ed.), *Empowerment through multicultural education.* New York: State University of New York Press, 125–41.

Boyte, H., and Evans, S. M. (1991). Power and the language of difference. *Liberal Education* 77, 20–23.

Brandt, G. (1986). Constructing an anti-racist pedagogy. In *The realization of anti-racist teaching*, 110–46. Philadelphia: Falmer.

Bright, C. (1987). Teaching feminist pedagogy: An undergraduate course. *Women's Studies Quarterly* 15, 96–100.

Brunner, D. (1992). Dislocating boundaries in our classrooms. *Feminist Teacher* 6, 18–24.

Butler, J. E. (1985). Toward a pedagogy of every woman's studies. In Culley, M., and Portuges, C. (eds.), *Gendered subjects: The dynamics of feminist education*. Boston: Routledge, 230–39.

Cannon, L. W. (1990). Fostering positive race, class, and gender dynamics in the classroom. *Women's Studies Quarterly* 18, 126–34.

Cross, T., et al. (1982). Face-to-face, day-to-day racism. In Hull, G. T., Scott, P. B., and Smith, B. (eds.), *All the women are white, all the blacks are men, but some of us are brave*. New York: Feminist Press, 52–56.

Disch, E., and Thompson, B. (1990). Teaching and learning from the heart. *NWSA Journal* 2, 68–78.

Fisher, B. (1989). The heart has its reasons: Feelings, thinking, and community-building in feminist education. *Women's Studies Quarterly* 15, 47–58.

Guy-Sheftall, B. (1991). Practicing what you preach: Strategies of an ex-English professor. *Liberal Education* 77, 27–29.

Klein, S. S., Russo, L. N., Campbell, P. B., and Harvey, G. (1985). Examining the achievement of sex equity in and through education. In Klein, S. (ed.), *Handbook for achieving sex equity through education*. Baltimore: Johns Hopkins University Press, 1–11.

Maher, F. (1987). Inquiry teaching and feminist pedagogy. *Social Education* 51, 186–92.

Minnich, E. K. (1991). Discussing diversity. *Liberal Education* 77, 2–7.

Olguin, R. A. (1991). Classroom culture and cultural diversity: Teaching in the crossfire. *Liberal Education* 77, 24–26.

Rakow, L. F. (1992). Gender and race in the classroom: Teaching way out of line. *Feminist Teacher* 6, 10–13.

Rothenberg, P. (1988). Integrating the study of race, gender, and class: Some preliminary observations. *Feminist Teacher* 3, 37–42.

Schniedewind, N. (1983). Feminist values: Guidelines for teaching methodology in women's studies. In Bunch, C., and Pollack, S. (eds.), *Learning our way*. Trumansburg, NY: Crossing, 261–71.

Shaw, L. L. and Wicker, D. G. (1981). Teaching about racism in the classroom and in the community. *Radical Teacher* 18, 9–14.

Shor, I. (1987). What is the dialogical method of teaching? In Shor, I., and Freire, P., *Pedagogy for liberation: Dialogues on transforming education*, 97–119. South Hadley, MA: Bergin and Garvey.

Spelman, V. (1982). Combatting the marginalization of Black women in the classroom. *Women's Studies Quarterly* 10, 15–16.

Suzuki, B. H. (1991). Unity with diversity: Easier said than done. *Liberal Education* 77, 30–34.

Criticisms of Feminist Pedagogy

Bilken, S. K., and Shakeshaft, C. (1985). The new scholarship on women. In Klein, S. (ed.), *Handbook for achieving sex equity through education.* Baltimore: Johns Hopkins University Press, 44–52.

Bunch, C. (1983). Not by degrees: Feminist theory and education. In Bunch, C., and Pollack, S. (eds.), *Learning our way.* Trumansburg, NY: Crossing, 248–60.

Diamond, A. (1985). Interdisciplinary studies and a feminist community. In Treichler, P., Kramerae, C. and Stafford, B. (eds.), *For alma mater: Theory and practice in feminist studies.* Urbana: University of Illinois Press, 199–208.

Evans, M. (1990). The problem of gender for women's studies. *Women's Studies International Forum* 13, 457–62.

Gorelick, S. (1991). Contradictions of feminist methodology. *Gender and Society* 5, 459–77.

Kremer, B. (1990). Learning to say no: Keeping feminist research for ourselves. *Women's Studies International Forum* 13, 463–67.

Rothenberg, P. (1991). Opinion. *Chronicle of Higher Education* 10 Apr., B1–B3.

Ruggiero, C.(1990). Teaching women's studies: The repersonalization of our politics. *Women's Studies International Forum* 13, 469–75.

Wexler, P., Martusewicz, R., and Kern, J. (1987). Popular education politics. In Livingston, D. (ed.), *Critical pedagogy and cultural power,* 227–43. South Hadley, MA: Bergin and Garvey.

Zinn, M. B., Cannon, L. Y. Higginbotham, E., and Dill, B. T. (1988). The costs of exclusionary practices in women's studies. In Minnich, E., O'Barr, J., and Rosenfeld, D. (eds.), *Reconstructing the academy: Women's education and women's studies.* Chicago: University of Chicago Press, 125–38.

Student-Teacher Interaction

Gender/racial issues may affect the ways in which students and teachers interact with each other in the classroom. The following works discuss the dynamics of that interaction.

Sex Differences in Student-Teacher Interaction

Basow, S., and Distenfeld, M. S. (1985). Teacher expressiveness: More important for male teachers than female teachers? *Journal of Educational Psychology* 77, 45–52.

Boersma, P. D., Gay, D., Jones, R. A., Morrison, L., and Remick, H. (1981). Sex differences in college student-teacher interactions: Fact or fantasy? *Sex Roles* 7, 775–84.

Brooks, V. R. (1982). Sex differences in student dominance behavior in female and male professors' classrooms. *Sex Roles* 8, 683–90.

Crawford, M., and MacLeod, M. (1990). Gender in the college classroom: An assessment of the "chilly climate" for women. *Sex Roles* 23, 101–22.

Dweck, C. S., Davidson, W., Nelson, S., and Enna, B. (1978). Sex differences in learned helplessness: II. The contingencies of evaluative feedback in the classroom. III. An experimental analysis. *Developmental Psychology* 14, 268–76.

Hall, R. M., and Sandler, B. (1982). *The classroom climate: A chilly one for women?* Washington, DC: Project on the Status and Education of Women, Association of American Colleges.

Kramarae, C., and Treichler, P. A. (1990). Power relationships in the classroom. In Gabriel, S. L., and Smithson, I. (eds.), *Gender in the classroom*, 41–59. Urbana: University of Illinois Press.

Lewis, M., and Simon, R. I. (1986). A discourse not intended for her: Learning and teaching within patriarchy. *Harvard Educational Review* 56, 457–72.

Sadker, M., and Sadker, D. (1994). *Failing at fairness: How America's schools cheat girls.* New York: Scribner's.

Statham, A., Richardson, L., and Cook, J. A. (1991). Conclusions and implications for teachers and administrators. In Statham, A., Richardson, L., and Cook, J. (eds.), *Gender and university teaching: A negotiated difference.* Albany: State University of New York Press, 122–39.

Sternglanz, S. H., and Lyberger-Ficek, S. (1977). Sex differences in student-teacher interactions in the college classroom. *Sex Roles* 3, 345–52.

Race/Sex Difference in Student-Teacher Interaction

Gay, G. (1975). Teachers' achievement expectation of and classroom interactions with ethnically different students. *Contemporary Education* 46, 166–71.

Grant, L. (1984). Black females' "place" in desegregated classrooms. *Sociology of Education* 57, 98–111.

Irvine, J. J. (1984). Teacher communication as related to race and sex of the student. *Journal of Educational Research* 78, 338–45.

———. (1986). Teacher-student interactions: Effects of student race, sex, and grade level. *Journal of Educational Psychology* 78, 14–21.

Jenkins, M. M. (1990). Teaching the new majority: Guidelines for cross-cultural communication between students and faculty. *Feminist Teacher* 5, 8–14.

Rakow, L. F. (1991). Gender and race in the classroom: Teaching way out of line. *Feminist Teacher* 6, 10–13.

Student Participation

Karp, D. A., and Yoels, W. C. (1976). The college classroom: Some observations on the meanings of student participation. *Sociology and Social Research* 60, 421–39.

Shapiro, J. P. (1990). Nonfeminist and feminist students at risk. *Women's Studies International Forum* 13, 553–64.

Tompkins, J. (1990). Pedagogy of the distressed. *College English* 52, 653–60.

Authority in the Classroom

Beck, E. T. (1983). Self-disclosure and the commitment to social change. In Bunch, C., and Pollack, S. (eds.), *Learning our way.* Trumansburg, NY: Crossing, 285–91.

Caughie, P., and Pearce, R. (1992). Resisting "the dominance of the professor": Gendered teaching, gendered subjects. *NWSA Journal* 4, 187–99.

Culley, M. (1985). Anger and authority in the introductory women's studies classroom. In Culley, M., and Portuges, C. (eds.), *Gendered subjects: The dynamics of feminist education.* Boston: Routledge, 209–17.

Grauerholz, E. (1989). Sexual harassment of women professors by students: Exploring the dynamics of authority and gender in a university setting. *Sex Roles* 21, 789–801.

Richardson, L., Cook, J., and Statham, A. (1983). Down the up staircase: Male and female university professors' classroom management strategies. In Richardson, L., and Taylor, V. (eds.), *Feminist frontiers* (pp. 280–87). New York: Random House.

Statham, A., Richardson, L., and Cook, J. A. (1991). Authority management in the classroom. In Statham, Richardson, and Cook, 103–22.

Mentoring

Fisher, B. (1988). Wandering in the wilderness: The search for women role models. In Minnich, E., O'Barr, J., and Rosenfeld, D. (eds.), *Reconstructing the academy: Women's education and women's studies.* Chicago: University of Chicago Press, 234–56.

Hall, R. M., and Sandler, B. (1983). *Academic mentoring for women students and faculty: A new look at an old way to get ahead.* Washington, DC: Project on the Status and Education of Women, Association of American Colleges.

Sheldon, Amy. (1990). He was her mentor, she was his muse: Women as mentors, new pioneers. *Women in the linguistics profession* 208–22. Washington DC: Committee on the Status of Women in Linguistics of the Linguistic Society of America.

Evaluation

Barnes, L. L. (1990). Gender bias in teachers' written comments. In Gabriel, S. L., and Smithson, I. (eds.), *Gender in the classroom.* Urbana: University of Illinois Press, 140–58.

Basow, S., and Silberg, N. (1987). Student evaluations of college professors: Are female and male professors rated differently? *Journal of Educational Psychology* 79, 308–14.

Feldman, R. A. (1992). College students' views of male and female college teachers. *Research in Higher Education* 33, 317–75.

Kaschak, E. (1978). Sex bias in student evaluations of college professors. *Psychology of Women Quarterly* 2, 235–43.

———. (1981). Another look at sex bias in students' evaluations of professors: Do winners get the recognition that they have been given? *Psychology of Women Quarterly* 5, 767–72.

Kierstead, D., D'Agostino, P., and Dill, H. (1988). Sex role stereotyping of college professors: Bias in students' ratings of instructors. *Journal of Educational Psychology* 80, 342–44.

Martin, E. (1984). Power and authority in the classroom: Sexist stereotypes in teaching evaluations. *Signs: Journal of Women in Culture and Society 9*, 482–92.

Tieman, C. R., and Rankin-Ullock, B. (1985). Student evaluations of teachers: An examination of the effect of sex and field of study. *Teaching Sociology 12*, 177–91.

Top, T. J. (1991). Sex bias in the evaluation of performance in the scientific, artistic, and literary professions: A review. *Sex Roles 24*, 73–106.

Vasquez, J. A. and Wainstein, N. (1990). Instructional responsibilities of college faculty to minority students. *Journal of Negro Education 59*, 599–610.

Bias in Testing and Textbook Materials

Feiner, S. F., and Roberts, B. B. (1990). Hidden by the invisible hand: Neoclassical economic theory and the textbook treatment of race and gender. *Gender and Society 4*, 159–81.

Ferree, M. M., and Hall, E. J. (1990). Visual images of American society: Gender and race in introductory sociology textbooks. *Gender and Society 4*, 500–33.

Lewin M., and Wild, C. (1991). The impact of the feminist critique on tests, assessment, and methodology. *Psychology of Women Quarterly 15*, 581–96.

Martin, E. (1991). The egg and the sperm: How science has constructed a romance based on stereotypical male-female roles. *Signs: Journal of Women in Culture and Society 16*, 485–501.

Peterson, S. B. and Kroner, T. (1992). Gender biases in textbooks for introductory psychology and human development. *Psychology of Women Quarterly 16*, 17–36.

Plake, B. S., Loyd, B. H., and Hoover, H. D. (1981). Sex differences in mathematics components of the Iowa Tests of Basic Skills. *Psychology of Women Quarterly 5*, 780–84.

Scott, K. P., and Schau, C. G. (1985). Sex equity and sex bias in instructional materials. In Klein, S. (ed.), *Handbook for achieving sex equity through education*. Baltimore: Johns Hopkins University Press, 218–32.

Whatley, M. H. (1989). A feeling for science: Female students and biology texts. *Women's Studies International Forum 12*, 355–61.

Language

These works discuss the means by which common linguistic practices place female speakers in subordinate positions while influencing the ways that men and women communicate. Some of the works address the linguistic differences that separate ethnic populations from the European American linguistic community.

Language Acculturation

Adamsky, C. (1981). Changes in pronominal usage in a classroom situation. *Psychology of Women Quarterly 5*, 773–79.

Borker, R. (1980). Anthropology: Social and cultural perspectives. In McConnell-Ginet, S., Borker, R., and Furman, N. (eds.), *Women and language in literature and society*, 26–44. New York: Praeger.

Davies, B., and Banks, C. (1992). The gender trap: A feminist post-structuralist analysis of primary school children's talk about gender. *Journal of Curriculum Studies* 24, 1–25.

De Lisi, R., and Soundranayagam, L. (1990). The conceptual structure of sex role stereotypes in college students. *Sex Roles* 23, 593–611.

Edelsky, C. (1981). Who's got the floor? *Language in Society* 10, 383–421.

Foster, J. D., Hannum, L. E., McMinn, M. R., and Troyer, P. K. (1991). Teaching nonsexist language to college students. *Journal of Experimental Education* 59, 153–61.

Kramarae, C. (1980). Proprietors of language. In McConnell-Ginet, S., Borker, R., and Furman, N. (eds.), *Women and language in literature and society*. New York: Praeger, 58–68.

Wolfson, N., and Manes, J. (1980). "Don't 'dear' me!" In McConnell-Giriet, S., Borker, R., and Furman, N. (eds.), *Women and language in literature and society*. New York: Praeger, 79–92.

Linguistic Imposition

Martyna, W. (1980). The psychology of the generic masculine. In McConnell-Ginet, S., Borker, R., and Furman, N. (eds.), *Women and language in literature and society*. New York: Praeger, 69–78.

O'Barr, W. M., and Atkins, B. K. (1980). "Women's language" or "powerless language"? In McConnell-Ginet, S., Borker, R., and Furman, N. (eds.), *Women and language in literature and society*. New York: Praeger, 93–110.

Ruiz, R. (1991). The empowerment of language-minority students. In Sleeter, C. (ed.), *Empowerment through multicultural education*. New York: State University of New York Press, 217–27.

Tannen, D. (1994). *Gender and discourse*. New York: Oxford University Press.

Thorne, B. (1989). Rethinking the ways we teach. In Pearson, C. S., Shavlik, D. L., and Touchton, J. G. (eds.), *Educating the majority: Women challenge tradition in higher education*. New York: Collier Macmillan, 311–25.

Treichler, P. A., and Kramarae, C. (1983). Women's talk in the ivory tower. *Communication Quarterly* 31, 118–32.

Walsh, C. (1991). *Pedagogy and the struggle for voice*. New York: Bergin and Garvey.

African American Discourse

Jordan, J. (1988). Nobody mean more to me than you and the future life of Willie Jordan. *Harvard Educational Review* 58, 363–74.

Stanback, M. H. (1985) Language and black woman's place: Evidence from the black middle class. In Treichler, P., Kramerae, C. and Stafford, B. (eds.), *For alma mater: Theory and practice in feminist studies*. Urbana: University of Illinois Press, 177–93.

Williams, S. (1991). Classroom use of African American language: Educational tool or social weapon? In Sleeter, C. (ed.), *Empowerment through multicultural education*. New York: State University of New York Press, 199–215.

Contributors

DALE M. BAUER is a professor of English and women's studies at the University of Illinois, Urbana-Champaign. Her book, *Sex Expression and American Women's Writing*, is forthcoming from University of North Carolina Press.

CARRIE BRECKE is the director of the Writing Center and an instructor of English and women's and gender studies at Roosevelt University in Chicago. Her current research explores the rhetorics of privilege in the documentary *An Inconvenient Truth* and "peerness" in writing center tutoring sessions.

PAMELA L. CAUGHIE is a professor and the graduate program director in the English department at Loyola University Chicago. She publishes on modernist literature, feminist and postmodernist theory, and pedagogy. Her current project extends her analysis in *Passing and Pedagogy* to class issues in literature, popular culture, and the academy.

ROBBIN D. CRABTREE is the dean of the College of Arts and Sciences and Professor of Communication at Fairfield University. Her research emphasizes understanding media in relation to social structures, revolution, development, and globalization. She has published widely about service-learning theory and practice, as well as feminist media criticism and pedagogical theory and practice in international contexts.

ANNE DONADEY is an associate professor of European studies and women's studies at San Diego State University. Her research focuses on francophone and anglophone postcolonial feminist literature. Her publications include a book on Assia Djebar and Leïla Sebbar, *Recasting Postcolonialism: Women Writing between Worlds*, and the co-edited volume *Postcolonial Theory and Francophone Literary Studies* with H. Adlai Murdoch.

MARY MARGARET FONOW is a professor and the director of women and gender Studies at Arizona State University. Her research interests include feminist methodology, transnational feminist labor activism, and queer labor organizing. She is the author of *Union Women: Forging Feminism in the United Steelworkers of America*.

ESTELLE B. FREEDMAN is the Edgar E. Robinson Professor in U.S. History at Stanford University. She recently edited *The Essential Feminist Reader* and published the collection *Feminism, Sexuality, and Politics*. She is currently writing about the politics of rape in U.S. history.

SAUNDRA GARDNER is an associate professor of sociology at the University of Maine. Her research and teaching interests include the sociology of family, domestic violence, sexual identity, and mental health.

LORI A. GOETSCH is a professor and the dean of libraries at Kansas State University. Her research areas include library workforce development and other topics in library administration and management.

ANNIS H. HOPKINS teaches in the English department at Southern Illinois University Edwardsville, as well as part-time at Rio Salado College in Tempe. During her thirty-year career, she has taught in middle school, high school, community college, and university settings, including in the women's studies program at Arizona State University from 1986 to 1999.

SAL JOHNSTON is an associate professor of sociology at Whittier College. sal's current research interests include gender and food systems research.

LILI M. KIM is the Henry R. Luce Assistant Professor of History and Global Migrations at Hampshire College. She is currently completing a book on the experience of Korean Americans on the home front during World War II and working on a project on the history of Korean migration to Argentina and remigration to the United States.

ADELA C. LICONA is an assistant professor at the University of Arizona where she teaches in the Rhetoric, Composition, and the Teaching of English Program. She is affiliated with the Institute for LGBT Studies and the programs in Women's and Mexican American Studies. Her research interests include borderlands rhetorics, Chicana theory, documentary film/media, and community literacies. She currently serves as president of board of the *NWSA Journal.*

DEBIAN MARTY is an associate professor in the Division of Humanities and Communication at California State University, Monterey Bay. Her current research interests include communication ethics, cooperative argumentation, and conflict resolution.

MARALEE MAYBERRY is a professor of sociology at the University of South Florida. Her current research foci include school-level change factors associated with high school Gay-Straight Student Alliances and identity formation processes associated with chemical education researchers.

JOHN MIHELICH is an associate professor of sociology and anthropology at the University of Idaho. His current research includes critical pedagogy, religious pluralism in the United States, and social class, culture and community.

RICHARD PEARCE is a retired professor of history at the University College of Saint Martin's College, Lancaster, England. He is also a Fellow of the Royal Historical Society. His publications include *Britain: Domestic Politics 1918–39, Britain: Society, Economy and Industrial Relations 1900–39,* and *The Unification of Italy.*

MARGARET N. (PEG) REES is a professor of geoscience at University of Nevada, Las Vegas (UNLV). She is also executive director of the UNLV Public Lands Institute and a member of her university's Department of Women's Studies Advisory Board. Her research explores globally significant events recorded in Cambrian-age strata.

STEPHANIE RIGER is a professor of psychology and gender and women's studies at the University of Illinois at Chicago. She is author of *Transforming Psychology: Gender in Theory and Practice* and co-author of *Evaluating Services for Survivors of Domestic Violence and Sexual Assault*. Her current research focuses on the impact of welfare reform on intimate violence and the evaluation of services for survivors of domestic violence and sexual assault.

REBECCA ROPERS-HUILMAN is a professor of higher education at the University of Minnesota. Her current research explores identity, diversity, and change agents in educational settings. She has published books focused on women's experiences in higher education, has served as Director of the Women's Center and as Director of Women's and Gender Studies at Louisiana State University, and is current editor of the *NWSA Journal*.

SUZANNA ROSE is the senior associate dean for the sciences and a professor of psychology and women's studies at Florida International University in Miami. She has published extensively on women's issues, including personal relationships and professional networks. She incorporates feminist activism into her teaching and her work as a consultant concerning strategic career planning in academe.

DAVID ALAN SAPP is an associate professor and the director of the Program in Professional Writing at Fairfield University. He is a workplace communication specialist with expertise in community-based and inter/transnational applications of communication theory and technology. His scholarship on intercultural cooperation and critical reflection explores ongoing struggles of disenfranchised populations.

DEBBIE STORRS is the associate dean of the College of Letters, Arts, and Social Sciences at the University of Idaho. Her current research explores rural health care activism, transformative pedagogy, and liberation sociology.

EVE WIEDERHOLD is an assistant professor of English at George Mason University. Her current research explores representation and democratic politics in relation to rhetoric and public sphere theories.

JULIA T. WOOD is the Lineberger Distinguished Professor of Humanities and Professor of Communication Studies at the University of North Carolina at Chapel Hill. Her current research focuses on intimate partner violence and the issue of voice in the lives of girls and women.

Index